# No Ordinary Son

## A Journey through Death & Living Again

Dr. Tanya McCoss-Yerigan

*Infinitely Yours Publications*

**Infinitely Yours Publications**
4857 Hwy 67, Suite #3
Granite Falls, MN 56241

Copyright © Tanya McCoss-Yerigan, 2014 (6)

All rights reserved. No part of this book may be reproduced or transmitted in any form or by any means without written permission from the author.

*No Ordinary Son:*
*A Journey through Death and Living Again*
Dr. Tanya McCoss-Yerigan

ISBN-10: 0996056505, ISBN-13: 978-0-9960565-0-2 (soft cover)
ISBN-10: 0996056521, ISBN-13: 978-0-9960565-2-6 (hard cover)

Edited by Olivia Bergeland
Photography by Frozen in Time (p. 281 and back cover)
Manufactured in the United States of America

**Infinitely Yours Publications**
*~ Making Our Story Yours ~*

## CLINTON ROBERT-DOUGLAS MCCOSS
*December 12, 1990 – November 5, 2006*

# DEDICATION

*"Faith is the strength by which a shattered world shall emerge into the light."*
~Helen Keller~

This book is written as a gift for all who loved Clint and for all who never met him. There is no in-between.

## CLINT

To my son, Clint, who I miss every second of every day. As few know, I made a promise to you on the day God took you home. I promised I would continue to live. I also promised not just to live, but to live a life that would make you proud. A life filled with love, laughter, and gratitude. I apologize for struggling with these things in the early years of your absence. The pain was just too thick. Today, I can honestly say that I have found a way to take my loss of you and make myself better and not bitter. Thank you for your hearence. I will explain this word to everyone else later. I love you, Kitty.

## MY OTHER CHILDREN

To my other children: Megan, Garrett, Briana, and Kayla. Without you, I am not sure I would have been able to survive losing Clint. In all honesty, during the first days, I waited for an opportunity to be alone so I could leave to be with him. Then I realized being with him meant not being with you. I could not do it. I loved him. I love him still, but I do not love him more than each of you. I loved him differently, and I love each of you differently than how I loved him. It's all of you who make me whole as a mother. So, on the second morning after Clint's accident, I made another promise to your brother and prayed that God would help me keep this promise no matter what it took. I promised Clint that I would get out of bed *every* day and live for you. I am writing this book so you understand my love for your brother and each of you. I love you guys!

## TIM

To my husband and best friend, Tim. Without you, I am sure I would not be here today. You never left my side in those early hours, days, weeks, and months. When you realized I wanted to leave this world and be with Clint, you made me keep the promises I made to him and the other children. When I would rage and try to push you away, you would pull me closer. When I did not know I was hungry, you fed me. When I had not bathed in days, you bathed me. When I would wander into the cold to lie where Clint drew his last breath, you would bring me inside so I would not freeze to death. When my hair was a mess, you brushed it. When I would look in the mirror and not recognize my own reflection, you helped me to see myself again. When I was so numb that I could not feel love, you showed me what it was. You made me promise that I would live until I could think again. You made me make the six-month promise. Ultimately, it was this promise and our children's faces that allowed me to be sitting here today. I love you, Tim.

## FAMILY & FRIENDS

Thank you does not do justice to my family and friends who held vigil over our sorrow. For months, my friends, parents, sister (Bobbie), brothers (Hollis, Todd, and Kyle), and their families made sure that I was never alone. They will never know how much this means to me. My dad reminded me that I will be with Clint again. My mom, whose love of Clinty rivaled only my own, looked into my eyes, and both of us knew no words were necessary. I will never forget the sound of my sister's voice when we talked on the phone, and I will never forget her hand on my knee as she sat in silence at my feet. I also remember when my big brothers wrapped their arms around me, and one of them said, "I love you, and it will be ok." Another brother shared his shock and sorrow by stating, "Why you? You are the best mom!"

My sisters-in-law were calling me day after day. Pam was nearly running across the room to hold me each time our eyes would meet. My nephews would come to hug me as though they were standing in for what Clinty could no longer do. They knew about the hugs he gave me and believed that someone, wherever they were, should come to hug me even if it was for just a few seconds.

Clinty's friends, who soon became our friends, would stop at our home whenever they could. They would unknowingly remind me that he *was* here. They were all such an important part of our lives and our home. They will never know how their presence cushioned the striking blows of pain that bombarded me.

To my closest friends, who kept calling even though I couldn't recognize the ring of a phone. Your hearts knew what my children meant to me, and you found a way to make me live.

To my family and friends, you did not just do this once; you did it day after day. Each of you gave me a piece of your strength so I could heal. Slowly, your acts of love and support helped to mend my shattered world so I could emerge and live again.

## COMMUNITY

To all of those who loved us through this or left us alone in our sorrow, this book is for you. Whichever side you were on, I have learned from you, and I love you for it. I hope my journey will spark some insight for you. Whether you supported us with your presence and prayers or were one of the town gossips, my hope is that my pain will bring you wisdom and compassion.

## GOD

Finally, this book is dedicated to my Heavenly Father. Thank you for your patience and everlasting love. You have granted me so many gifts: hearence, love, gratitude, and peace. I only hope I can do justice to these gifts and share your wonders with the world. I once heard this saying: "God can heal a broken heart, but He has to have all of it."

**God, my heart is yours!**

# TABLE OF CONTENTS

| | | |
|---|---|---|
| DEDICATION | | 4 |
| FORWARD | By Garrett McCoss | 10 |
| INTRODUCTION | My Journey | 14 |
| CHAPTER 1 | Let Me Introduce You to Who We Used to Be | 17 |
| CHAPTER 2 | He Prepares Me . . . But for What? | 33 |
| CHAPTER 3 | That Horrible Day | 45 |
| CHAPTER 4 | Unimaginable Decisions | 62 |
| CHAPTER 5 | A Mother's Goodbye | 74 |
| CHAPTER 6 | God? What a Hoax! | 87 |
| CHAPTER 7 | The Six-Month Promise | 96 |
| CHAPTER 8 | I Am So Lonely | 100 |
| CHAPTER 9 | My Groundhog Day | 106 |
| CHAPTER 10 | My Clinty Comforts Me | 110 |
| CHAPTER 11 | Anger Nearly Becomes Me | 115 |
| CHAPTER 12 | My Life Has Been Hijacked | 134 |
| CHAPTER 13 | Would Someone Please Tell Me Where He Is? | 137 |
| CHAPTER 14 | My Heart Opens & Hearence Reigns | 143 |
| CHAPTER 15 | My Fears Consume Me | 148 |
| CHAPTER 16 | Those I Once Loved to Hear About | 155 |
| CHAPTER 17 | Don't Hurt the Money | 158 |
| CHAPTER 18 | Knowing Clint | 170 |
| CHAPTER 19 | Clint's Friends | 176 |
| CHAPTER 20 | The New Us . . . Our New Life | 180 |
| CHAPTER 21 | Our Roots Run Deep | 216 |
| CHAPTER 22 | Ray of Hope | 237 |
| CHAPTER 23 | Holding On | 245 |

| | | |
|---|---|---|
| CHAPTER 24 | So What Happened Anyway? | 258 |
| CHAPTER 25 | Clint's Life & Legacy | 269 |
| CHAPTER 26 | See You Soon | 273 |
| CHAPTER 27 | A Son for a Son | 276 |
| AFTERWORD | Our Family Would Like to Hear from You! | 282 |
| EPILOGUE | Do You Still Hunt? | 285 |
| APPENDIX I | Infinitely Ours | 300 |
| APPENDIX II | Discussion Questions | 310 |
| APPENDIX III | Infinitely Clint Foundation: Donation Form | 319 |
| APPENDIX IV | Book Order Form | 320 |

# FORWARD
## By Garrett McCoss

∞

*"One doesn't discover new lands without consenting to lose sight of the shore for a very long time."*
~André Gide~

"Mom, what do we have, like, seventy years in this world without Clint? We will have an eternity to spend with him once we get to Heaven. This life will seem like a blink of an eye, and then we will see him again."

When I said that to my mother, I was just a young boy. When I told my mom that simple statement, I didn't know it would constantly replay in her head. It would become a statement that she would cling to, and it would help her through every hour, every day, every month, and eventually years. As I think back, I remember that it was a cold fall night. We were sitting in her office making small talk. I thank God every day because, in my eyes, I feel as though that statement saved her sanity and perhaps her life.

I've always seen my mother as being a strong, admirable, and indestructible woman. Life or not even this world could tear her down until that fateful morning. My name is Garrett McCoss, and I am the son of Tanya McCoss-Yerigan.

My mother came to me one day and told me that she was writing a book about our family: a book about Clint. At first, I told my mom I was not fond of the idea of the "whole world" knowing about Clint, about our family, and about me! As she wrote, months and then years went by. I started thinking more and more about it. I had to think about it from my mom's point of view. What if this book could help others who have lost someone they loved? What if this book could change people's lives? Through her point of view, I realized that my mom had inspired me in another way I had not yet realized. Knowing that Clint's death and the effect it had on our family would no longer be private, she still wanted to pursue it if it meant helping just one person.

I've found that, for me, keeping a journal can be emotionally healing. When I write, my mind sorts through what makes sense and what doesn't. The things that make sense become things I live by. They push me to be a better person. I feel like the more I've written, the more I've chipped away at the old me and opened my heart up to warmth, love, and life itself.

My mother and I were not always as close as we are now. When I was young, I loved my mother very much. I suppose I loved her about as much as every young child loves his or her mother. It wasn't until after my brother passed away that I grew distant and cold towards both the world and *my mother*! For years, my heart felt nothing but emptiness. My mom tried saving our relationship over and over again.

I've always kept a journal, but then, she wanted me to journal more with her. She also had me sit down with her and have long, deep talks about Clint, God, and the "what-ifs." I did as she requested, but it wasn't until I moved off to college when I finally realized she did it! My heart ached for the journaling and the deep thinking I only got with her. Journaling and then sharing some of my writings with my mom has helped me reach a higher level of understanding as well as touch emotions that were buried deep inside of me. Through writing, I've learned to be open-minded rather than simple-minded. It is through this deep thinking that I've learned to deal with the loss of my brother. Being simple-minded only allows you to focus on the negatives and not push for the positives. It is within this positive perception that we find truth. Once I was able to touch this part of myself, I've been able to live smarter and love stronger.

As time went by, I grew close to Mother again. I also let the wonders and joys of this world enter my heart. My mom always says to me "Garrett, it is God, family, and then friends. That is the order of importance in this life. If you keep a healthy relationship with all three, you will have an amazing life." To this day, I almost live by that!

As I get older, I look up to my mother a lot more. Her amazing belief in God and family and her passion for wanting to help others are characteristics I admire. I encourage others who know her and those who don't to be more like her. I challenge you to put others first!

I want to let you know that no relationship like mine with my mother comes easily. But once you have that special connection, you no longer have a traditional relationship with your parent; you have a best friend for life.

Once years had passed and the fog of grief had lifted, I was able to see miracles that happen around me every day. I had to realize the fact that there were too many extraordinary moments in life for God not to exist. In this process, I was able to find my way back to Him and realize where Clint truly lives.

I am ending this forward with a quote I made up to get me through a pain-stricken time in my life. If you don't know it already, I hope it helps you realize that nearly everything in life is a matter of perception.

> *"Ask not what time has taken from you*
> *but what time has given you."*

# INTRODUCTION
## *My Journey*

*"Time is a companion that goes with us on a journey.
It reminds us to cherish each moment,
because it will never come again."*
~Captain Jean-Luc Picard ~

Even though it's a cliché to write about life being a journey (in fact it might even be cliché to say it's a cliché), there really is no better way to describe the last several years of my life. It has been a journey to learn to live again without my oldest son. It has been a journey to write this book in an effort to share the lessons I've learned along the way. This journey has been long, painful, and full of surprises. Some of these surprises have obviously been very painful beyond what words can express. Yet, there have been pleasant surprises along this path as well. I call it a path because I believe with all my heart that God has placed me where I am. He's at the helm of my life both now and before I realized it. It has taken every bit of faith to trust that He will not leave me alone with this pain and that all will be worthwhile at the end of this path.

Of course, there are choices to make on this path. These choices are not easy and ultimately shape who we are and who we eventually become. That in itself is a choice. Who do you want to be? What legacy do you want to leave behind in this world?

Most people will probably have a hard time understanding what writing this book has meant to me. Only those closest to me will fully understand or comprehend the sacrifice that runs so very deep. In this life, you will meet people who fall on a spectrum of personalities that range from outgoing to reclusive. It may come as a shock, but I fall in the latter category. I'm private to an extreme and am perfectly happy interacting with the outside world on a minimal basis. I'm not one to talk about myself, let alone my most private moments and thoughts. This has only been compounded since losing Clint. After all, why would I want to share with a world that feeds off of needing something to talk about? Why would I want to share with a world that wraps its tongue around your thoughts and experiences, spewing them out in an unrecognizable form? I share because I want Clint's life and legacy to be free of subterfuge. I want each of you to know that forgiveness is real, and the reward is freedom from the weight of pain and hate.

Everything I do has a purpose. The cover of this book is no different and was not designed by accident. It's a rugged and rustic cover that appears to have been tattered and aged through time. It's much like me. Not only do I live a rustic life surrounded by antiques that have taken years to collect, but I also live a little on the rugged side. I like to experience everything in an effort to build the layers of my depth. There's also the buckle and the book's signs of wear. These are symbolic of the private me. To the public, my heart has been cinched so tight that it has left marks of anxiety on my soul and lines on my face. It has been pulled tight and closed for a very long time. It's through the writing of *No Ordinary Son* that the buckle has been released, opening my heart.

The morning after losing Clint, I begged God to make something good come from losing my precious son. Since that very moment, it has been heavy on my heart that God wanted me to write this book. No, He commissioned the writing of it.

Anyone who knows me, before and after losing Clint, knows that I live for my children. In this book, I detail the painful discovery of how *living* is even possible after losing one of your babies. In the hopes that something good will come from the loss of my son, I leave nothing out. Although I'm vulnerable and emotionally naked, I no longer fear your judgment.

On this journey, you will meet a woman with the world at her fingertips: she was happy and had everything to live for. She was blessed with an amazing husband, beautiful children, and by most standards, a perfect life. You will see this woman go from being a faithful servant and child of Christ to one who all but denounced His existence.

On this journey, you will find me in that place and, only by the grace of God, see life breathed into me again as I build a faith that is strong and unwavering, develop a love for God and others that is unexplainable, and feel a gratitude that brings me to tears every day.

I live for the promise made to me by my Father in Heaven that one day we will be together and that the perfect blend of my children's laughter will be reunited.

# CHAPTER 1
## *Let Me Introduce You to Who We Used to Be*

*"To my children...*
*If I had to choose between loving you and breathing...*
*I would use my last breath to tell you ... I Love You."*
*~Author Unknown~*

How do I explain who we were? We were a dream. We were great! We were a family blessed in every way. It was utter joy. It was a gift. We were a puzzle with each family member providing a special piece that blended perfectly with the rest. Every day, I prayed to God to keep our family "Safe, healthy and far from harm and evil, and to be with us every second of the day and every step of the way." This was a prayer I made up as a young mother and never let go of.

I'm scared to go back to that spot in my mind. I'm scared to return to that time of complete happiness. I'm scared to compare it to the new *us* that has the obvious gap of a missing piece. But if I don't go back, you will never understand the magnitude of our loss. You will never realize how one lost piece can destroy a puzzle. This puzzle couldn't be treated like any other puzzle that was missing a piece. This puzzle couldn't simply be put back in its box and returned to the game cupboard never to be opened again. And, no, it couldn't simply be thrown away. Not this puzzle, not us! You will never realize how painful the task was for those of us left behind. It was a nearly impossible task of recreating ourselves so that we can fit together again. But for you, I will go back.

## BLENDING OF A FAMILY

Many people in our lives don't realize that Tim and I have both been married before. For some, they don't even know that all our kids aren't biologically shared between us. Other people are fully aware that we brought our kids to this marriage to form our amazing and not-so-little family. Tim and I rarely segregate our children with labels such as *yours* and *mine*. They are just *ours*. In an effort to help you fully understand our family, I will break from that tradition so you can grasp the blending of *us*.

When Tim and I were married, I had three children and he had two. Megan is my oldest, Clint is my middle child, and Garrett is my youngest. For Tim, Kayla is his older child and Briana is his younger child. When we merged our families together, we ended up with an interesting dynamic. It was as though we had two sets of twins. Clint and Kayla are the same age, and so are Garrett and Briana. In order, Megan is two years older than Clint and Kayla, while they're two years older than Garrett and Briana. This was our perfectly blended family.

I need to explain that not only is *divorce* an ugly word but also an even uglier experience to live with. I purposefully say "live with" and not "live through" because when you have children, divorce is really never done. For both Tim and me, being previously divorced is the worst thing in our past. Obviously, the decisions were good for us personally because we found each other and have a beautiful life together. However, it has not been easy for our children. For them, as with all children of divorced parents, the experience has left its scars. They didn't ask for these scars, but they have to bear them. Their pain is among my greatest guilts in life. I pray often that they and God have forgiven me.

As I think back, I realize that Megan, Clint, and Garrett had only one request throughout the entire divorce. It was something they had thought about and hadn't taken lightly. Even though they were small children, they arranged a time alone with me to make their case. We were at our favorite place in the world, the family cabin. The four of us went for a paddleboat ride to do a little fishing. Between paddling and taking off fish, Megan, acting as the spokesperson, made their sole request. In a serious voice Meg said, "Mom, the boys and I have been talking. We want you to be our mom forever." Quickly and without thought, I explained how much I love them and that I'd always be their mother. She explained further, "But Mom, we don't ever want you to have a different name. Please Mom, whatever you do, don't ever change your last name. We want it the same as ours." Soon the boys joined in the conversation. Collectively, they made their pitch stating, "We don't want to be like other kids whose parents have a different name." There in that paddleboat, I promised the three of them I would keep their last name forever. Although it was a difficult decision that others couldn't fully accept or understand, I refused to cause further pain to my children. I've kept the promise and the name.

When Tim and I merged our two families, we merged for life. We knew the word *divorce* would never be uttered to each other, and it never has. We had found a friendship in each other that remains a pleasant surprise to this day. I still wake up every day and can't believe I'm married to my best friend. Again, I am blessed.

If only our life could be isolated from the real world. The world that is full of outside factors and influence. Being divorced with children means that somehow we've had to navigate the rough waters with the kids' other parents and stepparents. I will be the first to say that this hasn't always been easy. I have no ill feelings toward any of them and truly pray their lives are filled with happiness as well.

In this book, you will learn that Tim and I have spared nothing to ensure that our children have received what they need and most of what they desire. From the kids' perspectives, this situation is no different. True peace among all of their parents would be a dream.

## OUR HIGHEST OF HIGHS

Our life together has had the highest of highs and the lowest of lows. Let me take you on a ride through our highs.

As long as I can remember, I have dreamed of being a mother. I have never taken this job for granted. I haven't taken any sick days, any professional-development days, any vacation days, or any personal days. Yes, it has been a job I have taken seriously. I love my children!

### My Babies, a Dream Come True

When I was little, I would dream of having a little girl whose hair I would fix into cute pigtails. I would imagine that we would play with Barbies, have tea parties, and bake cookies. God granted me my little girl first. When she was born, I would always worry that I was going to do something wrong with her. She has been everything I've ever dreamt of having in a daughter. I wanted to repay God by being a good mother to her and any children that came after her. Megan has been perfect in every way. She has not always been perfectly behaved, but she has been perfectly mine. When Tim and I married each other, I was blessed with two more lovely daughters. All of the girls are smart and beautiful.

As a child, I also dreamed of blonde-haired, blue-eyed little boys. God granted those little boys to me, and I've never been disappointed. I've been frustrated at times but never disappointed. When they were younger, Clint and Garrett, who is lovingly known as Gar, were 100% B-O-Y. They were rough and tumbling, mischievous, loving beyond expectations, and sharp as tacks!

The kids have become some of my closest friends. It wasn't always that way when they were growing up. Tim and I figured that the kids would have plenty of time in life to make all the friends they wanted, but as far as parents go, they were pretty much stuck with us. They would get so mad at us during their manipulative teenage years when we reminded them that we didn't care if we were friends with them because we had to be their parents first. We would tell them that if we became friends when they got older, it would be a welcome bonus for all of us.

## Attitudes & Expectations

I'll be the first to say that the kids have always had what they've wanted from us. However, if they were *naughty*, their things could be taken away. Believe me, there were days when we had to take things away: the door from Megan's room because she slammed it too much, the computer from Clint when he played it too long, the CD player from Gar when he wouldn't keep the volume down, the cell phone from Kayla when she talked on it after bedtime, or Bri's right to sleep with her dog when she let it pee on her carpet. So, they were not perfect, but I wouldn't change them for anything.

They each had a list of chores just because they were part of the family. One mowed the lawn, and others would weed the garden, feed the chickens, do the dishes, clean the house, sweep the porch, feed the horses, and so on. Then, there was a list of paid chores that were first come, first served, and the children's eligibility for it required that their individual lists be completed first. To this day, those lists still hang inside our kitchen cupboard. It's a bittersweet reminder of when we were all together. I don't believe the day will ever come when I'll take them down.

**Just for Fun**

For fun, the things we did together were endless. We raced go-carts, had paintball wars, swam in the pool, climbed trees, built forts in the grove, and renovated our chicken coop into a cool hangout complete with couches, a television, and a gaming system. We played Ping-Pong, air hockey, and foosball, and we watched movies and played computer games.

Having long talks with my children was one of my favorite things to do. It was best to get them one on one. Megan and I would talk until late into the night. It didn't matter whether it was about a cute boy, trouble with friends, learning to share me with her stepsisters, or a spat with her brothers. Also among my favorite talks were those with Gar about life. Even as a little boy he has been such a critical and analytical thinker. Or my talks with

Clint, who was always filled with the greatest sense of humor. He still is and will always be the funniest person I've ever met. For example, when he wouldn't get his way, he would madly stomp away. I would remind him that his heart was too big and that he couldn't stay mad at me. He'd assure me that *this* time he was going to stay mad *forever*. As with all of our encounters, he was back within minutes, smiling and telling me he loved me. When he became a teenager, he would scold his siblings for sassing and being rude. He would tell them "we have the best mom in the world." Then, when the other kids were out of sight, he would break the serious atmosphere with an Italian accent: "Now toots, you better be good or you'll be swimming with the fishes," he would chuckle, and off he would go. I remember our talks with great fondness. Friends would often wonder why our children told us so much about their lives. It was, and still is, an honor that they have invited us into their most private happenings and thoughts.

**Work Hard**
Tim was a deputy with the Yellow Medicine County Sheriff's Office. At the time, he had been a deputy for nearly twenty years. It was not uncommon that he would go days without sleep, but he always made time for the kids. For most of the children's upbringing, Tim predominantly worked nights and half of our weekends. When he was not at the sheriff's office, he was attending the kid's sporting events, working on projects around the farm, or working at my brother's construction company.

When the kids were young, I worked for Lakeview Schools as a school social worker/in-home counselor and taught some social studies as well. I also worked nearly half-time in the education department at Southwest Minnesota State University. As though that wasn't enough, I began full-time graduate school in the fall of 2000 and became Dr. Tanya McCoss-Yerigan in early 2004. I can honestly say that because Tim and the kids were so supportive, the time flew by quickly. As soon as my Ph.D. was conferred, the university offered me a full-time teaching position. The kids would tease me about others having to call me "doctor" now. Some of Megan's friends even called me "Mama Doc." Mama Doc was ok, but I told them I shuddered at the thought of making anyone address me so formally. Somehow, it would feel as though I thought I was better, when in my heart I had never felt that I was better than anyone. To this day, my graduate students call me Tanya.

Finally, with a much more flexible work schedule, I had time to spend with the kids. I could begin making up for all those years of having multiple jobs and classes. Moreover, all their years of sacrifice had paid off, and I was all theirs. The next years were the ones I looked forward too with even greater anticipation. This would be a time when my focus could narrow even closer on my babies.

**Play Hard**

Our kids have lived the lives of adventurers. They have rafted down the Snake River of Wyoming, rode horseback in the Rockies, braved the white waters of the Colorado River, swam off the beaches of the Pacific, snorkeled the lagoons and underwater caverns of the Caribbean, parasailed above international waters, camped with grizzlies in Yellowstone National Park, snowmobiled the mountains of Wyoming, spent every summer at our family's Minnesota lake cabin, harvested trophy bucks in Wisconsin and Minnesota, braved the Canadian woods and waters, and dove off the Mexican cliffs of Xel-Ha. Yes, our children have had some of the richest experiences known to man. Some might say that my children have been spoiled. I say we are blessed as a family. Well, and maybe a little spoiled.

**We Were Real**

It was not the trips that mattered, it was the memories we were making. It was the laughter that was created. Recalling things such as our trips to the family cabin or the cliffs of Xel-Ha gave me the ability to close my eyes and fall asleep. No matter the air or water temperature, Clint was always the first one to leap from the dock at the cabin. Of course, it was usually prompted by Megan, Bri, Kev, Ethan or Garrett daring him to do it. Even so, it never took too much encouragement. Then, who could ever forget when they were standing on the cliffs of Xel-Ha. The kids were scared to jump, but when we promised we'd be waiting at the bottom, they trusted us and leapt into the air. It mattered more to them that we'd be at the bottom cheering. It was these timeless memories that we took from such excursions. It was these memories that would continue to exist only in our minds and photos. It was the smile on a face, the excitement of the unknown, the love of being together . . . wherever we might be. At the time, I never realized what peace those memories would bring in just a few short years. Those memories and photographs of my family forever frozen together remain in my mind as evidence that we existed, that we were here, and that *we* were real.

**The Absolute Best of Times**

Even though we had some great times traveling, those weren't the best of times. The best of times were at home where it was never quiet but filled with the constant chatter of my children's voices. It was the loud singing that permeated the floor boards and wafted into our great room. It was the disagreements that eventually worked themselves out and fit perfectly into our puzzle. It was all part of us, the incessant gas of the fartinator, the cockiness of a young athlete, and the crisis of one being the drama to another. Not one of us would've given it up . . . not willingly.

We had reached a point where our hopes and dreams were all coming true. Our home resounded with the occasional scuffles among siblings, but overall, it was filled with joy, caring, and stability.

I remember all those mornings having breakfast together. There really are a million ways to make eggs, and each of our kids had a different preference. So, we would be poaching, frying, and scrambling. Then there were the mornings I lived for. Those were the mornings when the kids would surprise us with breakfast in bed. Of course, Clint would make the eggs. That was his specialty. He never did let anyone know what went into them. Garrett has spent years trying to figure it out and is getting very close. Meg would get the antique serving tray ready while Bri poured orange juice, and Kayla and Garrett prepared toast and bacon. I never did figure out who made the coffee. The coffee that made me smile caused discomfort at the same time as the thick flow of grounds worked their way down my throat. They were so proud of being chefs, and they never let us leave a bite on the tray.

Many times, there was a note signed by all of them stating how much they loved us.

I can't forget our family nights with popcorn and scary movies. The coffee table would be shoved to the side, and the kids would lay out their favorite blankets and pillows. In our great room, a movie theatre was created and many memories were made. Even more special to me were the nights when Tim was on patrol. The kids knew I hated to be alone but didn't want to make me feel like a baby. So, they would bombard me in my bed and crawl under the covers. Sometimes we would watch movies, and other times we would just tell stories. Nearly every time, they would fall asleep with me. Thank goodness it was a queen-sized bed! When Tim would come home from patrol, he would spend an hour carrying those babies to bed and tucking them into their covers. It was part of our ritual but also necessary so he had a spot to sleep. Then without fail, I would fall asleep listening to Tim grumble how hot the bed was from the many bodies that had been piled among the pillows and blankets. I would smile as I fell asleep. A part of me was sad for him because he would never know the fun he'd just missed. Those were the best of times.

**An Abundance of Love**

The kids were never stingy with their love and affection, but some public displays of affection were prohibited. One day, I was driving the boys to the pickup site for summer wrestling camp. They were leaving us for a few days to attend camp at a lake in northern Minnesota. Most may not realize that the kids were rarely apart from us for long periods of time. This camp excursion, although exciting for them, was going to be hard on me. They knew this. Who would make sure they wore their life jackets and put sunscreen on?

When we were only a couple of blocks from the school, Garrett reached over the seat and hugged me. He said that it would probably be really busy once we got to the school, and he didn't want to miss saying good-bye. He told me he loved me and would miss me. From the passenger seat, Clint burst into laughter while calling Garrett out. He said that Gar was just embarrassed to kiss me in front of his friends. Gar tried desperately to convince him otherwise but to no avail. As we pulled into the parking lot, there were boys everywhere with their bags. Clint winked at me as he got out of the car. Trying to respect Garrett's need for independence, I stayed in the car and told him I loved him, to be careful, and that I'd miss him. I was expecting Clint to cheat me out of his usual hugs and kisses. However, he came around the car, threw his arms around my neck, kissed me on the cheek, and told me he loved me. As he pulled away, he smiled and mouthed to Gar "that's how it's done." As I watched them load their bags into their wrestling coach's trunk, I felt truly blessed.

## Where Did this Closeness Come From?

I think we were close because my parents raised my siblings and me to be close. I have four siblings: Hollis, Todd, Kyle, and Bobbie. Our childhoods were also filled with hard work, adventure, and love. If any of us have ever needed each other, we have always been there. The depths of this love would be made known when my perfect world broke into a million pieces of despair.

My home is located right across the highway from the farm where I grew up, and my parents still live there. The kids were lucky to have such immediate access to them, and as a result, they became very close. My mom would always joke that if she called one of them for help, she could hear their feet on her porch before she hung up the phone. The kids had a love for our family that was unrivaled. Mom and Dad had dinner nearly every Sunday after church. All of my siblings and their kids would be there. It was a joy for us all. Most of the time, my nieces and nephews would end up at our house. Heck, there were years when Kevin and Ethan pretty much lived with us or Clint and Garrett with them. Almost all of the cousins were inseparable. There really was no line between my children and my nieces and nephews. They felt like "ours." I love all of my nieces and nephews as though they are my own. I am close with each of them in different ways. I cherish them all.

**An Extra Special Touch**

To show the kids they were always on my mind, I allowed them to request special treats for after school. If they didn't request anything, I'd just have one waiting. One day, sports were cancelled, and they arrived earlier than I expected. I was finishing their favorite brownies. Clint had a special liking for my brownies and usually ate the entire pan. When Clint was a young boy, I would always find a little line down the middle of the brownies shortly after I frosted them. Although none of my children claimed ownership of the artwork, the spot of chocolate on Clint's lips and pointer finger were a dead giveaway. On one particular day, I was just dumping the mix into the bowl when I heard Clint shriek in dismay. I nearly dropped the bowl as I turned to see what was wrong. He lunged at me and gasped, "*Mom*, my brownies!" I calmly asked him what all the fuss was about and assured him they'd be done soon. I had assumed he was upset because they weren't ready. He paused and said, "They're not homemade!" I was confused and replied that "I've never said they were." He said, "But Mom, you make everything homemade." I chuckled and said, "Not my brownies, Buddy!" He shook his head, and as he walked away, he muttered to himself, "They will never taste the same." The other kids never had a problem with the boxed-mix brownies that awaited them. They dug in and enjoyed them just the same. It took Clinty a while to accept that his favorite brownies weren't homemade by his mother but by Betty Crocker instead. Although he accepted it, he never let me live it down. In fact, when his friends would come over, he would be sure to tell them and then flash me an evil eye followed by his quirky smile.

**Nighttime Rituals**

Every evening we had supper as a family, enjoying a meal that the children often helped me make or at least requested. Then, at the end of every day, these beautiful babies would kiss us good night, exchange "I love yous," and say their prayers. Some nights, after my nighttime rounds were done, I would go back to one of my children's rooms, and we'd talk deep into the night. Depending on the night, we'd laugh, cry, snuggle, and even have difficult discussions. I recited stories my parents told me. I shared my dreams for them and my hopes. I'd encourage them to be kind to others, show respect for all people, and be whatever they wanted to be in life. My most peaceful feeling as a mother was crawling into my bed knowing they were all safely accounted for in their beds. My heart could rest with my mind at ease that they were all where they were supposed to be . . . at home.

**God Was a Huge Part of Who We Were**

Every Sunday, we had our spot in church. The kids were involved in youth group and Sunday school. Tim and I were even youth advisors for years. Our children were taught about a God that is big enough for anything to be possible. I didn't know that one day, God would need to be big enough to endure our hate. I didn't know to teach them that. We loved our God and what He had blessed us with.

And so it was . . . the kids meant everything to both of us. Every spare minute was spent with them. Given the choice of having a social life with our friends or being with the kids, we picked home. It didn't matter whether it was going to a sporting event, going to a church event, watching a movie, doing homework, or having a tough conversation, we always picked being with the kids. If they needed it, we found a way to provide it.

At the time, Tim and I were so happy that we made the decision to expand our family by having a few more children. It had been a long and hard decision. For years, we'd pondered how to have more and yet make sure that the ones we had would still be special. We never wanted them to feel like less. In 2006, our family was close and got along well. Overall, we were in the perfect place. All the plans were in motion for a new baby that would never come because of the loss of another.

**Home Sweet Home**

Our home was a place the kids didn't have to be; they chose to be here. Their cousins and friends also chose to be here. It was our oasis . . . our own little paradise. Our house was filled with people and laughter. Oh, that laughter . . . such a perfect blend that made one unmistakable sound of sheer joy. People would ask how we could stand to have so many kids around all the time. My response was simply that I loved it.

Although we were blessed in all walks of our life, it was not the big house or the toys that defined who we were. The truth is we would've been just as happy anywhere as long as we were together. I knew it then, and I know it today. If I could've chosen anyone's life in the entire world, I would've chosen mine. I had the perfect life. Then, total devastation came.

**OUR LOWEST OF THE LOWS**

Our journey on the highs slammed into a dead end. It ended so abruptly that it was as though we stepped in front of a moving train–it was perfect one second and gone the next. We weren't presented with a fork in the road. We were jolted into a life we didn't want or ask for. This new life was one we had no idea how to navigate. It was a life in which nothing would ever be right or peaceful again. I am writing this book to share our deepest low.

# CHAPTER 2
## He Prepares Me . . . But for What?

*"In the silence of the heart God speaks. If you face God in prayer and silence, God will speak to you. Then you will know that you are nothing. It is only when you realize your nothingness, your emptiness, that God can fill you with Himself."*
~Mother Teresa~

There are times in life when you hear or know things, yet your mind instantly jerks with cynicism. What I'm about to reveal to you will tempt such a response. For your own sake, I urge you to keep an open mind about what you are going to read.

I believe God speaks to us, and we tend to pass His voice off as our inner thoughts, our fears, our imagination, or what have you. We tend to make reality whatever makes us feel better. The fact of the matter is that God has spoken clearly to me several times. I'm not ascertaining that He walked through my front door, introduced Himself, pulled up a chair, and shared a cup of coffee with me. It was something different. It's something I've struggled to find a word for. It turns out that there is no such word, so I devised my own. It's a term that I referenced in the dedication of this book. The word is *hearence*. My definition of this word is "the ability to hear and feel a presence that, for all logical purposes, should not be there."

## CHERISH HIM

My first experience with hearence was in 1990 when Clint was born. As far as labor goes, he was an easy birth for me. After sixteen hours of hard labor, there was my beautiful little boy barely weighing over six pounds, and he was perfectly healthy. It should've been a time of sheer happiness, but a sense immediately came over me. I didn't tell anyone but my mother about this sense, and I didn't even tell her about it until Clint was a few years old. I didn't know how to explain it to Mom, but she immediately knew what I was talking about because she had also experienced the same sensation. This sensation is what I call *hearence*. This is where you, the reader, may feel things starting to get weird. For me, it was confusing. God spoke to me the night Clint was born and told me to cherish him. He explained that Clint was special and that he would not be here forever. He explained that one day I would lose him. Of course, my mind made immediate excuses. I told myself it was my emotions because my pregnancy with Clint's older sister had been rough. After thirty-six hours of hard labor, she was born with a low Apgar score. Basically, she was all but dead. She recovered quickly, but I ended up with pneumonia and air around my heart. Not to mention, I needed several stitches where stiches have no business being. Anyway, you get my point. Even though I thought otherwise at the time, I now know that it was God Himself speaking to me. For fifteen years of Clint's life, that message lay heavily on my heart, yet there were no more incidents of hearence.

I was always careful with Clint, as well as the other kids. I was so careful that it drove them nuts. Heck, it drove my family nuts too. My brother Hollis gave me a lecture for scolding the boys for riding his four-wheeler without helmets. In fact, his lecture led to another lecture by Clint. Clint told me, "I live life to the fullest and when it's my time to go, it will be a great day." What he said to me that day struck my heart so profoundly that I scurried for something to write it on. I found a *Country Living* magazine, scrawled his quote across the cover, and dated it. I thought it would be a perfect entry for his scrapbook, which he eagerly checked for updates from time to time. I smiled inside because I could already imagine Clint's giggle when he'd see it in there. He'd know that his mother had listened and received the message. Instead, in a few short months, it would be inscribed on his headstone.

## TOTAL DEVASTATION AWAITS YOU

In the spring of 2006, God spoke to me again. I was home on the farm, sitting in my chair having a cup of coffee and enjoying the crisp morning air. I just can't explain *hearence* adequately. It's the sensation of knowing you are not alone. You actually feel someone in the room with you, and you hear them speak. But they don't speak like you and I would speak. It's different. It's as though there is a thin veil between us; they are here and yet not here at the same time.

That day, God told me that something devastating was going to happen that year and nothing would ever be the same. Again, I quickly began to think that it was my own mind running rampant with crazy thoughts. After all, it was early spring in Minnesota. Maybe we would have a fire because of the talk about dirty furnaces and house fires. Or maybe it was because the news was predicting an overactive tornado season; it was just my luck that we'd finished our remodeling, and our house was going to blow away. I was frustrated with God because the divorce had been hard. Visitation issues and what seemed like constant arguments had made life difficult. I thought to myself, "Don't we deserve a break?" My mind tried to pass it off as those types of everyday worries.

## IT WILL SOON BE TIME

In late October 2006, I was in church with all of the kids. Clint was actually lay reading. He loved to participate in church, and he loved Hazel Run Lutheran. As he stood reading, I remembered when he helped with the Easter play put on by the adults. He had been up front reading his part. There wasn't a member of the church that hadn't been lurching from side-to-side wiggling their heinies in the pews. Clint had forgotten his belt, and his pants were falling down. He hadn't wanted to make it obvious when he was reading. So he had kept pulling his sweater lower and lower as his pants fell further and further. As he wiggled, the entire congregation had chuckled, winced, and wiggled their backsides in sympathy.

As Clint stepped down from the podium, my memory of that Easter Sunday faded away. Clinty was walking toward us and flashed me a look as though to ask "How did I do?" I nodded to him in approval as God began to speak to me. "Oh no", I thought to myself, "I'm going insane". Tim was standing to my left, and Megan was standing to my right. The room started to spin as that familiar sensation of hearence returned. God told me that it would soon be time to take Clint home. My mind fractured as tears fell down my face. Tim grabbed me from one side as Meg did from the other while both whispered "What's wrong" in unison. I couldn't speak. My mind argued back. "NO, not Clint! This is meant for someone else." I was so confused. What was happening to me? Was I going insane? What did all of this mean?

## TIME TO REMEMBER AND TO WRITE

After a long day of writing, I decided to leave the comfort of my private cabin and venture out for some food. Just up the hill from my rustic bungalow is a restaurant our friends Harvey and Phyllis told us about. As I'm writing this, I'm sitting in a dinner lodge surrounded by antlers, taxidermy, and strangers. It's quite a grand place filled with both charm and class. It's beautiful and the service is outstanding, but I'm already missing home. My waiter, a young man working hard for a tip, is kind. He has no idea of the hurt that has spewed from my mind to my fingertips today. He reminds me of Garrett. He brought me the wrong salad dressing and quickly responded with "My bad." I couldn't resist asking him his age and telling him about my sons and daughters. He laughed as I told him of Garrett's frequent use of the same slang. As he chuckled, he scurried away to order up my prime rib.

The lodge has stacks of antlers clustered together with lights to form stunning chandeliers. This place immediately reminds me of our family hunting excursions. It makes me think of the trips to Tim's dad's house in Wisconsin. It makes me think of Tim's dad, Ray, and the difficulty he had with Clint's loss. It was hard for him to be strong for Tim when he didn't know how to deal with it himself. Just a few years later, Tim's parents would lose another grandson, Ian, in a swimming accident. We were estranged from them when they so desperately needed our support during those years. As I reminisce, my heart instantly aches for them and for Ian's parents, Mike and Kelly. I hope they felt even a small amount of love and support in the cards we sent. I needed them to know that we knew their pain and were praying for them. I hated that they had joined us in this gut-wrenching club in which even an amoeba would rebuke membership. My mind struggles to understand such senseless loss.

Oh my, this prime rib is fatty. I wish Tim were here. He loves this kind of meat. Oh well, I have nowhere to be. I will just slowly carve away at the fat as I interchange my bites with the clicking of the keyboard.

**IT IS TIME**

The next incident of hearence is eternally etched into my mind as though it's carved on placards of slate. It happened November 1, 2006, or since it was after midnight should I say November 2nd. This experience of hearence was different than the rest. This time, I felt God hold me as He spoke. I felt His arms around me while His grace and love filled the room. I knew this one would be bad. Why was it so different? It would soon be revealed to me. This time, it wasn't just a glimpse in time. My Lord and Father spent the entire night talking with me and holding me. It wasn't an angel or a disciple. It was God. He was there, in all His glory, just for me. Regrettably, I remember very little other than a tremendous respect for me and a full awareness of His extended presence. His words catapulted me into a cataclysmic state of denial. The words I remember the most stung my ears as if lye had been splashed in my eyes. He said, "It is time. I have come to take Clint home." I felt my heart fall from my chest, and only pain filled its place. My throat began to close, and I could barely utter words as the tears streamed down my cheeks. I felt desperate and betrayed as the room spun and my gaze went fuzzy. As I cried, I begged. I told him I had been a good mother to Clint and his siblings. I frantically pleaded . . . not my child . . . why my child? He simply replied, "Because you are strong enough to survive it." I argued with God that He was wrong and that I wasn't strong enough. That He had made a mistake. His assurance was unwavering and deafening. He stayed with me all night, but those are the only words I remember. More than the words, I remember the steadfast love He had for me. Even though my heart was filled with disobedience and denial, He comforted me.

## CLEARLY, I HAVE GONE MAD

That next morning, as Clint lay asleep in his bed, I sipped on my morning coffee and wondered if I should tell Tim. Do I tell him what just happened? Do I tell him God was with me last night? Do I tell him what God shared with me? I was tired from lack of sleep, but today I made no excuses as I had in my previous incidents of hearence. Today, I knew as He said, "It was time." Would Tim believe me anyway? Who in their right mind would? Why would God talk to me? Why would He warn me? I was lost! I didn't know what to do.

After sending the kids to school, Tim wanted to go for a morning drive to check the deer stands. I thought maybe a drive would take my mind off of last night. Maybe I was wrong but who was I trying to fool? There was nothing that could take my mind off of what I had just experienced.

Since we were going to drive into the pasture, Tim said we should take the truck. It was the same truck that we had used to bring the kids to the movies a few days ago. I couldn't help but remember that night and how I tried to reassure Clint on the way to the movies. He was worried about his friend who was in the hospital after a horrible accident. I remembered reaching into the back seat and rubbing his knee for comfort. While reminiscing, I could nearly feel his boney knee. It brought a smile to my face.

I pulled on my hiking boots, threw on my black-and-red plaid coat, twirled my hair in a clip, wrapped my earmuffs around my neck, and grabbed our coffee mugs. Even as I climbed into the truck, my mind was deep in thought.

As I stared from the window, the beautiful colors of fall were everywhere. There were miles of cornfields. Little did I know that this would be my last drive before these colors would hold new meaning and forever become a painful reminder of what was yet to come.

It was a quiet ride. My mind was far away from the inside of that truck. Years ago, we bought beautiful leather travel mugs. That morning, we filled them with hand-ground Starbucks coffee. It was the smell of coffee that pulled me back. In that moment, I would never have believed that I wouldn't even know what coffee was in a few short days.

As Tim was driving, he was singing along with the radio. He's the worst kind of singer: one that doesn't know he can't sing. His mother had warned me about this long before we were married. Without a doubt, she was right.

As we drove, I started telling Tim that I spoke to God last night. He joked, as he usually does when things get too serious, and said, "I hope he gave you the lottery numbers." Ghostly white, I turned to him and said, "I'm serious. He said it's time." Tim looked shell shocked and for once, lost for words. Somehow he knew it was about Clint. Somehow he knew that there was no margin for joking from this point forward. Rather, he tried to rationalize the situation. When he gathered his composure, he told me that with the recent loss of a boy at our school who was one of Clint's good friends, all of the mothers were worried about losing their children. He told me that my mind was working overtime with worry and that it was fear instead of God. I didn't tell him, but even in that moment, I knew it was God. I knew that God had indeed come to tell me that it was *time*. I knew my time with my son was limited.

I so desperately wanted to spend time with my kids that day. Although I'm an educator and know it's a cardinal sin to text your children during school, I texted each of them. I just needed to see them. I needed to see Clint. His phone wasn't working, but after school he called from a friend's phone. He said they were going to Montevideo to get some things together for his friend's funeral. I so desperately wanted to see him, but I knew his heart was in the right place. It was so much like Clint. He wanted to make others feel better. He wanted to support his friends with their loss. I told him it was a good idea, and I would see him later. He told me he loved me before we hung up.

Being the worrywart I am, I immediately bought him a new phone. I needed to be able to get ahold of him so I could support him through the tough days ahead. I was excited to give it to him. When he came home, which I might add was very late, he came into my room. As always, he hugged me, kissed me good night, and he told me he loved me. I tried to be mad at him for being late but just couldn't. I had the new phone next to my bed, and I picked it up and gave it to him. He screeched with excitement, jumped on top of me, hugged me again, kissed my cheek, and told me he loved me. He said he was going to stay awake all night putting numbers into it. As he turned to walk out of my room he turned back, and as his face filled with a smile he said, "Oh, Mom, I'm sorry for being late. I love you!" Again, I felt so blessed.

Obviously, Tim was right. I had been imagining things. Clint was just fine. He was under our roof, and at that very moment, he was in his room loading his friends' phone numbers into his new phone. He was perfectly healthy and happy. As I fell asleep, I let myself believe I had imagined all those ridiculous incidents of hearence. As Tim suggested, I was just worrying too much.

The next day, I told my mom and dad about the story in a roundabout way. I told them of my unfounded worries and explained that I feared if anyone in our family lost a child, it would be me and that it would be Clinty. My mom, with a tear rolling down her cheek, simply replied, "I know." In that moment, I knew that she knew. I knew that she and I shared a bond that I wished could be broken. A bond that I wished could be over anything else but my son dying . . . not that.

## WHY ME?

So, why did God choose to speak to me? I have no idea. Why did He choose to take my son home long before his time? To that, I also have no answer. I do know that my God and Father loved me enough to try telling me several times that my time with my baby was limited. Why did He tell me but not all of the other parents who have lost their children? I don't know. I only know that I should've listened. Why should I have listened? I'm not even sure. Would I have done things differently? Of course, I would've done some things differently. Do I regret being the mother I was to him? No, I don't. We had an amazing relationship filled with love and respect. Was it perfect? Not always, but it was close. We told each other that we loved each other every single day. In his short fifteen years, I know I received more hugs than most parents will get in a lifetime.

Garth Brooks wrote a song called "If Tomorrow Never Comes." I know the song was about a man who wondered if his wife would know how much he loved her if he died, but I often think about that song in relation to my Clinty. The answer is *yes*. I know how much he loved me, and in my sane states, I have little doubt that he also knows how much he was loved. For Clint, tomorrow never came, but my heart is fulfilled as though it did. Of course, that doesn't mean that I don't wonder. Furthermore, it doesn't mean that it doesn't feel good to be reassured by others. It just means that we loved deeply and that it *will* last us both until that amazing day when we meet again.

There will be skeptics who proclaim that God no longer speaks and that all we need to know is written in the Bible. I am no expert on the Bible, but I know that the

Father can speak to anyone He so chooses at any time for any reason.

So, when you have that nudging, niggling feeling that God is speaking to you, He probably is. Maybe He has been trying to reach you for a very long time. Do not make excuses or justify it as a crazy mind or as unwarranted worries. My prayer for you is that you will be brave enough to listen, bold enough to pay attention, and trusting enough to understand the path God has set for you.

# CHAPTER 3
## *That Horrible Day*

*"I loved you like there was no tomorrow.
Then one day, there wasn't."
~Author Unknown~*

This was the absolute worst chapter to write. Writing this chapter was coupled with the necessity to revisit a day I wish I could erase. The irony is it's the most vivid memory that lives within my brain. These memories flicker and flash through my mind hundreds of times each day. They pierce my chest with pain so extreme that no definition exists to describe it. I don't want you to fully understand it because understanding could only come with losing a child. My hope is for you to obtain a fragment of understanding from my words. To do this, I must replay the tape that has been locked away in my mind for safekeeping. This tape has caused my body to jerk, my eyes to roll back into my head, my fingers to turn to ice as they fumble for the keys, my stomach to feel as though it were being ripped apart, my eyelids to twitch uncontrollably, and my brain to seek refuge in numbness.

As I begin, the air in my office that generally has the pleasant smell of vanilla changes to odors of fall, and then it quickly changes to the smell of blood. I taste bile, my body trembles, and I feel nothing but cold. What I'm about to share is not for the faint of heart; it will sicken you, and it will hurt. For causing these things, I'm so sorry.

It was the weekend of the 2006 Minnesota deer hunting opener. We didn't get any deer on the first morning. When we went in for lunch, all of the kids decided they wouldn't go back out for the evening hunt. The girls decided to stay at the house to hang out with their foster sister, Sherreiea. The boys decided to head to a family birthday party in Fergus Falls with their paternal grandparents. No one was upset because there were still several good hunting days ahead. After a warm bowl of chili, everyone went their separate ways.

While the boys waited for their grandparents to arrive, they hugged and kissed me good-bye. I always gave them way too many kisses just to see if I could irritate them. Deep inside, I knew I really did it because I couldn't get enough of them. They were precious to me, and I wanted to cherish every second. Garrett took his kisses and ran outside. Clint laughed and said, "Geez, Mom. I'm going to be right back." As they got into the car, I noticed that Clint's grandpa let him drive. I was thankful for this. Clint looked so proud. I watched the boys drive away into the horizon. I often watched the kids drive away, never knowing if I would ever see them again. As it turned out, that was the last time I would ever see Clint. When the boys came home that night, they yelled "good night" and said they were headed right for bed. It was such an extremely rare occasion that I didn't go to their rooms and tuck them into bed. That night my parents were visiting, and by the time they left, I thought the kids were already asleep. Since we'd be getting up early the next morning, I didn't want to bother them. I would live to regret not tucking them in that night.

## EVERYTHING'S NORMAL

The next morning as Tim went to wake Clint, I tried to wake Garrett. Garrett was sprawled out in front of the great room television. He'd fallen asleep after sneaking up to watch movies late that night. When I wiggled his arm in an attempt to wake him, he could barely utter a response. He told me he wanted to sleep in but would probably go out hunting at noon. Then, I began to prepare our lunches and boil the apple cider. When Tim came upstairs, he told me that Clint decided to sleep in as well. I wasn't surprised by either boy's decision. They both said they would join us at noon. This wasn't uncommon. After all, they weren't die-hard hunters like Tim but rather two teenage boys who needed their sleep.

Sherreiea and Megan were also at the house. Sherreiea was going to make us dinner, and Megan was going to hang out with her. Both Kayla and Briana decided to come with us to our hunting stands. Bri would go with Tim, and Kayla would come with me. We were always careful to ensure that the kids had an adult with them. Because Tim is a firearms safety instructor, safety has always been of the utmost importance.

## WHY DID I SUDDENLY FEEL SO ILL?

I remember feeling terrible that morning. Everything in me told me to stay home. My stomach was hurting as though someone had cut a hole in it and was tearing everything out. As I hurried to pack our lunches, I could barely stand upright. I still remember how tempting it would've been to lay down on the throw rug in front of the sink. I didn't want to disappoint Tim, so I decided I would bear the pain and go with. Before quickly leaving the kitchen, I grabbed a pen and crossed November 5th off the calendar. Little did I know that the day was far from over.

I kissed Garrett on the cheek as he lay in front of the great room television. I walked to the stairs to give Megan and Clint their kisses, but I hesitated as I looked at my feet. We had recently laid new carpet, and I had been scolding the kids about needing to take their shoes off before walking on it. Since I had my boots on, I thought I should be a good role model, so I made the decision not to take them off. I broke from a strong protocol and didn't go downstairs to kiss Clint and Meg good-bye. I always kissed the kids good-bye. I never left home without doing so. I will never know why I made a decision to deviate that day. This simple and snap decision would later haunt me.

Just after arriving at my parents' north farm, we went to each of our stands. Tim had built me a beautiful stand the year before. He made sure it had everything exactly as I wanted it. It had two stools (one for me and one for a partner), a toilet, a roof, carpet on the floor, and a full shelf for my coffee cup, binoculars, snacks, camera, phone, and whatever else I might need. Since I sometimes make a little more noise than he prefers, he made sure to carpet the shelf to minimize the sounds that I'd most certainly make.

That morning was different than any other morning that I've spent in my stand. I felt horrible. I couldn't even concentrate on watching for deer. I felt so very ill. My stomach was in such severe pain that it felt as though my womb was being torn out through my belly button. I actually laid myself down on the floor in agony.

Around 8:00 a.m., I was startled by a shot in the distance. I thought that someone by our house was lucky and got a deer. Despite all the shots going off that morning, I've never forgotten the sound of that single shot ringing through the fields. For some reason, it spoke to me. Later, with all my heart, I would come to believe that it was not a deer that was hit with that shot. It was my son.

## WHAT IN THE WORLD IS GOING ON?

After a couple hours of lying on the floor of my stand, I got up to my stool. I saw a deer in the distance. It was a strange sensation. I took aim, held the deer in the crosshairs of my scope, and pulled the trigger. It was a textbook shot just as Tim taught me. The deer jumped and stood in the same spot. It was as though the slug never even left the chamber. I ejected the shell casing, adjusted my shotgun, and fired a second shot. Again, the deer never moved. With great mystique, it simply stared at me as though it was sad. Even though I never get nervous when hunting, my hands started to tremble uncontrollably. I felt as though I needed to throw up. Something was absolutely wrong. That deer only stared at me. Then, all of a sudden, black birds were everywhere! They started to fly through the openings of the deer stand right at me. I was both stunned and frightened by the eeriness. Not knowing what else to do, I grabbed my camera and took pictures. It was so different than anything I had ever experienced before; I knew it must have meant something. I wondered if something terrible was happening in the world. Was it ending? Even though

I knew it was too early to leave, I called Tim from his stand.

Tim came right away. He knew it was out of character for me to be nervous and upset. I felt so bad for the deer. It was still staring at me from a distance. Now, I could see a small trickle of blood running down its legs. It didn't take Tim long to spot my deer. Without speaking, he quickly took aim and fired at the deer. Even though it wasn't far from us, he also had difficulty hitting the deer. This was uncommon; Tim is quite a marksman. In fact, he ended up walking nearly right up to the deer to shoot it as it stood staring. Finally, the deer fell.

Tim dragged the deer over to the four-wheeler. He carefully tied a rope around its rack and attached the other end of the rope to the four-wheeler. I vividly remember my glove ripping in half as the deer was dragged behind the four-wheeler, bouncing across the field. I had Tim stop so I could recover part of my glove to sew back on later. All the while, I was still feeling so very sick. I told Tim it was like an evil omen had been cast over us . . . the difficulty harvesting the deer, feeling sick, and the swarm of black birds. Tim laughed it off as me being silly. He reminded me that the only omen in our woods was his gun, which we named after I had a dream about it. I dreamt we named it Nemo, which spells *omen* backwards.

As we loaded the deer, I could hardly wait to get home for lunch. As soon as we arrived, I would tell Clint I had won the bet and harvested the first buck of the season. I was already imagining his sheepish smile that would not only hide his own disappointment that he had not won but also beam with pride for my victory. I figured he would survive losing the bet. After all, he had harvested a trophy buck during Wisconsin's early youth season just a few weeks earlier.

## THE LAST TIME I EVER WENT "HOME"

When we arrived home, we were quickly met by my Garrett. He greeted us immediately so he could look at the deer in the back of the truck. He helped for a few minutes but then went chasing my dog that had found a rat the cats had dragged up. He knew I was scared of it, so he quickly covered it with a brick. Then he caught our dog, Belle, and put her back in her kennel. After seeing the rat, Garrett decided to go down to his grandparents' house to check on their rat-catching operation. He and Clint had been working with their grandpa to eradicate the rats.

Clint was nowhere to be found. I wondered if he was still sleeping. As Tim hoisted the just-gutted deer into the tree, I washed the deer's blood from the back of the truck. The smell of its warm blood and innards was nauseating. Little did I know that those smells and actions would forever be etched into my brain.

Glancing across the yard, I could see that Tim had located Clint. I smiled to myself. Clint was lying on the front yard watching the clouds. He loved those kinds of simple things in life and would often kick back and observe the shapes that clouds make.

## MY WORLD FADES TO BLACK

From the moment Tim found Clint, my mind faded to black. To help you understand, I will revisit the remainder of that morning just as it happened.

I can see him standing over Clint. Tim is slowly raising his head as he looks at me and waves me away. I can't imagine what they are talking about. Are they talking? I can't hear either of them or see Clint move. I wonder why Tim has such a look on his face. Tim and I have been married for a long time, but I have never seen that look before. Casually, my mind searches for what that look means. I don't know why, but time instantly stops and everything begins to move in slow motion. Things are beginning to make sense. After a recent accident of which a mother was kept from her son's lifeless body, I had told Tim that no officer better ever do that to me. I would need to be with my child. As though it's a fighter jet's radar, my mind locks in on what the look means. Tim is recalling that same conversation. Why is he recalling that conversation? I know something is *very* wrong. My only instinct is to get to Clint. I run to him, but it seems like I'm not moving. My legs won't move. They feel so heavy. It's probably only seconds, but it feels like minutes as I run to Clint.

Finally, I'm standing over my baby. Clint's lips are slightly blue, yet he looks perfect. His big blue eyes are gazing on the sky; one arm is across his chest, and the other is outstretched. What the hell is going on? Somehow I know he is gone, but at the same time, I feel trapped in a scene from a movie that I must just go along with. It's unreal . . . it's surreal.

As I stand over him, I instantly feel myself die. I know he's gone, but I don't understand yet. Even though only seconds pass, it feels as though it takes another ten minutes to touch him. My knees buckle and I feel myself on top of him. As I hold him chest to chest, he feels different. He feels like something solid and nothing like my baby. I feel no life. I would later realize it's what a body absent of its soul feels like. I hear somebody screaming, but I don't recognize the voice. I simultaneously feel something solid against my feet and something sticky on my chest.

What is going on? Where is Tim? I hear him in the distance, yet he's standing next to me. I think he's called 911. The exact words are bouncing inside of my head that is now filled with fog and barely processing. I think I hear him say that Clint has had an accident and shot himself. Just as he says it, I discover that the solid thing against my feet is Clint's shotgun. I notice his shoes are untied, there is dew on the grass making it slippery, his nose is blackened with a boney ridge, and there's a scope on his gun. All of this indicates that something has gone terribly wrong.

The stickiness against my chest is now on my hands, and it looks red. Red on my shirt, from what? Wait, his shirt is red. Maybe some of its dye has somehow rubbed off. No! That doesn't make sense. I touch his shirt and feel that it's a little cold and wet. I touch my chest and discover it's wet. What the hell is going on? I look closer at his shirt and discover it's soaked in blood but camouflaged by its original color. I'm confused, and my eyes will not focus. There is someone screaming. Would someone shut her up! There is a hole in his shirt. What the hell? I just bought Garrett and him these shirts. Why is there a hole? What has happened? Is he hurt? There is a shadow under the hole that looks even deeper. I look at his face and touch him. He's cold. Oh my God, he's been shot. I try to yell "HELP HIM! HELP HIM!" but I can't get the words out. My mouth is moving, but I can't get the words out. Wait, I hear that woman screaming again.

What is wrong with her? Can't she see what is going on? I look at Tim, and he looks lost. Everything is barely moving. My head hurts from that woman's screaming, and my mouth tastes of tears. Wait, I think I know that voice. She sounds so scared. She must think someone has died. Get her out of here. Someone get her some help. We need to help Clint.

I yell at Tim to give Clint CPR. I hear him whisper that it's too late. I tell him that it's not and to try. He tries. I see Clint's beautiful, flawless face spray with blood as air comes from his nose. Seconds before, Clint's face was beautiful. Now it has turned to horror . . . there is blood. Immediately, I desperately think about how I can make him better. My parents have always taught us that if we try hard enough, we can do anything. Yes, of course, then we can fix anything! I desperately wonder how I can help him. How can I fix this? He's cold, his lips are blue, and he appears to be dead. But wait! He looks so beautiful.

**PLEASE FIX HIM, PLEASE!**

I look for Tim and demand that he calls Kyle. Of course Kyle, my big brother, will fix this. Call him! Tim calls Kyle and tells him there has been an accident with Clint and to come right away. I later learned that Kyle was roofing at the time and that he jumped from the roof and drove over 80 miles per hour to get to me. Kyle later told me that he knew Clint was gone from my screams in the background and that he'd never heard such terror in my voice.

I turn my head and see Garrett running up the driveway. He stops at a distance and never comes closer. Why doesn't he come closer? This is a bad dream. If he came closer, he would wake me up. Months later, Garrett confessed that he came running to save me from a rat. He also said he had never heard anything worse than my screams. In fact, he said hearing my screams was worse than seeing Clint's body.

Soon, I see Sherreiea jumping off the deck with Megan. They must have heard that woman screaming. Would someone shut her up? She's going to scare everyone before we can fix this. They try desperately to give Clint additional CPR even though, deep down, we all know it's too late. We all know that too much time has passed. Yet, I'm still thinking that will all go away when somebody wakes me up.

## I HATE THOSE SIRENS

Although I never see him arrive, I feel my brother wrap his arms around me and pull me from Clint's body. To this day, I have no idea how he got there so quickly. I remember him saying "He's gone, Tan" over and over. I remember pleading "Fix him, Kyle . . . PLEASE!" It went back and forth as we sat on the ground with me between his legs, my back against his chest, and his arms holding me tight. We cried. I didn't realize until much later what I'd done to my brother by asking him to perform the impossible. I didn't realize the pressure I was unwittingly placing upon him. I was asking him to bring my son back from where you can't return.

I heard the ambulance screaming in the distance. Ever since, an ambulance siren evokes a physical reaction from me. My skin turns ghostly white, and I feel ill. It instantly makes my limbs grow stiff, and fear ignites within my soul. It mortifies me! I first quickly and desperately search to know where my children are located to ensure they are safe. Then, I seek to know where my husband, my parents, and my siblings are. If my mind lands on one and doesn't know their location, I must immediately find them. My children almost always know why I might be calling, but other family members have yet to figure out my nonsense calls. How odd I must seem to them because after I call them, we have awkward conversations. Then, all I can think of is getting off the phone and calling the next family member on my mental list.

Now, when Tim's on duty and responding to an emergency, he will turn off his sirens when he is a mile away from our house. He knows what the sounds do to my mind and heart. Just this small consideration has saved my senses more than he and I will ever know.

The ambulance is backing onto the front lawn. I think to myself that they should be careful. I would hate for them to crush the septic system as they back over it. I wonder why my mind would have such meaningless thoughts. When I wake up from this stupid nightmare, I will laugh about this. I never believed that I wouldn't wake up from this horror.

## WHY IS ALL OF MY FAMILY HERE?

In a short amount of time, family member after family member arrives. I see Mom and Dad pull up the driveway. My parents must have just come from church. My dad looks so handsome in his suit as he walks toward me, yet he has a face filled with terror. He momentarily stops as though he is scared to approach me. Mom never gets out of the car. This is my first realization that this is either a really stupid nightmare or a grave situation. My mom is a highly skilled registered nurse. If this is real, why isn't she running to Clint? I fear she knows that there is no saving him.

Soon, the paramedics ask me to step away. I don't want to, but Kyle tells me I have to. I trust him and do as he says. As I sit just a few steps away, my dad comes to hold me. Oh, no! Why is Dad so sad? What is that look on my dad's face. I can see him, but the earth is spinning so slowly. What is he saying? I can't understand. I scan the yard but can't see my sister, Bobbie. I look again and realize I can't see my brother Todd either. If this were real, they would be here. Maybe they are here. There are so many people. Why? Is Clint gone? Of course he's gone. No, he's not. This is a horrible nightmare that I will wake up from. Why else is everything moving so slowly in my mind? Why else is everyone's speech so sluggish? Then, I see them pull a sheet over his head. No! I run over and pull it down. Out the corner of my eye, I see my brother Hollis fall to his knees. What is going on? They cover Clint again. What? Why? I hear her screaming again. There is that stupid woman again. She does not belong here, not now. Wait . . . I do know her. Oh my God in Heaven, that screaming woman is ME!

Soon, they load Clint into the ambulance and ask me if I want to ride along. Of course, I do. They tell me I can go change, and they will wait for me. This is a dumb dream I'm having. In real life, they'd be trying to save him. I play along and go to the house. Who cares . . . soon I will be awake.

I remember everything as it was. The house was filled with our hunting gear, food was out for dinner, and people were gathering. So many family members are here . . . why? I quickly put a hair clip in and pull on a pair of jeans and a brown Henley T-shirt. These clothes will forever be frozen in my mind.

## OUR LAST RIDE

We are on our way to the hospital. Little did I realize this would be our last trip together in the same vehicle. Although this trip was much different than riding to the movies together just a few days earlier, I would later cherish these last miles together.

As I sit by his side, he lays still before me. I keep trying to close his eyes, but he is so cold. After a few attempts of gently brushing my hand over them, they close ever so slightly. It is the last sign of movement his body will ever offer. The blood on his nose bothers me because it wasn't there when we found him. I see a canister in the ambulance. It is a small tub of bleach wipes among the oxygen tanks, breathing hoses, and syringes. I grab it, pull out a wipe, and wash my son's face for what would be the last time. I feel uncomfortable as the crew member watches me. He may not be thinking this, but it feels as though he thinks I am not allowed. I gently wipe away the blood that had sprayed over Clint's face. My mind flashes to when I would wipe his nose when he was little. Then, he would struggle against me so he could run off and play, and maybe because it hurt a little. Today, I am careful not to hurt his nose. It looks as though it has been hurt already. It is blackened across the bridge and has a slight ridge in it. I wonder if it is broken. I can't help but wonder what has happened in the short time since I last saw him. I touch it, and it feels sharp under the skin. It feels so different. My mind flashes to his gun, that stupid youth-model gun. Clint has grown so much in the last year that he is nearly too big for it. Could he have misjudged its position when he pulled it to his face? Could the gun have recoiled, sending the sharp edge of the scope into his nose? I've had this happen myself. I feel his nose again. Yes, it is broken. I wish it could be like when he was little; he would've been struggling against me by now, gotten up, and run off to play. Instead, he doesn't move.

His hand lays on the gurney next to me. I pick it up and hold it like I have done so many times before. I would hold it when he was sad, when he'd gotten a boo-boo, to keep him safe when crossing the street, and to tell him I loved him. You see, my Grandma Weber had a stroke before she died, and she couldn't talk as a result. One day, I squeezed her hand three times while saying "I love you." To my surprise, she squeezed back to let me know she loved me too. When I grew up, I always did this with my kids. When I would squeeze their hand three times, they knew what I meant, and they'd squeeze back. We did it at lots of places. We did it if we were in a room with others, in church, at the movies, or passing by each other in a room just to be silly. So, now in the ambulance, I take Clint's hand and squeeze it three times. I wait and silently beg for a response, but his response never comes. There is only complete stillness and silence.

## HOSPITALS ARE FOR SAVING PEOPLE

I've grown up believing hospitals are for saving people. As we pull into the back of the hospital, I watch as they unload Clint. I realize, without hope, he won't be saved by this hospital's staff or by any others. With full clarity, I know that he is gone and that this isn't a nightmare I will wake from.

As they bring his gurney into a room, I am led into a waiting room. There, I find the rest of my family. I am not sure how Megan, Garrett, Kayla, Briana, and Sherreiea arrive.

God sends an angel to me this day. It is a woman named Verla. She works at the hospital and, in recent years, lost her son. She knows my pain and is careful to respect our loss. Through the intense fog, she makes me feel human. Although I am numb, her touch is intense. I know we will meet again.

I can hear screams from the hallway. Some I recognize and some I don't. I am too numb to care. My son is gone. The Bureau of Criminal Apprehension is here asking questions about the incident and Clinty. Really? This seems like such an intrusion during our tragic loss. Nothing they are going to do or discover is going to bring him back. Their work can wait.

Soon, I am allowed to see him . . . my Clinty. My mom and dad are with me. Why is an officer in here? Why am I being told I can't touch him? The officer appears to be uncomfortable. Even in my pain, I feel bad for him. Without words, it is as though he is apologizing for his presence. He looks the other way and allows me to touch and kiss my son. He, who shall remain nameless but forever respected, has the sense about him to know what I, Clinty's mom, needs. I need to caress his face, brush his hair from his eyes, and kiss his lips. I need to say goodbye. My last vision of my beautiful boy is of him on a gurney in a hospital's small emergency room with bags on his hands, a sheet pulled high on his chest, Megan and Garrett at my side, my mom and dad in one corner, and an officer in the other corner. Never for a moment do I realize that Clint will never look the same again.

After that, they take me home. Home . . . where is that . . . what is that? The home I knew had five children waiting for me. This place doesn't.

# CHAPTER 4
## *Unimaginable Decisions*

*"The loss of a child is totally different because it's contrary to nature,...when it happens, you question everything you've ever known."*
~Kyle Petty~

    When we pulled in the driveway, home felt different. It wasn't just because it was scattered with dozens of cars and what appeared to be hundreds of people; it was because I'd never been there without all my babies safely accounted for. Even in my fogged and distraught state, I already felt that so much was missing. Clinty was missing, my sense of peace was missing, and the way I thought of my family was missing. I got out of the car not noticing we'd even driven from the emergency room. We'd already travelled the six miles home, but nothing was moving, yet everything was moving in slow motion. There were people outside and inside, yet I couldn't really see or hear them. I looked at them, but it was as though they weren't there. I kept reassuring myself that I was stuck in a bad dream, and I'd wake up soon. Like an actress in a movie shoot, I anxiously waited for someone to yell "cut" so this scene could be over.

    There was food everywhere. I guess people were bringing food over for everyone to eat. The smell of it nauseated me. How on earth could people think of eating? I could hear their chatter and sometimes their laughter. Why were they laughing? If they wanted to laugh, they should go home. There was this noise. The sound kept shrieking, causing a burrowing pain in my head. Someone handed me something and said the phone was for me. A phone; what's a phone? It was obviously the source of that horrible noise. They instinctively put it to my ear. I recognized the voice right away. It was my friend Loddie. She lived out of state; why was she calling me? Is she part of this stupid dream too? All she said was "Don't talk Tan. I just want you to know that I am on my way and will be there soon. I love you." I put the phone down while my heart sank. Is this real? I convinced myself that it was ok and everything would be fixed when I woke up from this nightmare.

Some of the first people I recognized were our friends Harvey and Phyllis. They held me so tight. Why? Why would they do that? This is a crazy dream with so many people in it. It's like one of those feature films in which they bring all of the big stars together. This dream brought together those I love as well as some I would just see on occasion at the local grocery store. Yes, this is the craziest dream I've ever had. I want to wake up! If this were real, there would be no food, no laughter, and no people around. I didn't like having people around. I'm a recluse. Alright, I'm convinced this isn't real. My thoughts fade to what I know to be true. My thoughts fade to yesterday.

## I PROMISE, CLINTY

I couldn't have asked for a more amazing young man to call my son. He was kind, loving, and never missed a day without telling me how much he loved me. When I saw him yesterday, I must have kissed his face a million times trying to be silly with him before he left for a short day trip. He just laughed and told me he'd "be right back."

My mind flickers. I'm dreaming again. Clint was wrong. He would not "be back soon." The next time I actually saw him, he was lying on the ground. I knew right away he was gone. It wasn't a horrible scene like some might imagine. His eyes were open (beautiful blue eyes just sparkling in the sunlight); he was smiling with one arm outstretched and the other across his chest. There was really no blood at all. He had on a reddish shirt . . . so I couldn't see any blood. If the gun wouldn't have been there, I wouldn't have known what had happened. Even so, my mind still struggles to accept it.

A huge part of me died in that moment. I knew there was nothing I could do to make things right ever again. Not for me, my kids, anyone else who loved him, or Clint himself. I'd failed miserably as a mother. My job was to keep them safe. I always tried so hard. How could this have happened? I needed to escape this new reality!

That night as I lay alone without one of my babies, I promised that I would get up every day. I also promised that I would not drink or find other unhealthy escapes and that I would continue to be a good mom to the other children. I never wanted them to look back and feel that they'd lost their mom that day too. I was determined to live a good life for them!

**THE CALLS**

I'm not sure when I fell asleep that first night. The last thing I remembered was a phone call. I remember Tim asking me "Will you take a phone call?" I uttered, "No, I will not take a phone call." Tim said, "Tan, it's the organ donation center. They only have a few hours before donation is not an option." I instantly recalled taking Clint for his driving exam earlier that year. He passed and was very excited. We went to complete the paperwork so he could get his driver's license. As we filled out the paperwork, we came across the question "Do you want to be an organ donor?" Clint looked at me and said, "What do you think, Mom?" We briefly talked about it being a personal choice for him to make and how it would be a gift to a family who was faced with losing a loved one. After that, the decision was easy for him. He checked *yes*. My mind flashed back as Tim said, "Well, what do you want me to tell them?" I took the call.

Although it wasn't meant to be, the call was torture. It probably lasted for only thirty minutes, but it felt like it lasted for hours. There were so many legalities to approve Clint for organ and tissue donation. Many questions were asked to ensure he was healthy and that his donations would be safe for a recipient. Although they were necessary, I found the questions to be both frustrating and angering. Was he sexually active? Was he a homosexual? How many partners did he have? Was he an IV drug user? Has he ever been exposed to hepatitis? These were hideous questions for a mother who had just lost her son. I was frustrated because although I felt I knew the answers, I couldn't face the fact that I would never be able to ask Clint if my answers were right.

Not long after I hung up the phone, there was another tap on my shoulder. It was my friend Loddie. She had arrived. She told me there was another phone call for me, but I had no strength. All I could do was shake my head *no*. She told me I needed to take the call and that it was a mother who lost her son in an accident. As it turned out, I took the call. I'm not sure, but I think we talked for hours. I found it helpful. The calls kept coming from other parents. At first, I was annoyed. After all, I was *not* one of them. I was having a bad dream that I would wake from, and those poor parents had children who were dead. No, I wasn't one of them. Even though the calls gave me comfort, I hated those calls! Now, with hindsight, I know how courageous those parents were. I know the love and compassion they were extending. I'm forever grateful.

**SLEEP**

As I fell asleep that first night, I was utterly exhausted. I remember our good night rituals with each of the kids, and as always, I felt Clint put his arm around me, tap Tim on the shoulder, and say good night. I didn't realize what I'd just experienced until days later.

That first night was nearly sleepless. In the morning, I woke up believing I was drained from experiencing a horrible nightmare. I tasted vomit in my mouth. Wow, that nightmare was realistic. I dreamt I found Clint shot on the front yard of our farm. I dreamt that when we came home from the emergency room, I threw up profusely from the front porch. I dreamt some idiots in the background saying I must be ill. I thought to myself that it was clearly a nightmare because who would be so stupid to think that a mother who was throwing up after finding her son's body had some illness. Seriously, what a dumb dream! I was embarrassed that my subconscious had created it.

As I looked around, I wondered why we'd slept in the living room with the kids. I quickly passed it off by rationalizing that we must have fallen asleep while watching a movie together.

As I rose, I noticed that extended family members were scattered everywhere about the room. My brothers and sister never stay over. What are they doing here? Instantly, my brain was flooded with the events of yesterday . . . the deer, the lawn, the ambulance, Clint. Oh, my God! What happened? Even though I frantically scanned the room for Clint, I was silent and didn't move. He was nowhere among the sleeping relatives. I rolled over to Tim and asked him, "Where is Clint? Did he have an accident?" He didn't respond and only pulled me close. Without further words, I knew that yesterday was real. Tears fell down my face, and suddenly I felt faint. I put my arm around Garrett and Meg, who were lying next to me, and closed my eyes.

For many years, I would wake and ask Tim that same question over and over: "Where is Clint? Did he have an accident?" Honestly, I always maintained the hope that he'd respond differently. I'd even role-played it in my mind. He'd cock his head to the side, give me a sassy grin, and say, "Of course he's here. Did you have a bad dream?" That day never came.

**PROMISES! PROMISES!**

Later, I hear them whispering but am not sure exactly what they are saying. I hear the words *funeral*, *home*, and *bath*. I guess they must think either I stink or a warm soak would do me some good. Tim starts the shower, and my friend lays out some clothes. Clothes, I think to myself. Where do they come from? Soon, somehow I find myself undressed in the shower with water running down my face. The water, it's warm. Warm like . . . like Clint's blood. Oh, no! The rest of his blood is washing off my hands. My cheek and lips are being washed free of everything left of him. It's on me from when I placed my cheek against his and from when I kissed him yesterday in the hospital as he lay lifeless in the emergency room. I don't want it to go. It's all I have left. They won't let me out. They tell me it's good for me. I can hear more whispering. They are actually in the bathroom with me. What do they think I'm going to do? That's the problem. They know what I'm going to do. Every few seconds, one of them pops their head in. My old self would have hated this. I'm about the shyest and most private person I've ever met. Today, I don't care. I don't even feel life in me let alone care if someone sees me naked. I'm just a shell. It'll all be over soon anyway. Soon, I'll be with Clint. I feel myself slide down the wall and slip to the floor. I see a bottle that says shampoo, another that says conditioner, and yet another that says bodywash. What the hell are they? What am I supposed to do with all this stuff? I just want to be somewhere else. Someplace where I can hold my baby. Then, I see a razor. I know what that is and what it can do for me. I know that little blade stands between me and the arms of Clint. I reach for it as Tim calls my name. I tell him that I'm fine. This seems to assure him that all is well. What little he knows. He's not in control, I am. Just two seconds and all of this pain would be gone.

As I shut my eyes, my head rests against the wall. The water is hot, but I am shaking. I realize that I was in shock. Clearly, I was also shaking from the thoughts taking over my mind. Although it was probably for only moments, I held that razor for what felt like an hour. As the tears stream down my face and become one with the water, they swirl down the drain. Down the drain into that same mysterious place where Clinty's blood went after being washed from my hands yesterday. Why? Why is this happening to me? What have I done so wrong? I push the razor against my skin and feel that it's sharp. Yes, I think to myself, it can do the job.

My thoughts are interrupted by chatter. I hear the kids outside the open door to the bathroom. It's Megan and Garrett talking. It's my babies. I remember the promise I made to Clint and to God. This will have to wait for another day. Today, I'll live for my kids and leave a better legacy for them. I'll live so they know they are loved.

The razor falls to the floor, and the gateway to my son closes. Once again, Clint feels so far away. The sound of the razor hitting the floor startles me, and I realize I'm shaking uncontrollably from water that has now turned ice cold. How long have I been in here? It doesn't matter. I have nowhere to be. My life is over. Whose life is over? Who am I? The woman I know has five beautiful children she tucks into bed each night. The woman that has taken over my body is lost. Please, God, let me go back. I miss her already. I hate this woman I must now call *me*.

Every day, the scene is different, but the decision is the same. The difficult decision to shut that gateway to Clinty is too much power for someone who lives with so much pain. And the pain is just beginning.

## OBITUARY, FOR WHOM?

I hear Chris. She's a dear friend. They let her in the bathroom with me. We sit in the bathroom for what feels like hours. I sit on the toilet. She just sits at my feet. I tell her they're worried about a seemingly sad entry from Clint's journal. She reassures me it's nothing, that Clint is safe, and that we will deal with it later. She tells me how she looks up to me as a mom and how she is inspired by the love I have with my kids. She tells me what I need to hear. She tells me Clint loves me! She warns me never to doubt what my heart knows to be true about my beautiful boy.

    I hear talk outside the door about an obituary and a funeral home. I think to myself, why me? I'm not supposed to be doing this. Not my son! He belongs here! Chris makes me a promise that we will get through this and that she will not leave me.

    There are so many people around. I once thought I would hate having these observers in my home if I lost a child. That was so naive. These people have come to support us. They've come to feed us. They've come to wash our clothes and clean our house. They love us! I'm grateful to them.

    In the corner of our great room sits an antique square table I just refinished a month earlier. I had waited for Clint to come home from school to help me carry it in from the shed. He was such a strong young man. I knew it would be effortless with his help. That day, he also helped me carry in an old sewing cabinet I had refinished. It was my grandma's. Clint was sentimental. He told me that because he helped me, both would be his when I died. I had agreed with him! Unaware of what that table meant to Clint, my family sat at it waiting for me to write his obituary.

    My thoughts began to flow. We need to list all of his parents. He loved them, even the stepparents. We need to talk about his smile. Yes, his smile is the most important thing. That is what we need people to remember. Oh, we also need to write that he lived life to the fullest every day. We need that in there too. Things kept bombarding my thoughts and jumping out of my mouth. I urgently felt that everyone needed to know him as I did. Everyone there had input. My friend Loddie was home from Missouri to assist. She's a good writer. She was careful to clear every word with me. She knew I needed it perfect, and it was. I am forever indebted to her for her steadfast loyalty to me and Clint.

**FUNERAL**

The decisions were just beginning. What does he wear? Do we show him? Do we bury him? Do we cremate him? How much does it cost? Do you want flowers on the casket? How about flowers from the kids? Rent the casket or buy the casket? Who pays for what? What do we do with the cards? What do we do with all the flowers? What do we include in the program? Is the wake program the same as the church program? Do we have pictures? Where should we have the wake? Where will the funeral be held? Will someone sing? What songs did he like? Will someone read? Who will give the sermon? Will we allow open commentary or readings? What do we wear? Do the kids have appropriate clothes? Where do we plant all of these trees that are being delivered? Who keeps the gifts his friends are giving? Headstone . . . what goes on a headstone? Where do we put a stone? Where do we spread his ashes? Do we spread his ashes? What do we do with his room? What do we do with his clothes? How do we keep his memory alive? Most importantly, how can I ever love a God that could take my son?

The questions and decisions were literally endless and still pop up today. Each question has been encountered with grace and respect for Clint, his brother, and his sisters. I always asked myself . . . what would they want?

**I WANT CLINT**

That afternoon, I was feeling defeated, lost, and alone; I wanted desperately to be near Clint. I knew I couldn't literally be with him, so I wanted to go outside. Tim didn't want me go to where we found him, but I felt like I needed to. So, I went to the front yard where we found him just yesterday. Even though it was just over a day ago, it already felt like an eternity since I'd seen my oldest son.

People followed me to the front yard. It was so annoying. I just wanted to be alone where he spent his last moments. I wanted to feel him; I needed to feel him. I wondered where he had been found. I veered off to the east when I heard Tim call me back. He asked me what I was doing. I explained that I wanted to know where Clint had been. He told me it didn't matter and that the area had been cleaned by the deputies. Wrapped in a blanket and shivering, I was weak and could barely raise my head to look at him. He instantly knew from my swollen and pain-filled eyes that it did matter. No more words were spoken as he took me to the spot. There, I collapsed onto my knees, pulled my arms from the warmth of the blanket, and ran my fingers across the cold, hard ground. I was looking for proof that my baby had been there. I was looking for anything left behind. As my fingers caressed the lawn, tears fell down my face. I could feel the warm drops hit my hands. They didn't faze me. My fingertips just kept searching the grass. I knew people were watching me from the edge of the house as well as through the front windows. I wished they would've given me some privacy and peace. Why must they be here? Where is their grace? Soon, my hands found what I so desperately hoped not to find. It was wet and sticky. As I turned my hand over, there was blood. I parted the grass as though looking for lice on my dog. I searched for anything else. There was more blood, and soon there were fragments that I knew were once part of my beautiful Clinty. I pulled a Kleenex from my tank top, wiped the blood on it, and put the fragments inside of it. I continued to pick and collect what should've never been there. Only a mother would care about what was overlooked and left behind on the lawn. So there on my lawn, I picked until I could find nothing more. Then, I laid myself down where he had last lain. The cold of the ground chilled me to my bones. Maybe, I thought, I could get so cold that I would shatter into a million pieces, and the pain would end. Through my tears, I saw a mouse playing on the rocks. In a normal state of mind, I would have screamed and ran. I'm terrified of mice. Today, I chuckle to myself and wonder if Clint was trying to make me smile.

# CHAPTER 5
## *A Mother's Goodbye*

*"No matter what anybody says about grief and about time healing all wounds, the truth is,
there are certain sorrows that never fade away until the heart stops beating and the last breath is taken."*
~Author Unknown~

I woke that morning with the sun shining through my east window. It was one of those mornings when you can just tell that it was crisp outside. That's a kind way of saying it was cold. I hate the cold. Have you ever felt that moment when you pull back the covers and feel the rush of cold air that taunts you and dares you to crawl out of your safe, warm bed? That moment had come.

I prayed the thoughts running through my head weren't real. I prayed the last days were a compilation of one terrible evening of nightmares. I pulled back the covers and sat with my feet dangling over the edge of the bed. This morning was different because I couldn't feel the cold. We have one of those high beds with a mattress that is far from the ground. I often rest my feet on the large wood rails before turning onto my stomach to push myself off. Today, that rail doesn't stun my feet with the chill that settled overnight. This morning, I feel nothing. As I scoot off the bed just like I did as a young girl on the farm, I wished that I was a little girl again. I could start over. I could go back in time. I could protect Clint. He'd be here today. My thoughts quickly switch to my mom and dad. Maybe they could fix this. After all, they're among the smartest people I know. Mom's an RN, Dad's an engineer, and both are farmers at heart. Even in my mental fog, I knew this wasn't possible. I knew they wouldn't be able to fix Clint. For the first time in my life, my mom and dad couldn't help me. I was treading in water they had never swam in before. They had no experience with losing a child. I would have to face this road alone without the benefit of their wisdom. Even in this short time, the road was already lonely. For the first time in my life, I couldn't turn to them.

Before I get out of bed, I usually adjust my tank top to make sure nothing is hanging out for the world to see. This day, I don't care. This day, they tell me I need to bury my baby.

Bury my baby . . . that doesn't even make sense. Clint won't be buried. He will be cremated immediately following the service. There will be no casket in the ground. He will be free. That beautiful body that was his canister here on earth will be returned to the very earth he walked. He's no longer there. I'm not sure where he is. I mean, I know he's in Heaven, but where is that?

## I MUST WRITE

I see my laptop next to my bed, and I feel compelled to write. It's my first inclination that something else is happening. I don't like to write. In fact, I hate writing. Today, however, I must write. Over the years, I had planned so many things for Clint. There were birthday parties, sleepovers, confirmation, and campouts. This funeral is the last thing I ever get to plan for my Clinty. It has to be perfect. No one can do justice to my son at his funeral better than me. I was, no I *am*, his mom. This isn't a funeral today. This will be a celebration of his beautiful life. Clint was and still is a gift, and by the end of today, everyone will know it!

They hear me awake and come into my room. They never leave me alone. They still know that my thoughts are dangerous to my very being. They know I miss my baby. It's Tim. He tells me he loves me and adjusts my tank top. In these few short days, he has become good at dressing me. Honestly, it's hard to comprehend what clothing even is. I guess I should be glad he's here, but it's hard when I just want to be somewhere else . . . anywhere else.

Soon, a few of my friends and my brother, Kyle, enter the room. I can tell he's annoyed by one of my friends and her tendency not to leave my side. He needs to be alone with me. Tim can tell too, and he makes an excuse to call that friend away. Kyle hugs me and weeps. We've never been in such a vulnerable situation together. None of us knew what to do. He just holds me. I've always been able to tell when he needs something. I could feel it in his hug. He is nervous and filled with pain. He wants me to know there are rumors that Clint intentionally hurt himself. Our kids heard the rumor at school, and the town was seeking pleasure from such exciting conversations. He said our children and Clint's friends were being hurt by the rumors.

In that moment, I didn't care what those people were thinking. Kyle assures me that he would leverage the truth and that now isn't the time for worrying about such fodder. My big brother is here to take care of me. I know he will do what needs to be done. I feel safe.

I tell him I need some time alone. When I look into his eyes, I see only sadness and fear. He looks as though he's aged twenty years since yesterday. His eyes are puffy with his eyelids lined in bright red. He's been crying. Of course he has. He loves Clint. I can tell he is even sadder when he looks into my vacant eyes. "You need time alone?" he questions. I explain that I need to write a letter for the funeral. I need people to know about Clint. He knows his sister is stubborn and there is no use in arguing. Not even in my comatose state is there a chance he'll prevail. He tells me he will be in the other room if I need him.

Over the course of the next hour, several people kept popping their heads in and checking on me. My eyes never strayed from the keyboard. It was as though I was alone. I was alone in my memories of Clint.

## TIME TO GET READY

Soon, Tim came and told me it was time. I assumed he means it was time to get ready for the funeral. They put me in the shower: the same place I had been the day after the accident. I don't think I've been in there since then. Today, there was no blood to wash away. Instead, there were only tears that had dried in several layers on my face. I could taste the salt as they washed from my face and traveled down my body to the drain. The drain that now holds a part of Clint forever. The drain where I watched his blood swirling away just a few days ago. I didn't use any soap or shampoo. Looking back, I no longer knew what those items were. The water just washed over my stoic and hollow body.

They told me to dress in something black. Why black? To this day, I still wonder if I wore either my little black dress or a black skirt. All I know is that I wanted to wear my blue sweater. It was blue like Clint's stunning eyes. Somehow, wearing it made me feel close to him. I pulled it off the hanger and put it over the black I was requested to wear. As it slid over my arms, I realized I didn't dry myself off. That's right, when you get out of a shower or bath, you're supposed to dry yourself off. I'd forgotten. I'm sure I wore shoes, but I don't remember what they were. There was no makeup and no fancy hair. While I was still dripping wet, I pulled my hair up and twisted it around into a clip. As the water squeezed from my hair and ran down my arm, I wondered what the others would think of how I looked. Before my mind could finish the thought, a wiser part of my mind responded, *who cares.*

## IT DOESN'T TOTALLY LOOK LIKE HIM

We arrived at the church. There were so many people. The church was full, the entry was full, the yard was full, and even the basement overflowed with people. Did all of these people love my Clint? Of course they did. Who wouldn't? There were so many people, so many hugs, and so many tears. I know they were there, but I don't remember any of them. I just kept looking over at the casket. My boy can't be in that box. It kind of looks like him but not exactly. There is a lot of makeup, and he looks different after the autopsy and the transplant donations. Maybe it's not him. My wise mind argues with such stupidity.

My mind flickers back to the day we went shopping when Clint looked so dapper in his confirmation suit. It was the Saturday of Mother's Day weekend. It was just Megan, Garrett, Clint, and me. The afternoon started with stuffing ourselves on Chinese food, but the real mission was to find Clint a suit. As much as he loved dressing casual, he loved to dress up. He had only one request. His uncle Todd had teased him that he should really get me going by wearing a lime-green shirt on his confirmation day. Well, Clint had to have a lime-green shirt. Finally, we found it. A beautiful blue suit, a lime-green shirt, and a tie striped in blue and green. Perfect! It never crossed my mind that the handsome boy who stood before the church on his confirmation day would wear that suit for his own funeral.

My mind snaps back to the funeral . . . of course it's him. That's why you put his photo in the casket during last night's wake. You wanted people to remember him as he was . . . beautiful, full of smiles, full of life, and not like the person in that box.

## HOW DO I LET GO?

They're all watching me. I just want time alone with my son. They keep telling me I have to go downstairs. I don't want to go. I know that when I do, they will close that box, and I'll never see Clint on this earth again. I find myself touching every inch of him. At the time, I was annoyed knowing that people were watching me. Please, I thought to myself, this is my last moment with him, please leave me alone! I touched his hair . . . it was so soft. My mom was at my left, and my dad was at my right. Someone came to tell me that I needed to go downstairs. I witnessed something that made me so proud of my usually soft-spoken father. He told them, "My daughter is with her son and will take all the time she needs. We will be down when *she* is ready!" My husband stood behind my dad. He was trying to block the view of those who were watching. He was trying to give me space and privacy.

I crawled as far into the casket as I could while still keeping my feet on the ground. I hugged him and didn't want to let him go. I touched his cheeks, eyebrows, nose, ears, and lips. Oh, he had beautiful lips. I can't help but think of all the silly faces they had made and the words that had flowed from them. I kiss his lips and whisper to him that I love him and will see him soon. I hold his hands and take my ring from his finger. I always promised that it would be his. So last night at the wake, I placed it on his finger. With my hands trembling, I return it to my ring finger.

Even as I type, I argue with him, begging an answer... Why did you leave me? Why couldn't you just follow the rules? We had such a good life! What went wrong? You were just here! Please God, bring him back. I promise I'll be good! I bartered that I'd do whatever He wanted. There was no answer. I felt anger move into my heart.

As I played with Clint's hair one last time, I looked at my mom and said, "Isn't his messy hair beautiful?" She just cried and asked if I'd like some. Before I could answer, she told someone to get her a scissors. I had cut Clint's hair his entire life. Only once did he have someone else cut it. That turned out to be a mistake. The hairdresser massaged his head while shampooing it. After that, Clint thought I should provide the same service ... a wash and a massage along with his cut. My mom gave me the scissors. Even though I had cut his hair a thousand times before, this time was different. This time was the last time. While my dad stood behind to protect his little girl's privacy and last moments with her son, I ran my fingers through his golden locks, looked at my mom for her approving nod, and clipped a large piece. The old, black-handled, silver scissors were heavy and cut his thick hair with ease. I was careful not to miss a strand as I folded the hair clipping into my funeral program. I tousled his hair . . . he always liked it messy. I whispered again that I loved him, kissed him on his lips and cheek, and, using his childhood nickname, said, "Good-bye, my sweet Kitty." I knew it was time. It was time to go downstairs. As I looked back, I saw the casket being closed. It wasn't just the casket that closed. A part of my mind closed that day as well. It closed, and it has never fully reopened. It's a part of my mind that needed to be protected. It needed to be protected from the reality that was to come.

## FOR NOW, MY SWEET BABY, GOOD-BYE

The following is the letter I wrote the morning of Clint's funeral. A few years earlier, a friend of mine lost her son in an accident. At the time, we tried to offer support the best we knew how. To honor us, her husband agreed to read my letter to Clint. I needed people to know my son.

*Clint was the spark in my soul. From the day he was born, I knew he was a special gift. He had the brains of Einstein, a sense of humor that surpassed the world's best comedians, energy that had no end, and a smile that could warm the heart of anyone he met.*
*When Clint started to talk, we had GREAT talks. We talked about the importance of being kind to people no matter who they were regardless of race, size, smarts, or age. Clint must have taken every one of these words to heart. One day*

I was upset with him because he was hanging around some kids who I had heard liked to drink and smoke. Clint reminded me that inside they were good people and probably needed his help. Another time, I was complaining to Clint about a few extra pounds I had put on. First he joked and said that big butts were popular again. Then he got serious and told me that fat people were people too and no matter how fat I got, I'd still be special. This, of course, was followed by one of Clint's 20 second hugs. Whenever I was sad or upset with him, he'd grab me with his long ape-like arms and lock them around me. He'd whisper in my ear "20 seconds Mom and it'll all be better." Sometimes, if I were in the middle of scolding him, I'd struggle a little. He'd say "Oh, now the counting has to start over." Clint was right, whatever the issue was, when the hug was over so was the problem. I was left only with the smiles and laughter we shared.

 Clint was always happy go lucky. He'd wake up in the morning (usually 5 minutes before the bus would come or his sister was leaving). I'd ask him about his shirt that was backward, his pants that were wrinkly, his teeth that were unbrushed (he has beautiful teeth), or his hair that was uncombed. He'd usually look down over his body, shrug his shoulders, run his hand through the top of his hair, grab a tooth brush and run out the door…often with one shoe off and one shoe on. Once he got half way to the car or school bus, he'd come running back…"I forgot Mom…I love you" and he'd kiss my cheek and I'd kiss his. Clint's friends have often told me that only he could come to school dressed so goofy and get away with it. People loved it and many have said…ya know that kid would have been homecoming king.

 Each day the kids would leave for school, I'd watch him and the other kids drive away until I could no longer see *them. And every day as I watched them drive away I'd pray the same prayer..."Dear God, please watch over my babies today. Keep them safe, keep them healthy, and keep them safe - far from harm and evil. Be with them every second of the day and every step of the way" and I'd blow them each a kiss as they disappeared beyond the horizon. I did this and will continue to do this because I have always known they are a gift from God. The kids hug and kiss me good bye every day. Clint didn't care who would see. Sometimes he'd even spice it up with his mafia voice..."Get ov'er here toots, I wanna give ya some sugar. If ya don't hurry up you'll be swimming with the fishes". Clint was the spark that ignited my soul with the desire to be good to everyone. My father taught me to make every day better for those whom I crossed paths with and in turn I taught this to my children. Clint took this on not as a neat saying from Grandpa and Mom but as a way of life. He had the biggest heart this world will ever know.*

*Not long after Clint was born, I discovered that he was more than a special gift from God. Don't get me wrong, all of my children are amazing and wonderful gifts from God, but Clint had a different spark. The love and spirit of God was always around him. I swear sometimes I could even see a glow radiate from him. To me, this brought blessing and fear. Because of the way Clint was, I always knew God would want him back. When he was away from me, I was always scared. His poor friends were probably so sick of me. They'd go with Clint and his Mommy would be calling every couple hours just to make sure he was safe. Sorry Kevin, Andrew, Bobby, Anton, Dillan, Tom, Will, David, and the rest of you. Clint would be so patient with me, yet frustrated.*

*Early last week, my heart was heavy. I felt crazy when I turned to my husband and shared my fear. I told him God was sending me messages that we wouldn't have Clint for long in this world. I just didn't know it was going to be so soon. Clint is gone now but his love, the people he touched and his memories will live on into eternity.*

*Clint and I had a special ritual. I'd tell him I loved him and he'd tell me he loved me infinity. I'd say it back to him and he'd have to make it something bigger and better...so he said "Mom, I love you infinitely and beyond." He'd always follow that with a smile because he knew I remembered the first time he'd said this...he told me that there was nothing longer than infinity and beyond. When Clint was just a little boy and Tim wanted to marry me, as my oldest son, he asked Clint for permission. Clint told him only if you love my mom infinitely. Clint showed us the sign for infinity...a sideways figure 8. For our wedding rings, this sideways figure 8 was laid in diamonds. Clint always used to sneak the ring off my finger, pretend that it was stuck on his, and tell me that it was his when I died. I promised it would be. To pass the years until I would pass, for Clint's confirmation we had a goldsmith make a ring with the infinity sign on it so no matter where he went, he knew he was loved infinitely. Since God took Clint home before me, today Clint wears my wedding ring on his finger.*

*Clint always said his family and friends meant the world to him and he loved them each as though they were his very closest and most precious friend. He made everyone feel special. Clint loved life and had huge plans for each of us. Clint would want you to honor his memory by treating each other with love, respect, and sharing his stories.*

*The night of Clint's accident, he came to one of my family in a dream. He told her he was sorry that he had his gun out and knew he shouldn't have. He said he had tripped and was sorry about the accident. He said he is in Heaven and is happy but hurts for the pain we feel. He said God told him that he'd finally get to fulfill his life's dream of being in the army but a different army. He would be a peacemaker helping God to make things right in this world. Now, that gives us peace. If Clint is truly working from Heaven to make peace in our world, I know it will soon become a better place and in no time our Clint will be a 5-star general.*

*Just recently, after being a little careless, Clint told me, "Mom, I live life to the fullest so when it's my time to go, it'll be a great day."*

*So please, be kind to each other, help each other when you feel pain, kiss and hug your moms and dads no matter who's watching and never forget my baby and his beautiful smile.*

*"Until we meet again my baby, rest Clinty…Mom loves you infinity and beyond!"*

What I remember of Clint's funeral was that it was amazing. It was the most beautiful funeral I'd ever been to. It wasn't really even like a funeral. It was a celebration of his life. There were hundreds of pictures and flowers, the wrestling and track teams were dressed in full attire to honor their teammate, and police officers lined all the church walls in honor of our family. Stories and poems were read by his cousins, siblings, and friends; an Army ranger offered his beret to Clint, who had dreamed of being a soldier and should have served our country by his side. Glorious music was played, and a sermon that focused on a boy filled with kindness was given. It was a beautiful tribute to a beautiful boy. It all ended with Clint's lifelong favorite song, "Angels Among Us" by

Alabama. I can't help but reflect on its true meaning and the meaning it now holds for me.

# CHAPTER 6
# God? What a Hoax!

*"I will not cause pain without allowing something new to be born, says the Lord."*
*~Isaiah 66:9~*

After the funeral, we watched as Clint was loaded into the hearse and driven away to the crematorium for a process I won't even let my mind think about. His classmates released balloons into the air. I remember watching them fly high into the sky while thinking about the clothes Clint would be wearing soon. Knowing Clint would approve of his last wardrobe change, a smile crossed my face. Few people knew that his beautiful suit would be removed and replaced with clothing much more fitting for Clint. His last moments on this earth would be spent in his holey jeans, white tube socks, and a Hooters T-shirt. Ironically, Clint and his friends bought their Hooters T-shirts while attending a national youth church convention. There was a private letter from me in one of his jean's pockets, and the other pocket was filled with notes from friends and family. The hearse was no longer in sight, and the last balloon had drifted away.

People were gathered in the church basement for lunch. I've never understood this concept. I hate funeral food. One of my brothers, Todd, later confessed to me that he loves funeral food. He finds the same old salads and ham sandwiches both delicious and comforting. I imagine that the food is meant to nourish those who forget to eat because of grief. To each their own, I guess. At any rate, as I sat at that table surrounded by hundreds of people, I felt lonely. I was in a room full of people, but I was utterly and unequivocally alone.

Even as I sit and write this book, I feel alone and find myself wanting to tell Clint about my morning escapades. He would have teased me relentlessly. I've been writing this chapter away from home. I was totally enjoying my writing retreat at a beautiful little cabin in northern Minnesota. Knowing I love all educational topics, my husband woke me to see if I wanted to attend one of his emergency management sessions on creating safe schools. Mistake #1: I said yes, abandoned my writing plans, combed my Yeti-looking hair, and threw on jeans and a sweatshirt. After all, I was going to slip into the back row where no one would see me. Mistake #2: The keynote speaker asked if there were any educators in the group. It was out of character and stupid, but I raised my hand. I was the only one. Oh crap . . . I knew I was in trouble. Mistake #3: The keynote speaker asked me to come up front for a scenario to which I politely declined. I was urged by him and the group. I was actually shamed into it. It all went downhill from there. He brought me up front (yes, in front of 300 cops and emergency management directors) and made me answer school shooter questions for ten minutes. I'm pretty sure I experienced a stroke, a heart attack, and an aneurysm all at once. Yes, Clint would have found this hilarious!

**THE AFTERNOON OF THE FUNERAL**

During the afternoon after the funeral, I found myself standing in the bunkhouse. This was an old building that we had renovated for the kids just a few short years earlier. I can still hear them: "Please Mom, it would be so cool. We could clean it out, paint it, and put carpet in. We could have couches, a television, Ping-Pong, and air hockey. Oh Mom, we could even put our wrestling mats in here." So, I stood there in our once dirty chicken house looking at new windows, carpet, painted walls, couches, air hockey, foosball, a television with an Xbox, and stacks of games and movies. On the far end, blue mats that we bought from the Lakeview School auction covered the walls. The wrestling mat was maroon with a gold circle in the middle. Oh, what fun the kids had in this building. The floor was still littered with the airsoft pellets from Clint and Garrett's wars. They knew they weren't supposed to shoot them inside, but they did it anyway. Somehow, they'd even talked me into putting air conditioning in the building by stating "But Mom, you wouldn't want us to get too hot out there." They knew which of my heartstrings to pull. I never wanted anything bad for them.

My thoughts were interrupted by Dad. His voice was faint and sounded so far away. "Tanya, Tanya," he said. I could see him standing there with me, but I could barely focus. My eyes couldn't make sense of what I was seeing. There were plants everywhere. There were dozens of them. Then I heard another voice, it was the kids' dad and stepmom. Why were they in the bunkhouse? What were all these plants? They read the cards one by one. "The class of 1987, Tanya that is your class, what would you like to do with it? This one says the class of 1986, this is yours, David. Where would you like it to go?" It was the voice of the kids' stepmom, Terrie. Why did we have to do this now, I thought to myself? Deep inside, I knew that she was right and that it needed to be taken care of. So, the cards were read one after another. Someone was carrying plants away, but I don't know who it was. I just can't get my memory to focus. Names that I knew as well as names that I didn't know were read. I didn't care. They could take all of the plants and it wouldn't have mattered to me. Finally, after what seemed like a long and grueling workday, we were done. All of the plants were divided up and distributed to their proper places. Some went home with the kids' dad, some were brought into the house, and others went to local churches, schools, and nursing homes.

We met in the house next to repeat the process with the cards and the tangible gifts. With divorce nothing is simple, but this day it was. I don't know who decided how to handle the gifts, but I didn't care. Today it would be handled without needless argument. If something was from our family or friends, it would go to us. If it was from Clint's dad's family and friends, it would go to him. If it was from Clint's friends, it would stay with Megan and Garrett. If we couldn't decide who it came from, I really didn't care. They could have it. The gifts felt like blood money to me. They meant my son was no longer here and people thought of him as *dead*. I have never uttered that word in relation to my son. In the beginning, I didn't know why. I do now and will share it later.

Please don't misunderstand and take the thoughts of a grieving mother as unappreciative. My heart was overwhelmed with appreciation and gratitude. These things just became visual reminders of what I couldn't face.

So, the plants were sorted, and I was ready to head to the house to complete our next sorting tasks. Everyone had left but my dad and I. It was silent, and then it came.

I felt the touch of his hand on my shoulder. My dad and I have always been close nearly beyond words. We have a connection of the minds that needs no audible communication. He knew I was dying. He could see it and feel it. I could see it in his tired and puffy eyes. I could see more than that. I could see that he was crying without me. He was trying to be strong for me. Why? I knew he was devastated and could barely navigate the pain.

Because I was emotionally crippled, he must have felt compelled to find a way to save me. Save me from myself. I could see that he was searching his mind for that wisdom. It's a wisdom that he usually accessed naturally. Today, he struggled. I could see his hands shaking. They looked tired, slightly chaffed, rough, and stained from years of hard work, yet they were perfectly manicured. Clearly, nothing has been protected from this experience. It's as though even his hands have aged. Undoubtedly, in the last few days, they have shaken many hands, hugged many bodies, and reassured many with their touch. There is so much warmth coming from his hand that is now squeezing my shoulder. I must feel like poison to him. My very soul is shrieking hatred. He must have felt it. No, he had to have felt it ooze from me and creep into his fingertips.

Finally, he speaks. He praises me for getting through sorting the plants with grace and respect for Clint's dad and the establishments that would be receiving such beautiful gifts. I saw tears fall from his face. That was the cue. The cue that meant something profound was about to be shared. I knew I had to listen. He said, "You know, Tanya, a few weeks ago, I picked up the boys to go fencing with me. Honestly, I was frustrated with you. We were running late and the boys both quickly jumped into the truck so we could get our fencing done. You ran from the yard and made me stop the truck. I thought there must have been something important you needed to tell us. No, you just wanted to kiss your boys good-bye and tell them to be safe and that you loved them. I was annoyed that you had to do that. You'd never let them go without kissing them. I was busy and we needed to get going. Today, I understand why you always had to do that. You are a great mom; never knowing if you'd see them again, you wanted them to know how much you cared and that they were loved. How did you know to always do that?" I didn't know what to tell Dad. I felt as though he wanted me to tell him something wise, but I had nothing. I looked up at him and said, "I just love them Dad."

I didn't know it, but even in my state of severe, grief-induced shock, I was about to enter one of the most intellectual states the mind can enter: a state of cognitive dissonance. I was about to discover that something I had always believed to be true was actually untrue. My whole life, I had lived by this simple belief as though it were a code or covenant. I fell to my knees in the bunkhouse after our senseless sorting of funeral plants. I was defeated. I didn't know what to do. I felt rage instantly fill me. I cried, "Why has God done this to me? I have been a good servant, a good keeper of the children He has given me. Why would He do this to me? I believed if I was a good person, I would win favor with God and in turn, He would be good to me and certainly protect my children from harm. After all, not a day went by where I didn't hug and kiss those children, tell them that I loved then, asked God to protect them and thanked God for them. I was appreciative and careful. Now, this is how He repays me?" I looked at my dad and said, "Why Clint? I was a good mom!" With tears in his eyes, disappointment in his voice, and shock on his face, my dad said, "No, Tanya. God expects you to live a good life . . . to be loving and caring. You are not rewarded for it. You earn favor from God by bringing people closer to Him." I was stunned and dazed. As I kneeled next to my dad, I wanted to argue with him so badly, but I knew he was right. It was as though a switch flipped in my head. How could I have been so stupid? How could I have set myself up for such vulnerability? I instantly hated my Father in Heaven. I wanted favor for having been a good servant to Him and what He'd given me. I wanted Him to bring my son back!

With the benefit of hindsight, my thoughts and beliefs were ridiculous. Of course you don't gain favor for an expectation. It would be like showing up for work and expecting a bonus for being there on time. How stupid could I have been! If you don't show up, you get fired! If you don't live a life with Christ, you go to Hell! This state of cognitive dissonance and this discovery that a major guiding principle in my life was untrue rocked my world to the core. Little did I know this discovery would bring my world crumbling down. I, God's faithful servant, would step on a path of despise and hate for Him.

## LOOKING BACK

That day in the bunkhouse, my dad shared with me the most valuable lesson he has ever taught me. He thrust me into a state of cognitive dissonance that would forever alter my path on this earth. At first, it was a path that brought me through a valley of hatred so deep that I all but denounced the existence of God. In those moments of profound temptation, it was Mom's voice that saved my soul. I remember many of the Bible stories she read to me when I was little, but there was one that has always stood out in my mind. That thought, as though standing watch over my soul, has lingered in the forefront of my brain my entire life. I always wondered why this stood out to me, but I passed it off as useless information the brain automatically stores. It's kind of like remembering old phone numbers you no longer need. Mom told me that no matter where I go in life and whatever I do, there is only one unforgiveable sin. God could clear everything else away and make anew but this one. She told me life would be filled with great times and some not-so-great times. She said it was in these "not-so-great times" when I might get mad at God, and she said that was ok. Then, my mom shared this warning. She told me to *"Never* denounce God!" She told me to never cast Him from my life and never to deny Him. Sternly, she made it clear this was unforgivable. I don't know why my childhood brain clung to that story and held it in safekeeping until now, but I'm glad it did because I was about to embark upon a journey from which I would not have returned.

## HATRED IS BORN AND HEALING BEGINS

God became my enemy. I felt betrayed and alone. I was angry at God nearly every moment. I remember driving home from work one day and pounding the steering wheel with rage. I couldn't believe how stupid I'd been. I was an educated woman who was lured into this religious hoax. How ridiculous was I to believe that there was a God in Heaven. Clearly, I was wrong. In that moment, I had every intention of denouncing His existence and casting this *fake* Father from my life once and for all. Just as I was about to open my mouth and shout it out loud, I paused. What if He's real? What if I close a door that can't be opened again? I decided not being His any longer was enough. I appeased myself with the realization that if He's not real, I didn't need to tell Him anything. I didn't even need to tell Him that I didn't believe in Him. I chose to tell no one.

Although I was fully willing to cast Him away, a verse and a prayer arrived from one of my graduate students. I don't know why I held onto these, but I'm glad I did. The verse not only became a comfort to me but also a challenge to God Himself. *If* He were real, His compassion should be arriving soon. From that moment I first received this verse and prayer a healing began, and the challenge to my Father in Heaven was slowly answered.

> *"For the Lord does not abandon anyone forever.*
> *Though he brings grief, he also shows compassion*
> *according to the greatness of his unfailing love."*
> *~ Lamentations 3: 31-32 ~*

*Dear Lord,*
*Please help me in this time of loss and overwhelming grief. I don't understand why my life is filled with this pain and heartache. But I turn my eyes to you as I seek to find the strength to trust in your faithfulness. I will wait on you and not despair; I will quietly wait for your salvation. My heart is crushed, but I know that you will not abandon me forever. Please show me your compassion, Lord. Help me through the pain so that I will hope in you again. I believe this promise in your Word to send me fresh mercy each day. Though I can't see past today, I trust your great love will never fail me. Amen.*

# CHAPTER 7
# *The Six-Month Promise*

*"The woods are lovely, dark, and deep,*
*But I have promises to keep,*
*And miles to go before I sleep.*
*And miles to go before I sleep."*
*~Robert Frost~*

"The woods *are* lovely, dark, and deep." Yes, they call me to them. Why can't I go? That's right. I can't go because there *are* "miles to go before I sleep." Heaven must wait. There is much to be done.

I wake to the same reality day after day. Everything has changed. I can be surrounded by people and still feel utterly alone. My mouth is sore from gritting my teeth all night. Somehow, I must subconsciously believe that inflicting this pain on myself will ease the pain that lies beneath the surface. Not a day goes by when I don't want to die. Why can't we all be together? Maybe the world will just end. The voice in my head grows louder. He tells me no one cares about me. He tells me I should just be with Clint. I'm not sure who he is, but he scares me. He knows my weaknesses and plays on my pain. He offers a quick solution. He promises that I could feel peace in seconds. It's a peace I desperately long for.

Tim is sitting across the room. He doesn't ever leave me alone. He knows there is a darkness pulling at my once joy-filled soul. He knows if he leaves me alone, he presents an opportunity that I might take. Oh my goodness, he looks serious today. He's going to talk to me. I'm tired of people talking to me. What don't they understand? They *can't* make it better!

He's crying. I can tell he's tired. Maybe he misses Clint too. I'm not sure. He's so serious and stoic. He gets on his knees at my feet, yet another sign that this is going to be a serious effort to cheer me up. I couldn't have been more wrong. He's come to release me. Tears fall to the floor, and he bows his head. In a whisper, he simply says, "Ok, we will do it your way." He went on to tell me that he knew I wanted to die. He said he knew I was waiting for one of my loyal caregivers to slip and that I was waiting for him to slip. He also said he knew I must be in unspeakable pain to even consider such a selfish and permanent option. I was stunned at what he offered next. He offered me freedom from the pain. He said he would *not* help me die but he would no longer stand in my way. He asked for only one thing in return. He asked for a promise. That promise has become known as the "the six-month promise." It's also known as the promise that saved my life. It was a dangerous move on his part, but obviously his faith and love for me ran so deep that it was a risk he was willing to take.

He told me he knew the old Tanya would never disrespect Clint or her other children by leaving this world before her time. He also told me he knew that she would never destroy the lives that would be left behind to pick up the pieces and that she would never hurt her children in that way. He made me promise to give the old Tanya six months to return and see things from a different perspective. He made me promise that he could leave me alone during these six months and not fear that he would find me dead one day.

I thought it would be easy to pretend to agree to this promise and still ultimately do what I wanted to do. Even though I was grieving, he knew I have always been a woman of complete integrity. He knew I would never betray him if he made me give my word. He made me *promise*! In a faint, unassuming whimper, I raised my head and said, "I promise." I wasn't going to be cut short on this deal. In return, I made him promise that if I lived six months and still felt like dying, he would *not* make me live six months and a day. Without hesitation, he promised.

From that day forward, he returned to work and called off the caregivers. There would be no more guards to watch me go to the bathroom, check me in the shower, or sit with me when I ate, checked the mail, or fed the dogs. I would now be free. He trusted my word that I would live for six months. He gambled that I would be strong enough to see through the pain in six months. If not, he would turn away and let me die.

Ultimately, the six-month promise ended up saving my life. It gave a grieving woman something to look forward to. It gave me an expiration date. If I were to dig deeper into why I was able to survive those early months, the reasons were much more complex: I would not and could not dishonor Clint's life in that way, I would not and could not leave my children, I would not and could not hurt my parents and siblings, and I would not and could not leave that kind of legacy behind for all of them to bear.

Tim's gamble paid off, and the promise worked. I'm here today because of his love for me and my love for him and my children. I can't imagine what it must have taken for him to agree, at any point, to support me dying. To support me in ending my life so selfishly. His belief in my perseverance was stronger than his fear. His belief in me stood steadfast in the absence of my own strength. I won't lie; I hated those six months. They were painful and agonizing. The thoughts of escape were there, but the promise was honored.

After the six months were up, he knew we were operating with an expired contract. At times, I could see he worried when he asked things like "Is it ok if I leave you alone?" Tim was brave and continued to trust that I would find my way. Years later, he confessed that he didn't fear leaving home but that he feared what he might find when he returned. He was scared that I would succumb to my own weaknesses. Today, his fears have passed. Besides, I have "miles to go before I sleep."

# CHAPTER 8
# *I Am So Lonely*

*"You aren't crazy, you're just lonely
and loneliness is a hell of a drug."
~John Mayer~*

    What is that noise? It's so annoying! After Tim started going back to work, I'd hear it often. I now know it was the phone. It was a simple ringtone that I should've recognized but didn't. After I realized what it was, I had no desire to answer it. I had no desire to talk to anyone, yet I so desperately needed to.

    I had to deal with a change I couldn't understand. My naturally reclusive self actually needed to be around people. I couldn't understand why they didn't just stop by. I was so lonely. I was trying to keep myself alive. Why didn't they know I needed them?

    The pain was piercing. It felt as though I'd been stabbed a million times. My energy, my love, and my desire to be in this world leaked through these stab wounds. I needed people around me to bandage and plug these wounds. When I was alone, the pain would ooze through the bandages and then even more of me along with my desire to recover would drip away.

## PEOPLE AVOID GRIEVERS

    I believe most people tried to "be there" for me the best they could. The unfortunate part is that we're just not very good at it. Grief is an ugly monster that traumatizes not only its immediate victims, but also those who care by scaring them away from lending support. Grief tells them that they'll say or do the wrong thing, which in turn, will cause more damage. It's this fear of doing wrong that ultimately leads to wrongdoing. People care and really want to make things better for someone who is grieving. The problem is that the solution is so obvious that people often miss it. The solution is that there's no solution or cure for grief. You *can't* make it better and you *can't* undo it or take it away. Sometimes, all that can be done is to let the griever know you care and are available. But you should offer support *only* if you *do* care and *are* available. Never offer more than you can emotionally afford to give. We grievers are a drain.

Early in my grief, I learned that no one is immune from selfishness. One of my dearest friends betrayed me. It's still hard for me to face. This friend couldn't handle that I needed her 100% and that I couldn't be the friend she was used to. The friend she used to know was dead. This time, I was relying on her and could give nothing in return. She couldn't see that my tank was empty. She wanted to know what I did for her as a friend . . . I said, "*I live!*" I guess that wasn't enough. She was angry I didn't go to her oldest son's wedding, and she had no understanding that I couldn't; my oldest son would never marry.

She gossiped and couldn't respect my request for her to abstain from idle town chatter. She thought my request was controlling. Where was the love? She couldn't understand why I didn't answer the phone and why I'd dare ask her to call again or come over if I didn't answer. She felt that twenty miles was too far to drive. Our friendship experienced a slow and painful death. My grief compounded! Although I was able to eventually find it, forgiveness was difficult to grant to this naive friend. I remember Clint's words, "Give 'em grace, they don't know any better. It will make you bitter." In my heart, forgiveness is granted, but the inflicted pain and abandonment is not yet forgotten.

Nearly all our relationships changed. Many people didn't have the ability to give the help our family so desperately needed. It was strange to look to these people we had always been able to count on and realize we'd be walking this path without them this time. We'd be walking it alone. Thankfully, this was a very small group of people that comprised of only a few. These former friends weren't able to be there for us, and they still aren't to this day. Perhaps one day we'll be on the same playing field, and they'll look to me for guidance, help, and support. I hope I will be strong enough to greet them with grace and overlook the pain they caused.

Our family and friends were good for a very long time. For months, they came every day. Eventually, the visits turned to daily phone calls, and then their contact steadily lessened. The first few years, people were good about remembering the day of the accident as well as Clint's birthday. My siblings have been fairly good at remembering special events. Little has slipped by without their presence. There are days they seek me even when I hide from the world. There are days when they have an unspoken need to know I'm ok by looking into my eyes or by holding me. Their steadfast loyalty is never overlooked.

In recent years my siblings have supported me differently, but if I call, they drop everything and come to me. For example, my faithful friend Chris ordered pizza thinking people would stop over, but only Kyle and Pam showed. I called the rest, and they came. First Bobbie arrived, then my parents, and soon Hollis. Each of them came immediately after knowing how hard it was for me to make the call. Todd is a little more private with his affection. He once called me to let me know Clint is always on his mind. It has been years since Todd and I have talked specifically about my precious Clinty. That simple call meant more to me that he will ever realize.

For the most part, these special days I spend with very few people. Some of it's probably because of me. One thing grief has done to me is to compound and exemplify some of the worst in me. Weakness is like water to a withering plant. Weakness nourishes negativity and allows it to flourish. For instance, I've always had a tendency to retreat into myself. This weakness has been nourished by the negativity of grief; it has grown. Now, I am virtually a modern-day recluse that only leaves the farm when it's absolutely necessary.

## ESCAPING LONELINESS

At some point, I realized I didn't have to be alone. When I've felt the crushing suffocation of loneliness, I finally returned to what comforted and inspired me as a young child. I would read. I read nearly everything I could get my hands on including books about grief, Heaven, God, depression, and so forth. When I couldn't find a book and felt lonely, I decided that I would live by a quote. I read thousands. Those quotes gave me hope and comfort. Many were scriptures. These scriptures pulled me even deeper into the Bible on a quest to learn more.

In my loneliest hours, I found myself missing even the sound of Clint's name. Oh how I missed hearing people speak his name. I just needed to hear someone say Kitty, Clinty, Clint, Clinton Robert-Douglas, any of them, or, better yet, all of them. Just please! To this day, the loneliness that finds its way into my heart can still be cast away by the simple utterance of his name or by a simple inquiry about what he might have been doing today.

**AM I STILL NUMB?**

There is a numbness that you don't realize is there. It's like going to the dentist for a filling. They give you Novocain that leaves your mouth useless and totally numb. A short time later, you think the numbness is gone until you take a drink and half of it runs out the corner of your mouth. Then hours later, when you are sure it's gone, you take a bite of food and clearly discover it's still there when you bite your lip. Grief is much the same. You will go months, even years down the road and think the numbness is gone. You will think the shock has worn off. Then, you go further down the road and realize it was still there the entire time. I often wonder if it's still with me. This numbness provides a protective barrier that allows me to handle only what I am able to. When I make it through certain stages, it lightens a bit and gives me another dose of unrealized pain. In these times I may not know it, but the numbness, the Novocain, is still there. This protective numbness is what allows us to survive the unsurvivable. Even today, I wonder if there is any numbing agent left within me or if this is my new reality. I will only know as time passes and I reflect back.

There has been no pill or quick solution for me to begin experiencing joy again. It has been a long and lonely road. A road whose winding switchbacks I never want to explore again.

# CHAPTER 9
## My Groundhog Day

*"Whatever we plant in our subconscious mind and nourish with repetition and emotion will one day become a reality."*
~Earl Nightingale~

Have you seen the movie *Groundhog Day*? It stars Bill Murray and Andie MacDowell. At any rate, the movie is about a guy who wakes up every day having to repeat yesterday. I absolutely hated that movie. The thought of having to do that drove me nuts. I'm not even sure if I ever finished watching the movie back when it first came out in the early 90's. You're probably wondering why I would reference that movie. It's completely ironic that my life has become like *Groundhog Day*.

Sleep is something I used to do so well. What peace it gave me to crawl into my bed knowing my children were all safe in their beds. In their beds where I'd always kiss them good-night. They were safe at home. Sleep is something I miss, something I long for, and something I fear. I miss it because to rest would bring the refreshment, energy, and focus that I so desperately need. I long for it because I need rest so much. I'm tired. I'm tired from lack of sleep, and I'm tired of the fear. I'm afraid of the dark and afraid of waking up. I'm afraid of the dark because it holds the unknown, which is something my life has clearly become. I've been afraid to wake up because I've been waking up to the morning of November 6, 2006, the morning following Clint's accident, every day. Each day, I wake up fresh with a new hope that I just had a really bad dream. That I just had a cruel dream. No, a nightmare! A nightmare in which I found Clinty's lifeless body on the yard of our farm.

Every morning goes like this. I sit up, see a dried basket of flowers on my armoire, and my memory flickers. It flickers like an old movie in which the images come and go, sometimes in color, sometimes not. I see a basket of dried roses, daisies, and carnations. I remember selecting a basket and placing funeral flowers in it to dry. I think to myself that my nightmare must have been vivid. The flowers from the funeral look just like those on my armoire. From a funeral? I rub my eyes in denial as I roll out of bed and place my feet on the floor. I grab a clip and twist my hair up as I try to shake off the bad dream. I glance up at my fireplace and see my Bible. Hanging out of the corner, I see a piece of paper that looks like the funeral program I dreamt about. Could that be the same funeral program where I'd put Clint's freshly cut hair? Of course not, that was just in my dream.

I feel the carpet between my toes. The carpet the kids always used to crawl across when sneaking up to my bed to scare me. The carpet Clinty just walked across to lean over and kiss me good night. I smile to myself as I reminisce about their silliness. I'm eager to find each of them and start our day. I walk across the carpet and enter the dining room. I see a large picture of Clint on the refrigerator. I feel a chill come over me as my feet touch the cold hardwood floor. It takes only a moment to realize that the chill is not from the floor. I think to myself, why do I have a larger picture of Clint than everyone else? I would never do that unless, no, I won't believe it. I start the coffee pot. Yes, coffee is what I need to shake off this bad dream. As I walk to the bathroom through the great room, there are more plants. They are funeral plants. There is the small evergreen that was given to me by a close friend at the . . . funeral in my dream? My heart sinks as I realize it's true. Clint is gone!

That has been my morning ritual every morning since November 6, 2006. Why do I fear sleep, you might ask? The answer is simple. It's not sleep I fear. It's waking up. Waking up to a world where my son no longer lives. A world filled with the bitter reminders that he is gone. This is a reality that has become mine every waking day.

What's crazy is that I literally believe it really was a nightmare every day. Every morning, I wake up thinking that I just kissed him good night last night. Every morning, I wake up with hope. A hope that today I get my life back.

## HOW DO I MOVE FORWARD: AN UNBELIEVABLE PEACE

So, my world was seemingly perfect. I'd wake up each morning and a smile would cross my face before my feet could even hit the floor. Knowing I'd be able to spend another day with my children nearly gave me goose bumps. In the evening after we'd say the Lord's Prayer and our good nights, I'd tuck them in bed one by one and kiss their teenage cheeks. Each night, I'd fall asleep with a warm sense a tranquility for which there is no explanation. Just knowing that my babies were under my roof and safe in their beds was complete peace. This is a peace that comes naturally for a mother when her children are safe, but it's also a peace that can be shattered in an instant.

On November 5th, 2006, my perfect world did just that: it shattered. Since that day, nothing has been the same. My perfect life ended in an instant, and the peace that used to fill my heart was gone. After months of walking through an unbearable existence, I faintly remembered a verse I had heard many times before.

*"And the peace of God, which surpasses all understanding, will guard your hearts and your minds in Christ Jesus."*
*~ Philippians 4:7 ~*

As quickly as the words fleeted through my mind, I fell to my knees and prayed that God would fulfill His promise for that peace which surpasses all understanding:

*Dear God, please grant me a peace that surpasses all human understanding. Please take my pain and help me live for today.*

I prayed that day and have prayed nearly every day since for that peace, and He has continued to grant it. Through His peace that really does surpass all understanding, I'm slowly waking to a new day.

# CHAPTER 10
## My Clinty Comforts Me

*"In every life there is a turning point. A moment so tremendous, so sharp and clear that one feels as if one's been hit in the chest, all the breath knocked out, and one knows, absolutely knows without the merest hint of a shadow of a doubt that one's life will never be the same."*
~Julia Quinn~

It was late 2006 when a gate within my heart flung open. I felt hearence on a level I hadn't yet experienced. I'd felt God before, but I hadn't experienced hearence in direct relation to Clint himself. Today, God allowed the gate to open, and He allowed my son to share a glimpse of his life in Heaven. That day, for me, God lifted the thin veil that divides Heaven and earth; I could all but see my son.

It was a few days before our first Christmas without Clint. I was sitting in my chair after sending the kids off to school. I was sad, so sad, and I was missing my son. Tim was asleep on the couch next to me. Even though he was there, I felt so alone.

As I sat in my chair, I suddenly felt very warm. Even though Tim was still fast asleep, I no longer felt lonely. I began to hear Clint's voice. No, I thought to myself, now I'm going crazy. I begged for God not to make me crazy. I knew I couldn't withstand more issues to deal with, certainly not hearing voices. When I realized the voices weren't going to stop, I grabbed some scratch paper that was next to my chair and started writing what he was saying. I'm a fast writer with terrible handwriting, but I could barely keep up with the words I was hearing. I kept writing page after page. Hearing the paper flipping, Tim woke up. He clearly hadn't realized that he'd fallen asleep on his watch. After all, he was supposed to be guarding over my every move to ensure that I didn't slip from sight and hurt myself. Luckily, my mind was in a safe place that day. Tim asked what I was doing. As I continued to write, I turned my head slightly to the left and tossed him a look that advised him to be quiet. I heard Clint's voice for roughly five minutes. My hand only stopped moving when his voice ceased. Again, I felt alone. Alone with pages of scribble that I hadn't read yet. When I was writing, the words had been coming so fast that my mind hadn't chained them together into anything coherent.

Tim could tell the writing had stopped and asked me what I was doing. I responded that I wasn't sure but that I'd heard Clint's voice and wrote what I'd heard. I gathered my notes of scratch paper and put them in order. As I read them aloud, we were both stunned.

## WORDS FROM CLINT

*Tonight as we step forward through an evening where there may be pain,*
*feel that warmth all around you and believe that your loss is his gain.*
*For on a sunny fall morning God called me home.*
*Know that He was there in the yard.*
*I took His hand though it was hard.*
*I knew you would be sad, so I wanted to stay*

but the Lord was inviting and He promised He'd help you find
your way.
Instantly, I was filled with his love and incredible joys.
Believe me, it was better than a room filled with my favorite toys.
When I got to the gates they were all there . . . Grandpas and
Grandmas, Nick, Russ and Ray.
I have never felt such a glorious day.
We visited for hours and then took a tour.
The angels, the flowers, the sparkles of gold,
the Lord's great Kingdom and His love for the young and the
old.
As I sat by His side as one of his own,
He told me the story of why I was home.
He told me I was His long before life
and I was called home to end pain and strife.
He said I was a soldier of His and my dream had come true, for I
was in His army back when I was with you.
He said I did well and accomplished great things
and it was each of you that allowed me to go home with all that I
bring.
He said I'd returned with more than He thought
but there were still many battles to be fought.
He introduced me to Michael the mischievous one
and told me this was my place where Thy will be done.
I'll travel the Kingdom and the earth down below.
I'll bring His peace to those who don't know.
It may be a nudge for you to do right or it may be a path I lead a
lost soldier to safety in the night.
I'm proud of the lessons of courage, kindness and compassion
taken from you and I hope you are proud of me too.
For my life in the Heavens, while I wait for you,
will be spent helping others as you taught me to.
Please light my candle that I know Mom just bought,

*open your hearts and don't be distraught.*
*Please close your eyes and remember my smile.*
*I'm sure this will hurt as it's only been a short while.*
*Remember my presence that filled you with laughter and cheer.*
*That's not gone for I'm still with you sitting right here.*
*I'm always with you as your time passes slow.*
*But we will be together sooner than you know.*
*In Heaven, time passes quickly but it's never abrupt,*
*You just be sure to keep your faith and continue to look up.*
*So on this first Christmas that we are apart, just know that I'm with you deep in your heart.*
*You miss me and I miss you too, but know that I love you and this will always be true.*
*Cherish your time on the earth down below.*
*For it will soon be that you'll also be called to go.*
*Oh! Do you hear that sweet sound?*
*The angels are singing and God is around.*
*He's around you and He's around me.*
*He is rejoicing and is calling for thee.*
*I know this is short but I really must go.*
*For tonight, I sit with the King of the show.*
*Please share this night and all the days to come.*
*Know that when you're all together, we will always be one.*
*As you celebrate tonight, I know you'll ask "why?"*
*but please honor me and try not to cry.*
*Now Grandma; on with His story, sing songs and open gifts.*
*Pray to our Lord and your spirits He'll lift.*
*Enjoy this great evening, each other and all that it'll bring.*
*Know that tonight I'll be with Jesus our Savior and King.*

Unaware of the full context of what had just happened, I was in tears. I was left to wonder if that was really Clint with me just moments ago. I was left to contemplate and search for its meaning. Was God allowing hearence with Clinty? Could it be possible? It was so real. I could feel him, hear him, and smell him. What is happening to me? What is this thing I have come to call hearence?

# CHAPTER 11
# *Anger Nearly Becomes Me*

*"When we meet real tragedy in life, we can react in two ways—either by losing hope and falling into self-destructive habits, or by using the challenge to find our inner strength."*
~Dalai Lama XIV~

I felt so angry. I wanted someone to turn to. I wanted guidance and support. I wanted someone to ask me how I was doing and actually listen to my answer and not simply say "great" after I had just said I wasn't doing well. I wanted someone to tell me that God was real and that all would be made right again. Instead, we were hurt even further. Even more changes were in store for us. Why couldn't anything stay the way it was? Why did we have to lose it all?

**BROKEN PROMISES**

In the beginning, tragedy brings out the best in people. Everyone wants to find a way they can support you. In this state of being, you see the good in our little community. They brought food, visited us, or just sat with us while we cried. If that had been all they would've done, I would've been pleased. As the days passed, they made grandiose promises to us. People promised they would stand by us until we were strong; people said *we* would get through this together; people said they would stop by and see us soon. The fact is that we saw very few people after the funeral. We were nearly alone. My parents taught me that there is never a reason to break a promise; you keep it. So, I waited for all those things they promised, but most never came. When I started to return to the public eye and see some of those *promise makers*, I wondered if they even knew what they had given me and then taken away so quickly.

With hindsight, I believe people want to be all of these things that are popular to say. I just think we're not very good at it or simply don't know what to do. Maybe they thought we would call and ask. The truth is that proud Minnesotans don't ask; they won't ask. The consequence of this pride that is bred into us, at least for me, is loneliness followed by an unstoppable anger.

**BETRAYAL OR OPPORTUNITY?**

Other than family, they left us alone. Not all of them, but most did. A few faithful church friends visited, but even their visits dwindled to nearly nothing. I hardly left the house. Even though I knew I should get out, I couldn't. I couldn't even go to church. The pastors of my little country church came for a few visits, but they gave me spiritual advice that only made me feel more lost. They told me that God didn't know this was going to happen. They told me they had no idea where Clint was or what Heaven was like. I was enraged. In my mind, I compared them to computer technicians that didn't know the basics of a computer. Were they serious?

Another church family reached out and started visiting us. Pastor John and his wife, Tammy, sat with us for hours and answered our questions the best they could.

If they didn't have the answers, Pastor John would get out his Bible and search for the answers. I was in awe the first time I saw his Bible; it was held together with duct tape. I'd never seen a Bible that was so tattered and worn. At first, the strict Lutheran in me felt it had been neglected or abused. It didn't take long to realize that his was a Bible that was fully respected and well used. It quickly became clear that the answers to all of my questions were in it. This was new to me. I had been raised to listen to sermons for all of my spiritual advice. If I was taught to search the Bible for answers, the lesson had escaped me. After Pastor John's first visit, I made a request of Tim. I asked him to take me somewhere. He was shocked because I had been refusing to leave the house. I asked him to take me to the religious bookstore in Willmar to buy a Bible. It wasn't that I didn't have one. In fact, I had several: one the church had given me when I was a child and a second one my uncles, Russ and Ray, had given me when I was confirmed. There was even a third one I was given when I got married. There was nothing wrong with any of these. In fact, they were pristine and hadn't been used since the day I received them. I simply wanted to start anew. I wanted a Bible to start this journey of discovery and recovery.

At the bookstore, I pored over Bibles as though the outside world had disappeared. All that was left was me in the corner of that bookstore with all of those Bibles. There were big ones and little ones. There were so many versions to choose from: the New Living Translation, the New International Reader's Version, the New Revised Standard Version, the New American Standard Bible, the New King James Version, the English Standard Version, and so on. Yikes! Finally, I found the perfect Bible. For me, it would be the New Living Translation. When I was checking out, I was surprised at its cost. Over the years, I had watched my mother purchase beautiful Bibles and give them away as though they were free. So, in January of 2007, I took my new Bible home. The first thing I did was ink it up. Even as I write this, I feel a little naughty. I was raised to believe that we should not write in our Bibles. On that day, I wrote a dedication to myself in the front cover. The exact words shall remain between God and me.

Soon, I found that it was not only just a Bible but also a place to keep private notes to myself. Every time I'd pick it up, something would fall out. On that day, I designed and ordered a custom leather cover. It was open on the edges, but it had a leather strap that cinched it closed. Now my Bible was perfect. From that day forward, I combed through the Bible for answers and inspiration. I tabbed and wrote on every single page I read. I learned that a Bible was meant to be used. What an honor it would be to God if I wore it out. Isn't that what He hopes for?

Even when we attended the new church, we were expected to bring and open our Bibles during the service. Additionally, we found the church filled with people who were welcoming and kind. Even so, our attendance there faded. I was so angry at God that I couldn't yet see through my hatred. I just wanted to be home. I didn't want to leave the house. Over the next few years, we would go back and forth between two churches. I no longer had the time or love for this entity we call God.

One day, in a conversation with someone from my childhood church, I was told that we were no longer considered members. This person defended her stance by doing what cowards do. She stated that "others" thought it too. It was a harsh stance for a Christian woman to take. I wondered how outsiders felt, if as an insider I was left feeling like such an outsider. I felt sad for the entire church that I loved. She went on to say if we were going to be attending another church, then that is where we belonged. I don't know why I felt she deserved an explanation because she clearly didn't. I explained that we hadn't been there in months. In fact, I explained that it had been nearly a year since we'd been to any church. I further explained that we'd never changed our membership and had no plans to do so. I went on to tell her that we'd been lost and lonely. I explained that "her" church was also my church and that it was Clint's church.

I tried to explain what it felt like to be so lost. I felt like I belonged at my little country church because it's where I grew up and it's where my family had been whole. Obviously not fully welcomed by her, I couldn't help but wonder how many "others" felt the same way. Conversely, I was being welcomed by the new church, but I still felt like I didn't belong. It was no fault of theirs because they tried, and to this day, they still reach out to us. My heart just needed comfort and for something to stay the same. Unfortunately, it seemed like the church I grew up with was gone and simply no longer existed. I was lost, completely lost! Now, I could add the utter pain of rejection to my grief. I experienced complete betrayal by a church I loved. A church Clint loved. This created only more anger inside of me.

A new church was saying they'd take whatever part of us they could whenever they could. The church I grew up in was acting as though my absence was like a tardy from work for which I should be more than reprimanded. In fact, they acted as if I should be terminated. The consequence for my absence was that I was no longer considered a member of the church in which I had been baptized, confirmed, and attending for 38 years. My sense of belonging was ripped from me by a person that will never know what a thin thread I was hanging from. It was a thread that she thought nothing of slicing through with her words. Again, I was left wondering if more people felt like her. She said there were more that felt the same, but I couldn't help but wonder if she could've been a messenger of something that only she felt. Could it be possible that some members of my little country church missed me? If they do, where are they? Why don't they come to me? I miss them. I need them. Whatever the reason this woman chose to hurt me so terribly, I decided that I would pray for her.

After years of internal turmoil, my country church called a new pastor. This pastor was intriguing to me right from the start. He had people talking about how good his sermons were. Also, it seemed ironic that he, Pastor Owen, was Scottish. Clinty loved to act like a Scotsman. I couldn't help but reflect back to the track meet when he pretended he was a foreign exchange student from Scotland. The girls loved his accent and as a result Clint came home with many phone numbers. At any rate, Clint would've liked having a Scottish pastor. I didn't know it, but Pastor Owen, who had taken over our little church, and Pastor John would both make me whole again. Yes, it would take both of these faithful servants of God.

Pastor Owen stopped by one day to visit. He wanted to get to know the woman who was missing from the Sunday services. The woman he'd heard about through family and friends. The woman he wanted back in the pews of our little country church. As we sat and talked, my mind flickered to incidents of Clinty and his fake Scottish accent. Over coffee, we talked and cried for what seemed like hours. He was comforting and understanding of an angry and broken heart. He wept for my son and for a pain inflicted by a church that was now within the realm of his accountability. He explained that I would be a member of the church as long as it was my heart's desire. He told God mattered more than those few catty people and that He wanted and needed me there. Pastor Owen told me God was happy to have me worship with them anytime. He went further and instantly ended the torturous game of tug-of-war within my heart. He explained that they wanted me back at church even if I attended only once a year, once a month, or once every other week; he explained they wanted me back regardless of the frequency of my attendance. He also explained that not only did they want me, but also they would take whatever part of me they could. He went on to explain that both churches were God's houses. He also explained that God didn't care which house I worshiped Him from. Pastor Owen is a wise man. Of course he's right. God is bigger than everything else. Pleasing Him is what matters. This leads me to how Pastor John helped to heal my heart. He once asked me, "Is Jesus enough?" At the time, I didn't know the answer and quite honestly thought it was a strange question. Now, I do know the answer. "Yes, Pastor John, He is enough!" Is my heart healing? Yes, I think it is.

## AN OPPORTUNITY TO HEAL

It was, and still is at times, hard to go back. Rarely do I go without reminiscing on the words of both pastors. I also think about a saying I once heard, "He who kneels before God can stand before anyone." Although a church is comprised of the people within it, I go to church to be fed the Word of God. Yes, Jesus is enough. Sometimes, I find myself being fed at either the new church or my childhood church. I no longer feel torn. I know that *Jesus is enough* and that He will guide me to where I belong.

A few years back, my brother Hollis was telling me that they needed someone to give the sermon on Thanksgiving Sunday. Before I realized it, the words had escaped my mouth stating that I would consider doing it. Somewhat shocked, he replied with excitement in his voice, "Really?" Having come to my senses within those few seconds, all I could think to say was, "I really don't have time and am swamped with work." We joked back and forth and left it at that.

I didn't get any work done that entire day. I could feel God pestering me, for lack of better words. I liken His pestering to when the kids were little and repeatedly asked for more candy. The truth is that God had been working on my heart for a very long time. After losing Clint, I had a hatred brewing in my heart for my God and church. I spent a long time trying to convince myself that "church" and "God" were the biggest hoaxes of all time. Surely if there was a God, He wouldn't have betrayed me by taking my son. Surely if the church was real, it would have eased my pain. Over time, I realized that the person I had confided in about this hoax was Jesus Himself. I had to face that what I really believed was really real. Just as I had been taught my whole life, my Lord was alive and reigned from Heaven. To get to that point, He and I had many conversations filled with lots of tears. I was torn down to nothing and then restored. Through this process, my faith has grown beyond any explanation. Our Lord Jesus Christ is my Father, my confidant, my best friend, and my Savior.

Finally, one day in prayer, I asked a favor of Him. I asked Him to *please* let something good come from my loss of Clint. Looking back, I should've asked Him to make it easy. It should go without saying that it hasn't been easy. Jesus has pushed me in directions I've fought against. Through this journey, my relationship and trust in Christ have grown tremendously. Writing and publishing this book is an example of my trust in Him. Sharing so much personal information when I am private by nature is another example. Nothing would make me happier than shutting myself off from the world and just being home with my family. Rather, my life is guided by God's fulfillment of the promise I asked of Him, which was to bring good from the loss of Clint. I dislike talking about myself and hate the idea of doing it publically even more. Hate seems like a harsh word, but it's true. Yes, God has compelled me to share our story of loss. Because I have shared this story, many have expressed that they've turned closer to God and that their faith has been strengthened or restored. As if public speaking weren't enough, God has tested me with my second hate in life: writing. He has granted me a gift for writing that I didn't have before, and I simply can't explain how it operates. Hence, writing about Clint's loss is the second way that good can be accomplished through his loss. I've been told that my words have been inspirational and healing. If only I could find a sane way to explain that they are not my words but what God has put on my heart.

# THE SUNDAY MESSAGE THAT WAS NEVER SHARED

I never shared that message at church, but I did prepare it. At any rate, this is what I wrote for that Thanksgiving service at my little country church:

> So, I stand before you today not due to a love of public speaking or writing but by God's urging and desire. Thanksgiving...a time to spend with family, a time to reminisce, to consider, to ponder what we are grateful and thankful for.
>
> I don't think we, as a society, realize what a very, very important time this really is. Or maybe better stated, what a very important time it should be. It's a time to refocus! Yes, a national holiday, a day off from work for us to refocus and of course, eat. I'm sure most don't think of it this way. Many of you are probably wondering where I am going with this.
>
> Well, Thanksgiving...my memories instantly go the traditions associated with the Weber Thanksgivings. Mom, Bobbie and I baking a dozen pies Wednesday night. Mom always makes us prepare far too many. I think she has a secret deal on the side with my brother Kyle. You see, he never leaves without at least two for himself. I am not talking about pieces of pie. I mean full pies. The whole week building up to Thanksgiving there is an excitement in our hearts. Thanksgiving, at noon, we will all be together. No matter where we are, our parents, the kids, grandkids, and the great grandkids all make it home for those few precious hours where we will fill ourselves with turkey, Mom's potatoes and stuffing, my gravy, Bobbie's green bean casserole, Diane's sweet potatoes, Vera's vegetable medley,

and one of Pam's salads. But more than all of that, we come home for each other. Although unspoken, our hearts are filled with gratitude for one more holiday together.

In our society so much can and does happen. I might add, much of which is unexpected and hurtful. We are quick to jump to the negative in our lives. Whether it is crop prices being too low, an ache in the hip, another year without a raise, the car broke down, the cows are out, gas is too high, so-and-so did this or that, or the loss of someone we love. There are ALWAYS things to complain about. We even convince ourselves that we have some God-given right to do this. That somehow we are justified. That we actually have a right to complain and let the negative things that happen to us have rule and reign of our daily thoughts, conversations and overall lives.

I am guilty of this, and I know some of you are too. It's vital that we realize that it is in this state that we are the most vulnerable. To what, you ask? To evil…heck, let's give it a name…to Satan. He wants us to perpetuate the negative…the bad things GOD must allow. That's where Satan wants us to live. In a state where we see life through grey colored glasses, rather than rose. We emphasize the bad and not the good. We choose to see the worst in each other…to blame. We allow these things to pull us apart, rather than together. We infect others with negative rather than gratitude. We let it pull us down, rather than up. Down to where he lives. Down to where we become his.

Yes, during this Thanksgiving weekend, we will reminisce and ponder what we are thankful for! For health, for financial stability, a roof over our heads, for our families, for friends, for life! For one more day spent together in the presence of those we love and cherish. For these gifts that are only possible through Him!

*And if you want to do one better and go out on a big limb, one that won't break, count your blessings not just during the thanksgiving holiday. Count them often. Count them daily! Count them today! I urge all of you when you meet God in prayer in that beautiful place of solitude, where the Heavenly Father enters the room to spend time with just YOU, nobody but you. Where He sits before you, and His attention is all yours. Where He holds your hands and you bow your heads together. When you're in this place, don't just ask for all those things you think you need, but rather thank Him for the innumerable things He gives you each day. Do this every day and not just on special days like Thanksgiving. You will be amazed in a short amount of time how God will change your heart and refocus your world, our world. Through this, we can serve Him.*

*I thank Him. I thank Him for things I used to take for granted. Someone said to me "how can you love the Lord that has betrayed you?" The answer is simple, He has not betrayed me. It was written long before November 5, 2006 that Clinty would go home that day. So I was given a choice, hate God for the years Clint will be apart from us or thank Him for the 16 years we had him. Rather than loath Him for the son I can no longer kiss good night, I fall to my knees in prayer and thank Him for the children that I have to kiss good night and for His fulfilled promise that He now kisses Clint good night.*

*It isn't easy to concentrate on the positive. Satan would love nothing more than to win our hearts through negativity. Make no mistake, he is working against you. But know that by making a concerted effort to concentrate on what you've been given rather than what you've lost, you serve the Lord and His kingdom. You triumph over evil.*

*It has been this kind of thanks, this kind of gratitude that filled my heart for God, and in return He has strengthened my faith to the point at which my shattered world has emerged into the light. I stand before you today as a living promise that counting your gifts will strengthen you. So this Thanksgiving Sunday, thank you for letting me come home to what will always be my church; my son's church.*

*Please help us all to take this opportunity to change our hearts and minds. Let's train for a new day. A day where we take inventory of all the blessings that have been bestowed upon us. Not just for what we are grateful for, but also to whom we owe this gratitude: to our Father.*

## COMMUNITY

Incredibly, the anger began to subside. It didn't go away all at once. I would compare it to the ocean's waves. There were days when I was so angry, but those days became less and less.

There were community members that pleasantly surprised me with their support. Then, as I've said, there were others who stunned me with their abandonment of us. Some of the abandonment was intentional, and part was due to people just not knowing what they could or should do.

## CLINT

One of the last pieces of anger to subside was the anger at Clint. I was so mad that he just couldn't listen to the rules that day. After all, he knew better. He knew he wasn't supposed to touch that gun or any gun if we weren't with him. It took me years to realize that he never meant to hurt any of us. He was just a curious young boy who, with his ADHD, didn't think and acted impulsively. I have come to realize that although I wanted to share it with him here on earth, the love he's given me and the love I've given him will last forever. My anger can resurface when I let myself think about all we are missing without him. Selfishly, I've thought I had a right to live out our dreams *here* together. Instead, I will live with Clinty in my memories and in some make-believe visions and recreations that can never really be.

**TANYA**

The very last part of anger to subside is the anger over the death of *me*. I have said that I literally felt myself die when I found Clint. The old Tanya left this body behind, took Clint by the hand, and has never been fully seen again. Once in a while we will see glimpses of her, but for all practical matters, she is dead. The new Tanya does not think like her or act like her. With the exception of several more wrinkles from years of facing a painful reality, she might look the same on the outside, but without a doubt, the inside is different. This is a loss that has angered me beyond understanding. Why have I had to lose literally everything? How is it possible that everything can be taken from you including how you think? The unfairness of this has brewed a hatred in me that has been strong for years. I've understood how someone could take your belongings and maybe even kidnap your body, but how could your mind and thoughts be taken? This search for understanding has made for a slow recovery.

For years, I looked in the mirror searching for a match between what was on the inside and what could be seen on the outside. I would call Tim into the bathroom, have him look in the mirror, and ask him who that was. He would compassionately and consistently tell me, "It is you, Tan."

I so desperately wanted to die with her. I wanted to return to her. I constantly felt the pull towards a dark hole. It was like an old well one might find in the middle of an old farmstead. It was deep, and I couldn't see the bottom. It had a tremendous strength that pulled against me and my will. If I lost my grip even for a second, I would be gone forever. Every day, I fought against this vortex trying to take me away. One day, I realized it wasn't the old Tanya trying to bring me with her; it was grief trying to pull me down into a despair from which there would be no return. Living there meant not being a mother, a wife, a daughter, an aunt, or a sister. The entry fee was an acceptance of depression, alcohol, drugs, and maybe even death. Although it offered an escape from the pain and was tempting, the entry fee was too high. So, I fought every second of every single day against that sucking vortex. After years, the pull has become less and less. It still taunts me and offers a quick relief, but the new Tanya is growing strong. The new Tanya has been strengthened to the point where parts of the old Tanya have even been retrieved from the ashes within that black hole.

They say that "time heals all wounds." I don't know who *they* are, but *they* are stupid. Time does *not* heal all wounds. Time offers you a platform where you can recreate both yourself and your interactions with this world. It allows you to know what to share, when to share it, and with whom to share it. Time offers an open doorway to healing, but if you don't walk through it, time itself does nothing for you. I've had to start over building who I wanted and needed to be in this world. It has been a difficult journey that is painfully highlighted throughout this book. I can finally say that the ability to look in the mirror and recognize my face has returned and is refreshing. Finally, I feel a sense of me.

## ANGER BEGINS TO RETREAT

Finding peace with all of this is difficult. As parents and family members, we think we are entitled to certain things from each other. The truth is, we're not promised anything here on earth. To find joy without my son, I've had to decrease, and I've had to let God increase within me. I've learned to trust that He will be with me no matter what and that He knows what's best for me.

## TIME PASSES

Several months have passed since I last placed my hands on this keyboard. Another year has slipped away since I last sat in this chair. The chair in this little northern cabin has become the place I've chosen to write. It's a place where it's only me, my thoughts, and this laptop. There is no one around to stop me from pulling the bandages off and picking at the scabs that cover the wounds that are healing ever so slowly. You must wonder why I pick them. Everyone knows that when you pick a scab, it opens a wound and increases the risk of unsightly scarring. What they don't know is that I'm already scarred. You may not see these scars, but they run deep and hurt when touched. The marks that scar my heart are not much different than the scars that run around my eye.

When I was sixteen, I was a passenger in a car that rolled over. When the car began to roll, the driver and I bumped heads causing my sunglasses to deeply cut the skin around my eye like a cookie cutter through soft dough. Although it has been thirty years since that accident, I sometimes bump my scar when I grab the phone and pull it to my ear too fast. Other times, my grandchildren hug me and their little cheeks hit that spot on my face. These little bumps send breathtaking pains through my face as the tiny shards of glass that were left inside cut deeper. That is what picking at these emotional scabs and scars feels like. The pain can only be quelled by closing my eyes until the throbbing subsides. Yes, the scabs and scars that no one can see are much the same. Today, the scabs are itching. Just the thought of scratching at them is opening wounds that won't close easily and certainly not without even further scarring.

The phone has rung four times in the last hour. It's the kids checking in. Oh, how I love them. First it's Megan, then it's Bri, then it's Garrett, and then it's Megan again. They each have a reason for their calls whether it's something they need, a question that requires an answer, or an idea they want to bounce off of me. These are legitimate reasons, but deep down, I know they worry that I'm gone and are nervous about what I'm doing. Again, they want to know if I'm ok. Am I ok? Yes, finally, I think I'm ok.

It has been a tremendous fight to find the strength to defend against the anger that has so desperately wanted to win my heart and soul. I'd never really put it into words until I found myself sharing it with my friend Jessi, who recently lost her cousin. As I shared with her, I realized that my wounds were indeed healing. I wrote this letter to her:

> *You are heavy on my heart and thoughts. I wish I could take the horrific pain you undoubtedly must feel. How couldn't you? The loss you, and so many, have recently experienced could easily make you bitter. It could fill your joyful and once innocent heart with anger. I wish I could fill that spot with only love...love that our friend expressed in her mannerisms and interactions without forethought. A love that can only be surpassed by the unimaginable life she now lives with my beautiful Clinty and so many of our cherished others. The joy they have is undefinable and leaves us incapable of believing it could be better than life here with us. Understandably, our lack of knowledge of Heaven leaves us emotionally and intellectually naked in understanding the tremendous truth of God's grace and the gifts He now bestows upon them.*
>
> *That anger everyone (including me) is feeling is normal now but soon will become a poison to our very lives and overshadow our memories and what we know to be true for her future. Yes, her future...she LIVES!*
>
> *I know that anger all too well. I lived in it and with it after losing my precious Clinty. It can become you by gripping your soul and changing the essence of everything good within you. The weak will find comfort in being in that place. The strong—like you—will snatch away its power and remind the world that our loved ones are more than what happened the day we lost them. The strong will show the world that their love wins!*
>
> *I am praying diligently that God will grant you peace, comfort, and above all else the understanding to understand what simply cannot be understood. (Letter to JH, 2013)*

When I wrote this letter, I knew God had truly granted me a peace that surpassed all human understanding. Maybe that comes with time. I'm not sure. I do know it's something I asked of God every day. In the early years, I wish someone would've told me that my pain was solidifying into anger. That it was hardening my very heart. Truth be told, the shock of losing my oldest son created a paralysis of analysis. Simply put, I was unable to see my own situation and what was happening to me. It was as though my brain was paralyzed and couldn't process properly. I was unable to pinpoint what was causing changes within me as well as within the others that loved Clint.

I'm so thankful that God is big enough to handle our anger. I'm glad that His love is unconditional. He must look at us as parents look at their children. It's hard to have a favorite or imagine that any parent could. I would love a child that grew up to be a doctor but would also love their sibling if he or she ended up in prison. A parent's love does not discriminate. It doesn't matter how much one succeeds or how much one rebels. When they're bad or good, we love them. I've learned that God loves us in a purer, similar fashion. When I believed Him to be a hoax, God loved me. When I wanted Him back, He, to my surprise, was there waiting and loved me still.

# CHAPTER 12
## My Life Has Been Hijacked

*"Opportunities to find deeper powers within ourselves come when life seems most challenging."*
~Joseph Campbell~

Grief is like a kidnapper, a tormentor, and a terrorist! First, it snatches you from the life you once knew and loved, and then it terrorizes your every waking moment by taunting you about every memory of the past, everything you are missing, and every second that is lost. Slowly, it steals who you were and shapes you into something else. For me, it's a battle in my mind. It's a fight to keep bitterness, jealousy, and hatred from taking over and replacing the soft and gentle heart that used to fill my chest.

To control me, my captor plays with my mind and even withholds sleep from me. Since that day, I haven't slept a peaceful night. I haven't slept peacefully even though I've done all the things people promise will work. Remedies like warm milk, tea, or even medication haven't helped me. These hours of sleeplessness give my tormentor, my new enemy, grief, only more time to win against me.

Ah, the torture! It feels like pins are being pressed into my ears, like glass is being shoved under my fingernails, and like knives are sinking deep into my chest. Damn, it hurts. The enemy never retreats. He engages me in a battle where fairness has no place. He is a harsh opponent. This battle, my battle, his battle is one I may not win.

My captor keeps me bound and gagged. Certainly those around me can't hear my cries for help. They don't hear my painful pleas. My captor tells me to wear a smile and laugh so no one knows what he does to me inside. I look at those I love and can't believe they don't hear my subtle cries for help or see the sadness on my face: the sparkle that once filled my eyes has now faded, and there are lines that have been left behind. These lines have paved their way deep into my skin because of sleepless nights and an endless stream of tears.

Just when I think he's about to release me, my enemy pulls me back. He drags me back into the dark hole and slams the door. Silence! Only the clanking of steel and the visions of yesteryear flood my senses. In these moments, I see my sons playing with their sisters. I hear their laughter and watch them play as the sunlight bounces off their nearly white hair. They giggle together as they roll around in the fall leaves, undoubtedly planning some sort of mischievous act that most definitely violates the rules. They don't care, they're together! The fall air fills my senses, and my mind fleets to watching football games and drinking hot chocolate, growing up on the farm, bringing supper to my dad and brothers during harvest, and putting the kids on the school bus the first day of September. Fall has so many memories that are filled with the things we loved: each child picking out and carving their own pumpkin, Clint and I making corn shocks for the front deck, and hunting... my heart skips a beat, and I draw in a breath that I can't release. Hunting? My mind floods with blaze orange, the ambulance siren, my own screams, and Clint's lifeless body. The fragrances of fall turn to scents of blood. My moment of peace is gone.

As quickly as my captor allows me this moment of happiness, he steals it away. All the beautiful thoughts and memories of fall instantly turn to horror for not only this moment, but also for every moment when I recall all of these things that I once held so fondly. My mind has built a new pathway, a new association that will haunt these once cherished memories. This is yet another weapon that my captor uses against me.

He allows me these moments of happiness in which I can live. Then, cruelly he reminds me I am his. This life is not my own. It belongs to my terrorist, my enemy. He assaults my thoughts and sabotages my happiness. My life has been hijacked, and I am held captive by this terrorist named *grief*!

# CHAPTER 13
## Would Someone Please Tell Me Where He Is

*"Missing someone gets easier every day because even though you are one day further from the last time you saw them, you are one day closer to the next time you will."*
*~Author Unknown~*

Ever since the kids were born, they've spent the majority of their time with me. If I needed to get groceries, they came with. If I made a quick trip to Walmart, they came with. It was rare if they went elsewhere in their early years. As they got older, they obviously started to spread their wings and wanted to spend time with friends. When they went to the homes of friends, I always had to know who they were with, when they planned to be back, if the houses had fire alarms, and if they would brush their teeth, and I always reminded them to call to say good night and I love you.

After Clint's accident, I had an unquenchable need to know where he was. If he was out, I always knew where he was. I was a good parent who kept tabs on my children day and night. They were my children, my responsibility. Now, in an instant, Clint was gone. How was I supposed to shut off that need to care for and look over my son? Was it possible to just turn him over blindly to the unknown? The answer was and still is *no*, of course.

In order to feel some peace, I needed to know where he was. When someone passes away, everyone thinks their loved one goes to Heaven. I knew this simply wasn't true.

I needed to be certain that Clint was in Heaven. In searching for this answer, I reread his confirmation faith statement. When Clint selected his confirmation verse, many thought he'd made a mistake. His chosen verse seemed so serious.

> *"For the wages of sin is death,
> but the free gift of God is eternal life."*
> ~ Romans 6:23 ~

Now, I get it; Clint got it. He had a personal relationship with Jesus and lived a life with Him at the center. He approached every day so that others would know God by knowing him. Clint wasn't perfect, but he knew he didn't need to be. He knew the gift he'd been given for accepting Jesus into his heart and life.

After reading Clint's faith statement, I had no doubt that, between his expressed belief and the way he lived his life, he was with God. Now that I had confirmed what my heart knew to be true, I needed to know more about where he was. Simply, I needed to know what Heaven was like. I needed to be able to know and teach the truth.

I went on a quest to find out what Heaven was like. Even in the early days after losing Clint, I asked many of the various pastors that visited me about Heaven. In general, I was told that very little is known. One of them, who I didn't know very well, annoyed me completely. He was unwavering in his belief that the Bible reveals nearly nothing about the afterlife, about Heaven. To me, this was such lazy theology. Even as he spoke, my heart rebuked his commentary while my brain categorized it as ignorance. To be fair to him, my mind was in a state of partial functioning, and I struggled to follow his bleak explanation. To be fair to me, I couldn't get past his incessant farting on my couch. I glanced at my siblings, Kyle and Bobbie, several times to see if they noticed. If they did, they were relentlessly stoic and never let on. As for the pastor, I chose to believe that he thought that I didn't notice because I was in such a state of shock. When in actuality, my mind was being catty and already planning to disinfect the cushion that supported his tush. I couldn't help but think this was an ironic twist of fate. His response was *full of shit* and so was he. Of course our Father in Heaven wouldn't promise us an extravagant afterlife without sharing any knowledge of it. I knew better than this. I hope God forgives me for those ungracious thoughts and that He too has a sense of humor.

As an avid researcher, I refused to believe the Bible didn't reveal a glimpse of Heaven. I refused to believe that the God I was raised to know wouldn't reveal more about a place where we all hope to live one day. Even in my fogged state of mind, I was determined to research this for myself. I thrust myself into studying the views of Bible scholars as well as reading the Bible and other reputable resources. What I found both intrigued and angered me. I was angered because the visiting pastors should have clearly known more. I was intrigued because the Bible reveals a great deal about Heaven. Through my research, the following is a partial list of things I found to be true of Heaven. All of these things are rooted within the Bible itself:

- *Heaven is a real place.*
- *Heaven is fascinating and not boring.*
- *In Heaven, we will be reunited with our perfect bodies.*
- *Heaven provides us with an eternity of discovery.*

- *In Heaven, we worship and serve God.*
- *Heaven is purposeful with work to do.*
- *Our loved ones in Heaven are aware of and pray for us.*
- *Those in Heaven do not feel sadness for the rest of us left behind.*
- *The people in Heaven prepare for the day we join them.*
- *In Heaven, there is everything we desire and nothing we don't.*
- *Although relationships in Heaven may not be as we understand relationships to be here on earth, we will know our loved ones in Heaven, and they will know us.*

Ah, what a relief. Now I can rest with a glimpse of where my son lives. I can close my eyes and, ever so slightly, envision his new home. He's happy, he's busy, he prays for us, he's in a real place that is fascinating and full of discovery, he feels no sadness or pain, he has everything he ever dreamed of at his fingertips, he waits for me, and we will be together again. My son lives in a *real* place. He is *not* dead.

At the beginning of this book, I stated that I do not use the word *dead* in relation to my son. I've cringed at every single place in this book where I've had to use the terms *dead* or *dying*, and I've only used them for your understanding. To me, I believe 100% that Clint lives in another place that is maybe near or maybe far from earth. He is happy and healthy. The body that he lived in here may have passed away, but his spirit did not. In fact, even the Bible promises that his beautiful body will be restored to its perfect form and reunited with his spirit. I sense Clint's existence so strongly that I feel him alive every day. Somehow, my spirit is connected to him, and I've never felt his light go out.

I have even discovered some new, emerging scientific research that validates this sensation. Scientists have found that the energy within the human body does not dissipate when a body dies. The energy remains unchanged. The laws of physics say that energy can't be killed. Could it be that this energy is the spirit or soul that lives within the physical body? Could this be real scientific proof that the spirit is real and lives on? I like to think so and will be researching it further. It's refreshing to know that someone's life can't be blown out like a candle. This energy, the soul, is eternal. I take comfort in knowing that my son lives in paradise. In paradise, there are no phones, no e-mails, no text messages, and no other means of physical communication to earth.

When a heart is filled with hurt from missing a loved one, we must try to remember God's promise that we will be together again! Until that day Clinty, I will miss you! I try to remember that the 5th was not just the day we lost him, but rather it was the day he really became alive in Heaven. Although it's a day of pain for us, what an amazing day it was for him. I tell myself that Clint lives; I just can't see him.

I used to plead with God to return my son. I would stay awake and cry. I would promise Him almost anything and everything for that trade. One night, after realizing what Heaven was really like, I dreamt of Clint. It was more than a dream. I believe with all my heart that God allowed him a few moments with his mother. Clint shared that he was happy and had lots of friends. They were with him, but I couldn't make out their faces. I didn't really care. All I wanted to do was look at him. He hugged me and rubbed his prickly cheek against mine. He put his hands on me, one on each shoulder, looked into my eyes, and said, "Please Mom, don't ask me to come back. It's amazing here." He hugged me again and said he had to go.

In that moment, I truly learned the extent of the sacrifices a parent can and must make. As much as I wanted Clint with me, he belonged with God. I love my son, but there was no way that I could ask him to leave his Father in Heaven after looking into his beautiful blue eyes. I knew I would never plead with God again to return Clint to me. I knew he was home. Instead, I wrote and repeated this prayer . . .

> *Dear God, when the pain of missing someone we love consumes us, please be with us and remind us it is only temporary and that we will have eternity together. Help fill our hearts with a peace that knowing those who believe in and follow you WILL be together again. Help our hearts and minds to visualize the great feast they prepare for our homecoming. Amen.*

As I've written, the last time I saw Clint, as I kissed his face a dozen times, he said, "Geez Mom, I've gotta go but I'm gonna be right back!" I believe with all my heart that he will be right back. He won't come back to live with me, but he will come for me. Until then, I will be sure to live a Christ-centered life so God allows him to take me with him.

I've realized that Clint is still with us and that we are a whole family. For now, Clint lives somewhere else. He lives in Heaven and prepares the celebration for our homecoming.

# CHAPTER 14

## *My Heart Opens & Hearence Reigns*

*"Faith is to believe what we do not see;
and the reward of this faith is to see what we believe."*
~St. Augustine~

As I sat in my chair overwhelmed with an emotion I couldn't find words for, I prayed to God that He would bring some good from the loss of my son. Hearence filled my senses once again. This time, it was Him. It was God. Again, I felt warm and at peace. God promised me that good would come from Clint's loss. I found myself arguing with words that hadn't been spoken. You can imagine Tim's fear and confusion. His wife was sitting in a room with just the two of us, and I was arguing with someone else. I said, "No, no, no, no! I do not like to write, and I cannot write! I will not write!" Again, God told me that I *would* write about everything and that He would help me. He told me that this was the good that would come from losing Clint. I argued, "I don't even know what I would title a book." Hearence, in its strongest form, firmly returned. My mind was flooded beyond recognition. The following words penetrated every aspect of my senses: *No Ordinary Son.* That was to be the title of my book. As I still fought the possibility of hearence, I thought to myself that my crazy mind somehow came up with a perfect title. Of course, my son was extraordinary!

Prior to that moment, God had left the gate slightly ajar. It was as though He were asking me to walk through it. I would imagine He was trying to ease me into this thing I now call *hearence*. From that moment forward, He has swung the gate wide open. He didn't just do this for me but for others who didn't know the gift they'd been given. Over the years, I have collected their stories.

**HEARANCE**

After Clint's accident, my friend Loddie came from Missouri to spend the first few weeks with me. As she made the long trip home, she experienced hearence. She felt something serene and then heard Clint say, "Lod, tell my mom I'm with her. She can't feel me, Lod. Tell her I am with her." When Loddie called to share this with me, I could tell she was physically shaken and had experienced something extraordinary. I had no doubt it was my son.

I began gardening to keep myself busy. There were many days when the tears fell so profusely that I couldn't see through them. During one calm, hot afternoon, I felt a breeze that gave me chills. I could feel Clint first touch my shoulder and then wrap his arms around me. After that day, I would often feel something strange, smile to myself, and say aloud "I know you're here, baby! I love you."

Gar had been frustrated that he'd never felt Clint after years without him. However, when Gar was driving to school one day, he said he got a strange sensation that Clint was with him. I remember the day well. It was October 28, 2010. Gar said there was no need to look because he knew Clint had been there, sitting next to him in the passenger seat.

One day, I felt like I couldn't go on. I was struggling to keep myself out of the vortex of depression and fell asleep in my chair. I remember drifting into sleep while smelling the most beautiful flowers. The smell was followed by a warm sensation. I knew this feeling from previous incidents of hearence. During this experience, Clint said that he was "sorry and that nothing went right the day of the accident." He held my hand and touched my face. He told me, "You will be ok." He promised that he would always be with me. He promised! He told me we would all be together soon.

One of the most profound incidents of hearence came to me before I even knew what it was. Certainly, it happened long before I had given it a name. It was Clint's 16th birthday and our first without him. We went to Marshall to get Christmas gifts and groceries. We were in the checkout line at a major discount store when I literally felt a push. As a parent, you know which kid does something without even needing to look. Well, I turned around to scold Clint and realized he wasn't there; he couldn't be there. Even so, the nagging feeling remained with me. I felt as though Clint were whispering to me to go to the front of the line. Now, remember that I'm a shy person who wouldn't go willingly out of my way to seek out attention. For some reason, I did it at my son's urging. There, at the front of the line, was a poor old man being humiliated by the checkout woman. She told him he didn't have enough money to pay for his cart of groceries and gifts. She was making him choose items to be taken off of his total. Suddenly, it was clear to me. I had been prompted to intervene. I walked up to the checkout lady and asked what the issue was. She rudely and condescendingly said that the man didn't have the funds for his "heaping cart of food and gifts." I told her to run his items through. She refused and told me she wouldn't. The man looked at me with surprise. I couldn't help but notice he was frail and dressed in tattered clothing. The woman continued to scold the man. I stepped up to the counter as close as I could get to her, showed her my checkbook, told her I would be paying for his bill, and politely asked her again to run them through. She told me I couldn't do that. Feeling very annoyed at the young woman who obviously enjoyed humiliating this man, I told her I wasn't making a request of which she had an option. She asked me what he could buy. I replied, "Everything." She said, "Do you know how much that is going to be?" I told her I didn't care and neither should she. She ran all of the items as I stood watching to ensure she didn't put one thing back. The elderly man was shocked and told me he would pay me back. He asked for my address. I pulled a business card out of my pocket, looked at it, and quickly put it back. I told the man there'd be no need to repay me and to have a Merry Christmas. After writing the check, I turned to walk away. The man stopped me and thanked me profusely. As I went to complete my own transaction, another man approached me stating that he was the elderly man's son. He thanked me. He said his siblings were all home for the first time in years, and he said his father was excited to have a Christmas together. He said now his father's wish would come true.

 To this day, my heart feels full when I reminisce about what happened that day in the checkout line. I know God was at work for us to do something good for the elderly man and maybe even for all who witnessed it, including my own children. I am thankful to have been His servant that day. It ignited a flame inside of me to do more for those that suffer around us. That man who anxiously planned the return of his sons for Christmas will never know how I suffered that first Christmas without one of my sons. He will also never know the peace it gave me to know that I had sparked some happiness elsewhere on that very special night.

# CHAPTER 15
## My Fears Consume Me

*"In the English language there are orphans and widows, but there is no word for the parents who lose a child."*
~Jodi Picoult~

### FEAR OF LOSING MY CHILDREN

I left home one day with all of my babies safe in their beds. *Home* is where they were supposed to be safe. I now know that is not a given right. Ever since that day, I've struggled with leaving home or my kids. I have a very founded and rational fear that one of them may not be there when I return. After all, that is exactly what happened in the fall of 2006. As a result, it's hard for me to be far from home, my kids, grandkids, parents, and siblings.

There are people who say this is irrational anxiety. That would have been a simple diagnosis if Clint's accident would have never happened to me. The fact of the matter is that for me, it's real. All I have to do is close my eyes and see Clinty on the front lawn to know that it can and does happen.

It's hard when the kids are away. Even though I have lost a son, it wouldn't be the same as losing a daughter. It's different for each of us. Most importantly, I know the intense pain of losing a child, and it's a pain I never want to experience again. Losing one of the girls wouldn't be easier, but it's a different loss than what I'm familiar with.

In talking with a close friend of mine who lost her daughter, I find that her experiences are different. We both lost children, but our experiences aren't nearly the same. Some of that's because she and I are different people, but some of it's because she lost a daughter and I lost a son. Although both losses were severe, our expectations for their futures and our personal relationships with them were different.

I'm learning to live with the fear that is in my heart as being part of the new me. To me, this fear is as evident as having a third eye. It feels like this fear is so out of place from the old, peaceful heart I used to have. I was so content being surrounded by my babies each night. I never took them for granted. Now, that old place where peace used to live holds only fear. I haven't felt *complete* peace since the night of November 4th, 2006, when I kissed them all good night. I miss it, and I hate this anomaly that has replaced it. It feels foreign and, at times, not real. It still feels like a movie. The fact is, it's my life. I wonder if amputees feel that way when they miss their arm or leg. Like it should be there but isn't.

**FEAR OF THE DARK**

My fear of the dark increased exponentially. I used to be a little afraid of it, but after losing Clint, the fear became crippling. It was so severe that not only could I never be alone after dark, but I also couldn't walk into my basement or my own bedroom once the sun had set. For months, I slept on the couch until Tim would get home from patrolling. When we'd go to sleep in our bedroom, I'd pile pillows along the edge of the bed so I couldn't see the windows and the blackness that lay beyond them. The fear was so intense that I would have to wake Tim to even use the bathroom for nearly a year. He would have to walk me to the bathroom door and wait for me. I was so angry about this. I had already lost so much. Why did I have to lose my independence too?

It was my birthday that following year. I was cynical and angry with God. I prayed that He would gift me with peace from this unrealistic fear of the dark. I prayed that He would take it away. That night, as with every night for nearly a year, I carefully piled four large pillows on the edge of my bed. As though I were a brick layer, I carefully flattened the first two pillows so they made a solid base. It was roughly eighteen inches by four feet. Then, I stacked a fluffy row of pillows on top of them. As I always did, I got into bed and made sure I couldn't see over or around them. That night, as though to test God and His ability to answer my prayer, I pushed all of my pillows onto the floor to prove the fear was still there. To prove He was a hoax. To my shock, there was no fear. All that was left in its place was peace. Part of me was angry that this was so easy for God. I was angry I had suffered a year and all I had to do was ask. He was supposed to be my Heavenly Father; He should have known I needed His help. Right? Even though I was angered by how simply He could solve my fear of the dark, I couldn't help but thank Him for bringing me a light that no darkness could overcome.

## FEAR OF BEING ALONE

The fear of being alone persisted for several more years. This was nearly crippling with Tim working so many nights as a deputy. After I progressed from going to bed on the couch to going back in the bedroom, I would literally throw myself into bed, cover my head, and leave the television and lights on all night. I don't mean just one or two lights; I mean every single one in the house. One day I was talking to Pastor John, who had now become one of our close friends, and I was telling him about this crippling fear of being alone at the farm. He asked me if I had asked God for protection. Of course I would have done it if it were that simple, I thought to myself. Then, as immediately as the words came out of my mouth, I remembered what God had done when I asked Him to take away my fear of the dark. In an instant He had done it. Now that my attention was peaked, I asked Pastor John what I needed to ask for. He simply replied, "For angels." He must have noted a lost look on my face and told me that God would send angels upon my request. He went on to say that they weren't the white-winged fairies we read about in storybooks but rather muscle-bound warriors. He told me to ask God to send them whenever I needed them. Again, filled with cynicism for a God I felt betrayed by, I pondered it.

    That night, as though daring God again so I could prove Him wrong, I asked for these muscle-bound angels. I didn't ask for one of them. I thought if I was placing an order, it was going to be a big order. If God had this kind of army at his disposal, I wanted it, and I asked for several warrior angels. I asked for one to be placed at each corner on the roof of my house, for one to sit on the front porch by the bedroom window, and for one more to sit on the edge of my bed. That is how I imagined them as I fell asleep that night. I fell asleep? Yes, I fell asleep all alone, yet I sensed that I was no longer alone. The funny thing is I could feel them there. Everyone has probably had that sense of not being alone. We just intuitively know when someone is in a room with us or when someone is watching us. That is the feeling I had. I knew my angels were there in all their glory to protect me just because I asked. You're probably wondering if my fear of being alone went away. Yes, it did; however, it did return easily.

In these times, I would often call my husband while he was on duty. I would be frantic and beg him to stop by and check the house. He would remind me that God's angels were with me. He would laugh that as big and burly as he was, he couldn't provide more than they could. Tim would tell me to close my eyes, pray, and ask for them.

We found that my angels or maybe God, much like us, like to be recognized for their service. If I simply expect them to be there, sometimes fear can return when I'm alone. The key is remembering to ask God to send them and thank Him for it. When too much time passes without doing that, He must assume I no longer need them. Then, He reallocates His resources elsewhere. Sometimes, I feel rude and have had to go soul-searching because of my poor behavior. If I had hired bodyguards, I would never walk right past them night after night without acknowledgement. Of course not, I would probably even cook meals for them and bring them late-night snacks. I would appreciate their service and their presence. Why would I be so callous to angels sent from God's own army? Of course I needed to acknowledge them! When I need them, which is still often, I ask for them, and then I thank them and God. When I do this, it never fails. I feel safe, and I *am* safe.

## FEAR OF THE "SCARY TUB"

In our basement we have a craft room. Tim hates when I call it that. It doesn't sound very manly. It's a room where he and I can retreat to partake in our hobbies. He has his guns, his reloading equipment, and his hunting things. I have my scrapbooking, card-making, and jewelry-making supplies. In actuality, he has a small area while I have the rest of the room. He jokes that we'll build a shed one day so he can have a man cave for all of his things. Then he quickly laughs and states that I would probably fill that space too.

In the corner of this room sits a storage tub. It has become known as the "scary tub." I hate this tub! It's a Rubbermaid tub that is grey with a matching lid. It's fairly large and looks as though it has never been touched. If you lifted that tub, you would say it's heavy. If you took off the lid, you would say it's sad. For under that lid is everything from that horrible time period. It contains cards from the wake and the funeral, extra funeral programs, the LifeSource donation center letters and paperwork, the beret from the soldier at Clint's funeral, the poster from his classmates, and everything else I can't bear to see. Some ask why I don't just get rid of it. I don't throw it out because I will also face this fear someday and go through the scary tub. Inside of it, there are cards from those who loved and supported us, there are items cherished by others that were given to us, and there are letters of thanks from people who Clint so graciously donated his organs and tissues to. Someday, I will go through the scary tub. Someday, I will find a way to face this fear.

## FACING MY FEARS

People say they're proud of me for facing so many fears. The reality is that perseverance has been forced upon me. I'm nothing special. Life is a mystery. I have no idea why God has brought such pain into my life. I can only imagine its purpose is to give me an experience to share with others who are hurting. I trust that I'll know the reason for this pain when I find it. Who knows, maybe I've been sharing my experience with others all along and I just don't realize it. People's words give me hope that this is true. I do know there must be a profound reason why I'm living without my son. There is no explanation or description for the dichotomy that takes place in my mind. That dichotomy is comprised of the desire to be happy, yet it's surrounded by an intense pain. It's shattering to my spirit. It's in my lowest times when I focus on the fact that if anything good is to come from the loss of my amazing son, it will have to come through me. I owe Clint that tribute.

Life is full of things we don't anticipate, and sometimes the only thing we are left to do is to face it and take a lesson from it. From the loss of Clint, I have learned a great deal about people, life, grief, death, living, and grace. Although another fear of mine is the public, it has become a goal of mine to share whatever wisdom I can from this horrible experience.

# CHAPTER 16
## *Those I Once Loved to Hear About*

*"Envy comes from wanting something that isn't yours, but grief comes from losing something you've already had."*
~Jodi Picoult~

There is such a dichotomy in my mind. I'm happy for all those I love as I watch their lives move forward, yet I feel such pain. As I watch proms, graduations, weddings, babies being born, and so forth, my heart aches as my face smiles. Every time, I tell myself it's not their fault that Clint isn't here and that they shouldn't have to stop living in order to honor my son's life. Yet at times, I wish they would. Quickly, my mind refocuses itself and tells me just how selfish this really is. No, I don't need my mind to scold me. I already know. I just don't know what to do about my feelings.

I know that Clint would want me to promote and share in the happiness of others. If he had a mantra for life, that would've been part of it. When he was little, I always told him to try making someone else's day better. This is the same lesson my parents taught me. Certainly, part of making someone's day better is caring about what they do. We show this by being interested in them and by supporting them. This is a goal of mine. It's something I've worked hard to regain.

It wasn't until roughly the sixth year after losing Clint when it no longer hurt to see friends and family enjoying life. I've been able to sort through my hurt and pinpoint its real source. It doesn't hurt to see my friends and family enjoying life; it hurts to see Clint absent from living with them. Although this difference seems small, it's helped me to regain a realistic and reasonable approach to life. Clint is a puzzle piece that's forever missing. As a mother, Clint's absence is one of the first things I notice. I often wonder if others notice it to. Part of me hopes they do.

Clint is remembered at many events. For instance, his classmates laid a cap and gown on his chair at their high school graduation. At Megan's wedding, she had a special bouquet of flowers placed on the altar. I have no doubt that the other kids will do something similar when they marry. However, when it's an event for someone or something else where I feel he would've been, it's not our place and, in some cases, it's not even appropriate to do such things. During these times, I've learned to have a piece of him there with me. For instance, I wear either his cross or my necklace with his picture in it, or I wear something of his. I realize that he's not really there, but it makes me feel like he's a part of the event.

It's still hard when we're at an event and people talk about life as though Clint never existed. Even so, I'm finding ways to cope with it. Again, these are times when I escape into my own mind and remind myself that he's still with me and just lives somewhere else. He lives somewhere beautiful, and he awaits my arrival home.

So, why did God take Clint home far before we thought it was time? Why did he leave this world so young? While searching the Bible, I found a verse that made it clear to me. Isaiah 57:1 says, "The righteous perish, and one ponders it in his heart; devout men are taken away, and no one understands that the righteous are taken away to be spared from evil." To me, that verse brings sense to nonsense. Clint was pure of heart, and he was taken home to Heaven before the evils of this world could hurt his innocence. He was taken home to Heaven before this world could harden his heart.

# CHAPTER 17
## *Don't Hurt the Money*

*"Never mistake knowledge for wisdom.
One helps you make a living; the other helps you make a life."*
~Sandra Carey~

I must confess I chuckle as I type the title of this chapter as "Don't Hurt the Money." Ever since I was a little girl, my parents have encouraged me to learn. They encouraged all of my siblings as well, but it was different for me. As I interviewed my parents for the writing of this book, I asked some questions I have always wanted the answers to. In general, I wanted to know why, out of the five of us, they chose me to become a scholar. Mom simply answered, "Maybe it was you who wanted it." Dad expanded by saying that it was easy to inspire me to learn because I always loved learning. When I would go to my Grandma Weber's house after school, I would have her drill me on spelling words. We'd have our own little spelling bees. Whenever my grandma and I were bored with our spelling bees, she, who had been a teacher for nearly 70 years, would teach me Latin. My friends and siblings would play after school or watch cartoons, but I wanted to learn.

It wasn't like that during the school day. As far back as I can remember, I wanted to be in charge of my own learning, but I also wanted to be guided by those who knew more. I wanted them to facilitate my learning by pointing me in the direction of knowledge but not by filling me with their own knowledge. I wanted to be forced to think differently and more deeply. My parents did that for me. They were the perfect artists of my brain, slowly molding it by facilitating my learning. They were and still are an inspiration to me. Those long nights when my mom worked as a registered nurse, Dad and I stayed up until the wee hours of the morning. In those hours, Dad pushed me to think outside of the box and troubleshoot life. As I grew as an educator, I found a name for what my dad was doing. He was promoting higher level thinking; he was facilitating the emergence of a scholar. I guess I've always been a geek.

They told me to read the encyclopedias one by one because knowledge would give me power. This is a power that comes from knowing a little about everything. It's also a power that takes the fear out of the unknown and creates a foundation of familiarity with math, science, geography, animals, and so forth. I read those encyclopedias until I wore the pages thin. The more I read, the more I desired to learn. An unquenchable thirst was born.

I was reading books before kindergarten. When I was a first grader, my mom was ordering not just one or two books from the school's book flyers but cases of books. The other kids would tease me about this. The teacher would call out the students' names and give them one or two books with their order slips. Then, the teacher would come to my name. The other kids would interject, "Tanya Weber, your parents need to bring the truck to pick up yours." I knew they were teasing, but it made me sad. I didn't understand why they thought it was funny. I soon learned that my quest for knowledge would be a private matter. I decided not to try hard at school. I determined that mediocre grades would suffice. While my private quest to learn only grew at home, my public quest was squelched. It would remain dormant for years.

Maybe this was because my parents always told me to make life about the others around you. They stressed that the attention should be placed on them and not me. It should be "you" and not "I." So, I learned to listen more and talk less. Dad always told me that his father told him, "It's better to keep your mouth shut and appear stupid than to open it and remove all doubt." I grew up thinking that the grandfather I never met was a wise man. I'm sure he was, but I found out later in life that it was Mark Twain who originated that quote.

It wasn't until my sophomore year of college when I realized that it was alright to publically express knowledge because I was nearly kicked out of school. From there, I finished my undergrad with honors, completed my master's with a 4.0, and rocked my doctoral program with a perfect record. Although I like to say my grades are public knowledge because they're on my transcript, I have never even told my parents. I guess they will read it in this book and be proud. Yes, I know they will be. To me, their pride will be prejudiced and targeted at the wrong individual. While their minds are praising my accomplishments, they should be praising their parenting and the inspiration they instilled in me for learning.

I tell you all of this not to brag because that isn't me. I tell you so you can fully understand the impact of the loss I endured. On that fateful fall morning, I not only lost my son, but also I lost "the money" due to the trauma.

Being a college professor has never been enough for me. I've never been shy of any kind of hard work. In addition to teaching at the college, my husband and I also run an international research company, own several rental units, and love to renovate old houses. My parents always tell me that I work too hard. They fear that the workload and stress will cause my mind to slip. Over the years, my dad began to joke with me saying "Don't hurt the money!" What he means is to be picky about the kind of work I do so I can continue to be an educator. He thinks I should cease involvement in the other labor-intensive tasks. You see, my parents have always worked multiple jobs. They each had their professional jobs: Dad was an engineer, and Mom was a registered nurse. In addition, they also ran (and still do run) a farming operation and gravel corporation. Their point in saying "Don't hurt the money" was for me to use my mind and not my hands to make a living.

Although the saying has been a joke among us, my parents have always said it with a hint of warning. In my naive mind, I thought that if I were physically careful, then my mind would be fine. I promised not to get hit in the head while working on projects with a two-by-four, not to sniff the lead paint I was scraping, and certainly to wear a mask when abating mold. Also, I would drive carefully to avoid accidents and wear good shoes so I wouldn't fall and bump my head. There, the *money* would be fine.

When someone dies (I hate that word) you expect to be sad and to have your world turned upside down. What I didn't expect was for my world to be *destroyed* in ways that impacted much more than just my emotions. It impacted my functioning. I had *hurt the money*. I didn't realize it at the time, but I now know what I experienced has a name. It's called post-traumatic stress disorder (PTSD). Not only did PTSD onset with the trauma I experienced that day, but also it caused significant brain damage. Some of the brain damage was temporary, and unfortunately, some of it was permanent. I didn't hit my head. Nothing physical happened, but I'd definitely "hurt the money." I know there will be skeptics, but I challenge you to open your mind and understand the power of our brains. I am a highly educated, doctoral-level professor who has studied the brain and mental health for years. I understand it, or should I say I thought I did until I experienced the unimaginable firsthand. Not only did I "hurt the money," but also I catastrophically demolished the bank that held it.

Yes, I sustained brain damage without receiving physical injury. My brain damage was induced by the trauma surrounding my son's death. As strange as it sounds, I could almost feel some of my mental functions fade to black when I found Clint. The best analogy I can give is what would happen when we shut off one of the older televisions, the ones from the 1970s. After you turned the television off, the screen would go from grey and quickly shrink to the center until it faded out. That is exactly what I experienced with my mind. Of course, when I found Clint's body, I didn't know I'd lost more than my son. In that moment, nothing else mattered.

In the days and weeks after losing Clint, reality set in, and life had to resume having some resemblance of normalcy. For instance, I had to be a caregiver for my family, and I had to return to work.

The researching scholar in me recorded these changes in my brain functions, and I asked others to monitor for me what I couldn't monitor myself. Through journaling, observational logs, and ability logs, my brain's damage and functioning were recorded. Although these records are informative to me, what mattered is what I'm about to share with you.

Overall, the areas of my functioning/ability that were most impacted were bathing/dressing, cooking, professional work abilities, writing/spelling, and the collaborative use of my hands. As I alluded to earlier, some of these abilities came back fairly quickly, others took years, and some have never returned. It's like hearing a song on a scratched CD. Because the CD is damaged, it catches on nothing. Throughout this struggle, my mind has been like a scratched CD. It has spun looking for something that had been there, but because of damage, it clearly wasn't. When dealing with a bad CD, you can toss it away, but when it's the human brain, we tend to be stuck with it.

At first, there were losses in basic functioning. I didn't know what some fairly automated functions/abilities were. For instance, when I was first told to shower, I didn't know what a shower was. I knew it was in the bathroom because my husband and friend walked me in there. I watched Tim turn the water on and realized a shower must have something to do with that little booth-looking thing the water was running into. As I was about to step into the booth, he grabbed my arm and told me to take my clothes off. Clothes, I thought to myself. What are they? The way he said it and, more importantly, the look and nod he gave me when he said it indicated that *clothes* were the things I was wearing. Ok, so I take my *clothes* off and get into the booth and let water run on me. That is a shower. Ok. After taking my clothes off and getting into the shower, I saw bottles with words on them. I could read them but had no idea what the words meant: shampoo, bodywash, conditioner, and shaving cream.

What are they? When I got out of the booth, now known to me as a shower, I stood there shivering and dripping wet. Tim came in and dried me off with a towel. I had no idea that the water from the booth needed to be taken off of me. My mind struggled to understand why they had put me in the booth, dumped water on me, and then wiped it off. I wondered what all those bottles were doing in there. Was I supposed to use them? Once I was dried off, I wondered what I was supposed to do now that I was *showered*. Just as I was about to walk into the great room filled with people, Tim told me to put clothes on. Ok, I thought to myself, what are clothes? Thank goodness he had some sitting on the counter and grabbed them. I was even more grateful when he put them on my body. Slowly, through repetition, I learned that we need to shower our bodies (after taking our clothes off) and dress ourselves with clothing to cover our body parts. This ability was the quickest to return.

The next loss was my ability to cook. For that matter, I didn't even know what food was. How is this even possible? I tried desperately to make supper for our family. Before the accident, we always ate supper together. Now, no one would sit at the table. No one said it, but not one of us could bear to see Clint's empty chair. At least we can eat, I thought to myself. I'm a great cook. The problem was I had no idea what the word *cook* even meant. My kids have always joked that they wished they knew what some boxed foods tasted like. They had never even tasted Hamburger Helper until junior high, and that was at my sister's house. She, unlike me, would rather not cook. For months, I would open the cupboards and try desperately to *cook*.

The main issue with cooking concerned the loss of another function, my vocabulary. The jar spells S-A-L-T. I know I have seen it before, but what do you do with it? I had no idea. The freezer? That is where I'll find something to make. I see H-A-M-B-U-R-G-E-R. I slowly sound it out in my mind. The package is red and white, and it's familiar to me. Yes, my dad and oldest brother, Hollis, raise cattle. It's beef. I remember it being something the family would brag about–top-grade Angus beef. Helplessness fills me as I wonder what you do with it. I shut the freezer. I feel defeated. I think maybe there is something left from the week of Clint's accident. Some frozen food, maybe? I turn back to the freezer and quickly recall that the food is gone. People only brought food for that first week. I clearly remember the extended family members commenting about eating the last hotdish the day after the funeral. Reality hits; the food is *gone*.

I decided I would go to the grocery store. As I walked through the aisles, I was overwhelmed by the thousands of words that were bombarding my mind. The words were everywhere: butter, milk, ham, eggs, spice, beans, rice, coffee, and bread. I had no idea what they were. I stood in the aisles of that grocery store as the room started to spin. I felt dizzy and wanted to throw up. I saw foods that I knew I'd made for my babies, for my Clinty, but I had no idea what they were. There were even some foods I knew only Clinty liked, and I knew I would never be able to put them in my cart again. I was, once again, sad, alone, and lost.

My ability to understand the meaning of even simple words was gone. Even with my speech, I would often stop in the middle of a sentence while the wheels in my brain grinded against each other. My mind couldn't hit the cog that would bring sense to the senselessness. My ability to process meaning was severely limited. Not only did this impact my ability to function in my everyday life, but also it impacted my ability to perform my professional duties.

I no longer knew what a computer was or what it was used for. I would try to go to my office and find that hours had passed while I was staring at a blank screen. I kept thinking over and over, "I know how to use this. I just worked on this machine a few days ago." The fact is I had no idea how to navigate the software or files that I had previously become so adept at using. To confuse matters even further, the way my mind viewed my desktop computer was different than my laptop. I could understand aspects of my laptop but those same understandings did not transfer to my desktop computer. These discrepancies in how my brain processed information caused even further confusion and frustration. There was no rhyme or reason to the way my mind recognized or remembered information.

Once I returned to the college classroom, I would be in front of my students (I teach practicing educators), and my mind would go blank in the middle of a sentence. I would not only lose my place in the lesson, but also the words my mind naturally wanted to say disappeared as though they were deleted from my vocabulary database. Imagine talking in front of a room full of teachers and, all of a sudden, your mind goes blank. All eyes remain on you as though waiting for you to continue, waiting for you to regain your composure, but you cannot because your mind is empty. My co-teachers, Scott and Jay, who are also dear friends, finally put together an informal plan that would ease my anxiety about the possibility of this happening. They never let on about the anxiety and embarrassment it likely caused them. They would watch for such incidents and simply step in and take over for me. Professionally, these two amazing educators and friends stood steadfast in their support and belief in me.

To this day, my vocabulary has not totally returned, and what has returned did not come back easily. I have literally had to fight for every word by learning it over again. Not only just learning the word but also the context in which it belongs.

I also lost much of my spelling ability. Unlike the meaning of words, which I had to relearn, the ability to spell slowly returned on its own. It was a struggle for nearly two years. During those years, I patiently looked up words and used spell-checker on all of my documents.

The ability to put together a compound word is a total anomaly to me still. The ability to understand this concept is absent. I have read about the concept of compound words, and I've asked my family, friends, and colleagues. Additionally, I've even been tutored by educational experts. Finally, seven years after the loss of Clint, I had to face the fact that my ability to understand, put together, and properly utilize compound words was gone forever. To compensate for this, I had a grammatical expert put together a list of compound words. I took the list, laminated it, and placed it by my computer monitor. Rather than fight this loss of brain function, I have finally adopted a strategy to circumvent it.

I had no idea what to do during this time. Tim would often tell me not to worry and that he'd take care of it. I was sickened. I'd lost my son. I'd lost my productive role as a mother and as a provider. I couldn't work, and I couldn't cook. I didn't know what common food items were. I didn't know what a computer was. I just wanted somebody to help me!

Many told us to call them if we needed help. In fact, they told us to call if we needed anything. Yeah, *we* could call. For stupid! I was and still am a proud woman. I'd never call. Why couldn't they just call me? So many things no longer made sense to me. I was so confused. Why did people bring the food when there were so many people around that could have cooked it? Why didn't they bring the food when all of the people there to help were gone? Why didn't they visit when all of the visitors had returned to their lives? Why did I care? The old me liked being alone. Now, I fear being alone. The old me hated to be helped. Now, I needed the help, but my voice wouldn't ask for it. Where were the hotdishes, and where were the visitors?

My mind was broken, seriously broken. The world had no idea of the losses I'd experienced. I had been well-educated, smart, and professionally on top of the world. In an instant, it was gone. Some of the losses impacted my mental abilities, such as the ability to spell or retrieve vocabulary, and other losses were more physical, such as one hand being forever faster than the other. All of these were things that few people realized or understood. Top all of this with trying to make sense of losing my son so tragically. With a normal functioning brain, it would have been hard enough, but it was nearly impossible with the amount of damage my brain had sustained. Most people expected me to slowly piece my life together and return to normalcy. That alone is unrealistic, and only those who have lost a child would understand. There was an expectation that all of my other brain functions were still intact. After all, my head hadn't slammed against a windshield in a head-on collision. What they didn't realize is that it just as well could have been. I was dealing with the same type of traumatic impact to my brain.. Maybe they would've been more understanding if my head was bound in gauze with blood seeping through. Maybe they would have given forbearance. No one expects the brain to become damaged from witnessing something traumatic. How would I navigate among them with my secret? This secret damage to my brain had to take the back burner. Later, I'd find a way to share this with my family and the world. Later, I'd tell educators what I'd discovered in the hopes that they could help their students. All of this would have to wait until later.

Most importantly, I lost my oldest son, who is a part of my very being. Just beneath the surface of my pained face were a broken spirit and a severely damaged brain. I suffered silently and alone. How could I ever tell the world that I did nothing wrong and yet still *hurt the money*?

# CHAPTER 18

# *Knowing Clint*

*"In this life we cannot always do great things. But we can do small things with great love."*
~Mother Teresa~

From the time Clint was born, he was full of smiles. He always had this angelic look about him with his blond hair and his glistening, perfect teeth in an ear-to-ear smile. He was happy, energetic, and full of life. There wasn't a day when he didn't make my emotions range from sheer joy to frustration and anger. The anger almost always came from his mischievous deeds that were well-intended. They were well-intended to produce fun for him or those around him. Most of the time he did just that, but on occasion, he got himself into trouble. His silly interactions were always coupled with his own special vernacular comprised of words such as *shibee*. To be honest, I'm not even sure what it means let alone if I spelled it right.

In his times of mischief, generally he'd laugh it off and tell me to "lighten up and have some fun." Then, he'd throw his arms around me and smother me in hugs and kisses. Even as a young man, that's something he never stopped doing. To add to how special this was, he didn't care who saw him do it. He loved, and he loved proudly!

All of this is just part of who he was. He had a kindness that anyone can grow within themselves. For Clint, it was a priority. From a very young age, he knew that a smile was all it took to leave a mark on someone forever.

To fully understand my son, you need to realize he wasn't perfect. As he grew up and attended high school, he was generally a C, a D, and sometimes an F student. Because I'm an educator, you can imagine my dismay. During his freshman year, I began to wonder if Clint had a learning disability or if he was just academically lazy. So I did what most educators do, I had him assessed. I didn't want to label him at school, so we had him privately tested. Clint's test revealed an extremely high IQ. What this meant was that Clint could've literally done anything. Certainly good grades were within the realm of reason. When I sat down to talk with Clint about it, he wasn't surprised about his test scores. Actually, he showed little interest in them at all. He simply replied by telling me that he knew he was smart.

It was what he told me next that was profound and has never left the forefront of my mind. Clint said that grades weren't everything and that most people were so wrapped up in attaining high grades that they forget what was important. They forget to focus on the people around them.

Clint told me he'd much rather spend his time making the day for others. He said he'd put his brains to work later when he attended college to teach history. He cautioned me that the teaching would be delayed a bit because he planned to enlist in the United States Army after college graduation. My heart sank for fear that this would be far too dangerous for my soft-hearted son. He quickly reassured me that he promised Grandma Weber that he'd quickly rise to the ranks of an officer with a degree and would be much safer. He joked that he had too many plans for him to die. He said once his tour with the Army was up, he would attend graduate school for his doctorate in U.S. history. Oh my goodness, he was a genius when it came to U.S. history and world history. He and Garrett would spend hours researching and reenacting famous battles. In the last year of his life, Clint even began collecting memorabilia for his future classroom. He had ordered an original Army trench coat from World War II, an Army helmet, and a set of Nazi uniforms. He had planned to place all of them in glass cases inside his future classroom. You see, Clint was a hands-on, experiential learner. He hated paper-and-pencil tests. He planned to have his students learn by living and interacting with history. He would have been an amazing teacher! At any rate, the day the Nazi uniforms arrived, Clint couldn't get off the school bus and into the house fast enough. When he opened the package, inside it was a Ziploc bag containing doll-size uniforms. Clint was mortified. He quickly darted his eyes at me and exclaimed that it wasn't a funny joke. I told him I didn't do it. He flashed a look at Garrett who was laughing hysterically. Clint quickly realized that it was no joke and that he had been had by an online scammer. He vowed to never be fooled again.

Growing up, Clint and his siblings were always told to try to make *every* day better for someone else. We always knew Clint was a great kid. I'm not saying he was a perfect kid. Like all kids, he certainly had days when the weight of the world bore down on him. However, he somehow honed the art of being a perfect friend to those who crossed his path.

It wasn't until after we lost him that the true impact of his presence was made known to us. The stories others have shared with us have been endless and remarkable. Some stories were as simple as Clint giving out candy in his school's hallways to make others smile, or Clint visiting those who didn't have any friends at all. He was famous for giving hugs. In fact, he coined his most famous hug as "The 20-Second Hug." He fiercely ascertained that if he hugged you and you hugged him back (without struggle), your worries would fade away at the end of those 20 seconds. I don't know what magic he put into those hugs, but it worked.

There were simplistic stories about him lending a helping hand, and then there were grand stories such as when a classmate dropped out of school. He asked her to return to school. When she said she couldn't because no one cared, he told her that he did and that he was her friend. Or maybe even more touching was when he was at the National Youth Convention and a friend didn't want to leave the room because he was bound by fear and anxiety. Clint went into the room to get him and told him not to fear because he would be at his side the entire time. Turns out they both had a great night.

It wasn't just kids he was a friend to. There was the story of an adult family friend who was going through a divorce. Clint asked her for a ride to town for a pop, and then he lured her to his paintball course. There, he sat her down, held her hand, and told her, "It will be ok. God has big plans for you." She laughed and shook his hand away. He took her hand again, looked into her eyes, and said, "No, I promise you. God has big plans for you. This *will* be better." An instant later, he jumped up and skipped out of the paintball fort while sipping on his famous cherry Pepsi. The stories were endless.

It wasn't a story about him that impacted me the most; it was something I observed over and over. It was a statement made by kids that came from every background regardless if they were jocks, nerds, geeks, or outcasts. They kept saying the same thing, "He was my best friend."

After losing Clint, those closest to him (siblings, close friends, and cousins) felt frustrated that so many people claimed to be friends with Clint or know him well. To me, that became the hallmark of my son's heart. What a gift he'd given. He treated them so well that they all considered themselves his best friend. What a legacy to leave: pure and uncontaminated friendship.

I'm a lifelong educator with all the perfect degrees: two bachelor's, a master's, and a doctorate in education. All of that is supposed to make you smart, right? Yet the greatest wisdom I've ever attained was from a boy with a tremendous love for life, a smile that glittered like gold, and a huge heart that is clearly just as valuable.

As you go through your days busy with the tasks of life, don't forget about what is truly important. All the education and money in the world are nothing without a heart filled with gratitude and grace.

Clint probably wouldn't have won an academic scholarship or a sports title. He probably wouldn't have even made the honor roll. He even had a few detentions on his record for mischief, attempted drinking, and more. It was his character, his humanitarian efforts, and the way he lived that made him flawless. What he did better than most adults I've met is evangelize through his actions and the way he lived his life. He didn't just evangelize through his words.

Clint loved being home. If I could surround you with his favorite things, they would include his friends, his siblings, his parents, his grandparents, his cousins, and his aunts and uncles. Of course there would also be brownies, pumpkin bars, Pepsi, paintballs, and the game of Risk. On a table somewhere would be lilacs, daisies, or dandelions that he'd picked for me. There would certainly be uncontainable laughter, jokes, and hugs.

One of Clint's favorite sayings was "I love you infinitely." Many of us simply remember Clint with the infinity symbol. It has come to stand for so much more. In fact, those who've received Clint's scholarships had it on their checks, their plaques, and their certificates. Others have tattooed it on their bodies or adorned themselves with infinity jewelry. When you see that symbol in relation to Clint, let your hearts, minds, and behaviors be filled with kindness and compassion. Know that you are changing lives *infinitely*.

# CHAPTER 19
## Clint's Friends

*"Though miles may lie between us, we're never far apart, for friendship doesn't count the miles, it's measured by the heart."*
*~Author Unknown~*

    During a time when it has become customary for society to quickly criticize youth, I find myself pondering whether I should share something good about them. Would people understand their good deeds? Would people care to understand? Would having a positive understanding of youth be as exciting as having something to gossip about? Would people want to know? These are just a few of the questions that bounce around my mind even as I write this. In the hope of making someone else's day, as my son was so famous for, I have decided to share my thoughts.

    Although some don't realize it, 2009 would have been Clint's senior year. Somehow, even though it was unimaginable that the pain could've gotten worse, his senior year was like salt in a fresh wound. It included all the things he would've been doing and should've been doing, and I was watching it all happen without him. I tried to attend as many of the senior year events as I could because I knew Clint would've wanted it that way. He loved his classmates. In spite of Clint being gone, the students at Clint's high school, especially his class of 2009, were amazing. They remembered Clint and found ways to make his spirit present in all of the year's milestones. Whether it was a banner with his name in the senior class picture, a slideshow at homecoming, a tree planted in his memory on the high school's front lawn, letters in his memorial site's journal, gifts by his headstone, visits to our house on his 18th birthday, or just a hug in the grocery store, his class and his friends always remembered Clint. The innumerable ways they chose to grieve and remember Clint brought unspeakable support to our family.

The night of their senior prom, as with so many other events, I went to watch Clint's friends and classmates. They were all growing up into such beautiful young adults. On prom day, there was no corsage for me to pin, no bow tie for me to fix, and no pictures for me to take. I only thought about what goofy pranks he would have played to make his fellow students all laugh at "drive up." The next day, like so many others, I walked down my driveway to Clint's memorial site. What I saw when I opened the gate filled my heart. There, at the base of his headstone below the picture of his smiling face, lay two prom corsages. They remembered! When these kids could've been anywhere else, they came to remember and include their friend.

I really don't even know how to put into words how proud we should all be of our youth. Not only for what they've done for Clint and our family, but also for the tremendous respect and compassion they have within them. Even though they were children, it was us who should have taken a lesson from them. Now I know why this class meant the world to my son. So, to the class of 2009, I thank you from the bottom of my heart.

Even though it has been years since his class graduated and moved on in life, there are several who remember us and what Clint meant. It doesn't matter if it's Anton stopping by to tell a story and hang with Garrett, if it's Tommy sending me a letter from college telling me Clint is always with him, if it's Andrew hugging me at the grocery store, if it's seeing Amber waitressing with Clint's cross still hanging from her neck, if its Shelby Facebooking to remind me that she remembers Clint, if it's Blake laughing about all the big bucks they could've bagged, if it's Kevin hugging me tight, if it's Darcy bringing me a notebook of Clint's she found in a box, if it's Alexis faithfully writing in Clint's book by his headstone, if it's the other Amber leaving a plaque, if it's William telling me he loves me and that Clint was really a brother, or if it's the rest of you who have shared a piece of yourselves. All of their efforts have been cherished and carefully cataloged in my mind. For your loyalty to my son and his family that was left behind, I thank you.

    It helps me to know how much he meant and still means to each of you. There are no words to explain how much Clint loved his friends. One might think that everyone loves their friends, and this would be true. However, it was very different for Clint. He really lived for each of you. I know he's looking down from Heaven, and he's extremely proud of what you're doing and how you've grown into adulthood. For those of you who've taken the time to help us, I have no doubt that you hold a special place in his heart even today.

    I'm sorry for the pain you've gone through and continue to experience without him. It's hard to know how to smile when it was that beautiful boy who knew how to brighten our days so well. Every so often, I want to call him, text him, or go down to his room to ask him how to help one of you. I usually make it a few steps before I remember that he's not there to answer and that we'll have to figure this one out on our own.

The stories you share are truly gifts. Again, thank you for the tears, the smiles, and for continuing to keep Clinty present in your lives. It means the world to me. As each of you know all too well, we were blessed with someone extraordinarily remarkable if just for a brief moment in time.

# CHAPTER 20
## *The New Us ... Our New Life*

*"We must be willing to get rid of the life we've planned, so as to have the life that is waiting for us."*
~Joseph Campbell~

The best way I can explain what losing a child feels like is to explain how the members of my family and I virtually lost our lives. Our lives split into two realities; there's the life before when Clint was here, and there's the life without Clint. It's an unfair existence because others compare our new selves to an unfair standard, our old selves. For some reason, they choose to compare us to who we used to be. They don't understand, or perhaps they can't understand, that my family no longer exists. So, for those who wanted us to "get back to normal," there was no longer a normal. Early in the book, you read about who we were before the tragedy. Now, I will tell you about who we've become.

Before November 5, 2006, my world was seemingly perfect as I've written. I'd wake up each morning and a smile would cross my face before my feet could even hit the floor. Knowing I'd be able to spend another day with my children nearly gave me goose bumps. In the evening after we said the Lord's Prayer and our good nights, I'd tuck them into bed one by one and kiss their teenage cheeks. Each night, I'd fall asleep with a warm sense of tranquility for which there is no explanation. Just knowing they were under my roof and safe in their beds brought me complete peace. This is a peace that comes naturally to a mother when her children are safe, but it's also a peace that can be, and was, shattered in an instant. Since that day, nothing has been the same. My perfect life ended in an instant, and the peace that used to fill my life was gone. Life was forever changed. None of us are who we were before that horrible day. In a way, a part of our souls left with Clint in that fateful instant. It's the physical part left behind that sometimes gets transformed beyond recognition.

A dear friend, Wendy, sent me a portion of a Beth Moore Bible study: "Plead as we may, sometimes we have to go on living in the absence of someone dear and even find that hearts over time can actually heal. We also find immeasurable comfort in knowing that our fellowship with those in Christ will resume one happy day and nothing will ever interrupt it again!" This quote only solidified what my heart already knew. The hope of seeing Clint again came to mean *everything* to me. It became just *one more reason* to survive.

You see, I've heard, smelled, touched, and seen things no mother should ever see. In the middle of a thought, a conversation, or a task, my attention fades, my eyes see nothing, sound disappears, and my mind fades to memories of Clint. In these moments I see him, hear him, touch him, and feel him. As quickly as these moments come, they're gone! Reality returns, and I face it all over again. Yes, he's really gone!

I've come to realize that living with sadness isn't easy, but it *is* easy to be sad. It's difficult to fight sadness and the grips of depression. There are choices we must make every day, but none are greater than the choice to live. It would be easy just to exist. I don't mean that. I mean to live a good life with love and gratitude. I've made that choice. In fact, I make it every day. Sometimes, I make it every hour, and other times, I make it every minute if necessary. If I'm going to live in this world, I'm going to live the best life possible for myself, my children, my husband, my extended family, and God.

Some people think happiness is a gift that is given or not given. Many unhappy people go through life disgruntled that happiness wasn't given to them, and they're jealous of those who have it. That couldn't be further from the truth. The truth is that happiness is a choice. Every day, you have the right to choose to be happy. You have the right to make the best of the circumstances you're given. This was something I've always believed but had lost for quite a while. Happiness used to come easily for me. Now, life is different. I must earn happiness by choosing to work hard for it. That doesn't mean there aren't simple joys that come naturally in this new life because there certainly are. It only means that we have a choice to select the lens with which we see this world through. My lens shows me that I'm still a very blessed woman. I have a happy marriage, beautiful children, extraordinary grandchildren, an amazing extended family, and stellar friendships. Is it perfect? I used to think it was perfect. My view of perfection has changed. To be perfect would mean my life would be beyond penetration by anything imperfect or bad. Certainly losing a child falls into the imperfect category. So maybe, just maybe, life can't be perfect. Or maybe it can be. The truth is I don't really know. What I do know is that for me, life will forever be different without one of my children. It's not what I dreamt for myself or, for that matter, anyone I love. Even so, it's the life I've been given unmistakably, and I will fight negativity and sadness every day for it. Why? Because it is a choice I've been given.

When you lose a child or anyone you love, you aren't given a choice in their fate. You are forced to live without them. I *hate* that helpless feeling of being powerless, and I never want to return to it. It's from this hatred that I've learned to take back control over myself and, more importantly, my thoughts. I've learned to control the negativity that wants so desperately to take over my brain and replace it with love, kindness, and compassion. I've learned to share love with those I love and those that love me, but I've also learned to love those who seem to know no love. I've learned to extend kindness to those who are easy to be kind to and also those who are not. I've learned to give compassion to those who are compassionate to me and, more importantly, those who haven't been compassionate. Yes, these are all choices. It isn't our talents or abilities that'll ultimately define who we are; it'll be the choices that we make.

It was during one of the first incidents of hearence that God granted me when I heard Clint's voice. It was as though a warm blanket were placed gently upon my shoulders. I felt wrapped in only what could be described as perfect and pure love. The closest I can come to a definition of the love I felt is agape (a-gah-pay) love. Agape love is unconditional and given freely and extravagantly to others even when it's not returned. I've read that it's a combination of all other virtues including faith, friendship, justice, and hope. It's pure and true love. It's this kind of love I was engulfed with that day. When Clint spoke, it was with these words, "Mom, grant them grace. They know no better, Mom. It will make you bitter.

Forgive them." I shook my head in dismay as though I'd certainly be certified as insane now. There, in my great room on a regular winter day, he gently repeated the words. In that moment, I understood the words and what they meant, but I couldn't fully understand what I was supposed to do. Time is a wizard because I've learned that Clint's words are ones to live by. I need to grant grace to those who know no better and forgive them for it. In doing so, it's a gift given to myself. This gift to myself slowly helps me to restore a heart that had become bitter. This gift helps me to restore my very soul so it could sparkle within me once again. This gift helps me to spread faith to those who have lost it. This gift helps me to share and spread a love that can't be understood by definition but rather, it must be felt.

I often get asked, "How do you keep it all together?" That's a very good question. I'll be honest, it's difficult and, at times, I don't. I always had the best of intentions, but it got to the point that I had to schedule and plan a time for only me. This would become a time of great reflection and focus. At first, I felt selfish but soon found that it made me better in every way as a mother, educator, sister, friend, aunt, and person in general.

For me, it was hard because I've never really taken time for myself. In the beginning, it was almost more work to figure out what I should be doing. Finally, I sat down and made a list of the things that filled my inner tank. Initially, I was surprised by what those things were. Some were things I'd do just for my benefit, and some things benefitted both me and others. Whatever it was, I'd schedule the time and find a fun place for my kids to go.

## A NEED TO WRITE TAKES ME NORTH

As we drive north down the winding road, the light flickers through the trees as I gaze into the woods. It's almost as though nature is giggling at its beauty as the tall and boastful trees change their leaves to the oranges and reds of fall. I think to myself that this ride has been long. It's been a long trip but also a long ride. This fall marks far too many years without Clint. We've had so many trips north for pleasure as a family, Clint included, but this trip was different. On this trip there are no laughing children and no carefully planned itinerary of events. The purpose of this trip is to finish a long ride of another kind. This trip is for finishing my book. As the light continues to flicker between the trees, my trance is broken. In the woods there is a beautiful cabin with fresh corn shocks on the deck. Corn shocks that look just like the ones Clint and I used to build every fall, and they're neatly tied around the poles of our deck with pumpkins resting at their bases. It sounds simple, but my mind fills with so much more. It fills with the trip to my brother's field to cut the corn that he grew on our parent's farm. I remember the rough leaves that left both Clint and me itching and complaining, and I remember the old machete that was left on the barn wall from the previous owner when we bought the place. A machete that I'm sure could tell many stories from decades past. I remember Clint begging to use it while I worried that he would somehow hack off my leg with it or, worse yet, his own. We would load the corn into the truck and slowly drive back to our farm where we'd carefully count the shocks into five separate piles. He would hold them around the post while I'd tie the twine and secure them in place. I recall the impatience of my teenage boy if I moved too slowly. Then, the pumpkins would be put in their place. We would hand select five pumpkins; one for each of the kids. My thoughts draw back. I think to myself that I still buy five pumpkins.

That next morning, I arose from bed after a nearly sleepless night. We arrived late to a resort just north of Pequot Lakes, which is in central Minnesota. Surprisingly, we were put in a private cabin instead of a hotel room. It's the perfect place to write. It's filled with log furnishings, a private patio, two bedrooms, a private hot tub, full kitchen, and it's quiet. I immediately think to myself that God is so good to me. Not only does He sustain me every day, but also today He provides me with the perfect environment to share the story that I know in my heart He has commanded me to write. As I settle at the table alone with my laptop and a fresh pot of Starbucks Breakfast Blend, my thoughts race. They race to places I don't want to go, but I know that He is with me and that I must begin.

## MEGAN

After a short walk on a wooded path, my mind is focused for writing again. I can feel the texture of the log chair as I sit down. Just as I reach for the keyboard, Megan calls to let me know all is well back home. I tease her because she calls me nearly a dozen times on any given day. Although we joke about it, I know she needs to know that everything is ok with me. As much as she needs to know that I'm ok, she needs to know that *we* are ok. She needs to know that our family is ok. As with most of our phone calls, she tells me how my grandbabies are doing, and then she asks about us. She asks about Gar-Bear and Bri to make sure I've heard from them. If there's something exciting going on, she likes to be the first to hear about that as well. Our family means the world to Meg. Since that day, Megan has gone through a lot of changes. She became afraid of leaving home. She desperately needed to know that her loved ones were with her.

I know she's always felt that Clint would be ok if she had kept him close by that day. I desperately wish I could reach into her brain and take that thought out to make her realize there was nothing she could've done to change the outcome. If I could only make her see how that day was written long before any of us were ever born. I've told her the story of my own heart being filled with guilt. It's a heart filled with guilt because I'm Clint's mom, and I should've taken better care of him by keeping him safe. It's a heart filled with guilt because I should've been able to make him ok. I've always been able to fix things. But why couldn't I fix Clint that day? The answer leads to even more guilt. I feel guilty for marrying a man that hunts and brought guns into the home. I feel guilty that someone threw a coat over Clint's gun and that it was missed when the guns were being locked up that evening. My guilt never wants to subside. It's a guilt that I pray God will take away and replace with the truth. So, even though I wish and pray I could take Meg's guilt away, I understand it only because I live it.

Within a few months of Clint's accident, Meg changed again. She decided that she'd push us away and maybe that would protect her heart. Right after her high school graduation, Meg moved out of the house and into her own place. She still called every day and came to the farm, but my home was different again. There was one less child living there.

For many years, I couldn't even cry in front of Meg let alone bring up Clint's name. With time, that has changed. Now we're able to have precious moments of talking about it. She has a few rules for this though. It can't be in front of people, before someone is coming over, or before she is going somewhere. If it is, she can easily explode with anger and have a snappy attitude. Conversely, if I follow the rules, I can talk about him and say his name all I want. I can even cry in front of her now, *but* I can't expect her to share in the story. She can only listen.

Although Megan has difficulty recalling her brother with stories, she has found a way to honor him. She has chosen to honor him in a way that many from her generation have done. She has chosen to tattoo her body with things of Clint. She has a full-faced tattoo of Clint's smiling face on her back and the signatures of her brothers on her wrists: Garrett's on the left and Clint's on the right. Across her shoulder are lilacs to represent the trees she, Clint, and Gar used to play in as young children and the flowers they would proudly bring to me. Down her arm is an antique pocket watch that appears to have been battered with age. It is surrounded by the quote that Garrett shared in the forward of this book. It is a reminder to us all not to concentrate on what time has taken from us but, more importantly, on what time has given us.

Meg still struggles with opening her heart. She doesn't want to love and be hurt again by losing someone close. She also struggles with finding enjoyment in nearly everything. I think she unknowingly seeks that perfect joy of all of us being together. She struggles in believing that we'll have it again. She has her doubts that we'll return to our home in Heaven where Clinty waits for us even now. Meg struggles to believe in Heaven. She struggles to believe there is a Heavenly Father that can be so cruel. She often questions, "If He is real, what has He ever done for me?" When Meg's in her soft and vulnerable moments, she'll admit she believes in God but feels like she owes Him nothing for taking her brother. I pray every day that God will soften her heart so she can return to Him. She must so we can all be together again.

As an adult, Meg has been a certified nursing assistant to the elderly and a massage therapist. There's so much she wants to do in this world. She wants to be a nurse, a social worker, a cop, a probation officer, or an emergency medical responder. As I look at the list, I realize that my little girl wants to serve others. I'm so very proud of her. Does my daughter have a big heart? Yes, she does!

Although it's hard to admit, there's a coldness that lies within her that's so frigid it could freeze you solid with a single touch. What few people know is there's a warm and beautiful fire that burns within her heart. It's like a small cabin that is deep within a mysterious forest. After searching for safety, you see it through the pines. It's obscured, hard to see, and surrounded by danger; however, once you get to it, it's well worth the treacherous pursuit. Inside there's a fire crackling to warm and comfort you. There, you're relaxed, safe, and engulfed in love and protection. That's the spot that lies within my Meg. In those rare instances when she invites you inside, you never want to leave. It's when we are in that place, together, that I know my daughter *will* fully return to us one day. I love that place.

Megan has two children, Maddie and Tanner. When she's with her children, she lets her guard down once in a while, and the old, soft-hearted Meg shines through. They've healed her heart. They've forced her to face unconditional love and, more importantly, to show it. They've been good for her flickering fire; they've been good for her soul.

## MADDIE

Madelyn Rae Weber. Can you say "sunshine?" Can you say "salvation?" When Meg told me she was pregnant, I reacted how most mothers of an unwed daughter would: not very good. The timing was wrong! There wasn't enough money and so forth. It turns out the timing was perfect. To this day, I believe God sent Maddie to save us. I was so lost and hadn't experienced sheer joy since Clint was with us. That beautiful little girl opened a window in my heart that invited all the wonders of this world back inside it.

When Maddie was born, I made her a quilt out of Clint's clothing. On it, I placed the following poem I'd written.

*Soon a mom my big sister will be. I'm sure you'll dress her in pink and all girly.*

*I've seen her already…little fingers, fat toes and don't forget that big Weber nose.*

*I'm sure as you wait, you wonder if you'll be a good mom. I know you'll be perfect and before you know it, she'll be going to prom.*

*I know you hurt that I'm not there but please always know how much I care.*

*I love you and I've loved your baby too. They say it's time for her to go because she's leaving Heaven for you.*

*Yes, I know her. We've played and we've laughed and I've kissed her good bye. She's the cutest thing I've ever seen and that's no lie.*

*Even though I won't be there to hold her and give her kisses at night. Know through life, I'll be at her side and squeezing her hand so tight.*
*Tell her stories of me and make sure she knows who I was and where I live now. Make sure to teach her of God our Father and to His feet she should bow.*
*When you take her home, love her and snuggle her in the quilt of my clothes. Be sure to tell her the stories of us and make sure that she knows.*
*Tell her that Uncle Clint is only a prayer...just a whisper away.*
*I'm so excited for you Meg and know I'm with you each day.*

When I wrote that poem, I had no idea of what was to come. When I look back, I can't help but think that those were Clint's real words and that I was only a vessel for placing them in ink.

When Maddie was a toddler, she would hold hands and talk with someone that wasn't there. It started when she was about 18 months old. One day, when she was 2 years old, I went to get her from her crib, and she was talking up a storm. I asked her who she was talking to, and she responded, "My fwend Clinty." After picking her out of the crib and setting her on the floor, she took my hand and said, "Come Grandma, I show you." She climbed to the top of the steps near my office and picked up an 8 x 10 photo of Clint, and she said, "Dat my fwend, Clinty." My heart nearly jumped right out of my chest, and tears fell from my face. I couldn't believe that this little girl, who had no reason to know Clint, knew him. From that day forward, I knew without a doubt that my son was with her and that she could see him.

One day everyone in the house was excited for the day's activiites, but I was so sad Clint wouldn't be with us.

I was putting my makeup on when Maddie came into the bathroom. She'd been running around the great room playing cops and robbers. She stopped, looked at me, and said, "Grandma, are you sad?" I told her I was. She said, "Clinty says you miss him." Startled, I dropped my eyeliner into the sink. I put my hands on her shoulders and said, "What?" She replied by stating that Clinty had told her I was sad because I missed him. I asked Maddie if Clinty was with her. She told me he'd come to play cops and robbers with her, and she pointed to the other room. She asked me if I could see him. She put the toilet seat down, sat on it, and said, "Clinty says you look pretty." With tears falling from my face, my heart knew he was there. When he was a little boy, he'd always come into the bathroom when I was putting on makeup. Every time, he'd put the toilet seat down and talk to me. The last time he came into the bathroom while I was putting on makeup was about a week before his accident. He'd told me he'd made a decision about what he was going to do after high school. He was going to college and then he would join the U.S. Army. He said he'd return to college for graduate school after his military service. Then, out of nowhere, he looked at me and said, "Mom, you look pretty." Of course! He came today knowing I was sad. I got on my knees in front of Maddie and asked her again if he was still there. She told me that he was. I asked her if she could tell Clinty that "Mommy misses him and loves him so much." As she ran off, she said, "I will Grandma but he heard you! He loves you too!"

In that moment, I understood that God had allowed and continues to allow my son moments among us. I knew that I needed to listen and watch for those moments.

In that moment, I was certain we could also see and hear Clint if that innocent child could.

## TANNER

Before Tanner was born, Meg was scared that she wouldn't love him like she loved Maddie. She was afraid that we wouldn't either. Tanner was born as a perfect little bundle of joy. As with Maddie's birth, I got to be in the room when he was born. It was amazing! This time, his dad was brave enough to cut the umbilical cord himself. He didn't even seem like he was going to pass out.

Tanner has a smile that could fill a room. It reminds me of Clint's smile. As Tanner grows up, he loves to give hugs and kisses too. His favorite words are music to our ears: Gram, Pops, and "I wuv you." What a delight! Tanner doesn't have private little talks with Clint nor does he claim to play with Clint. He does, however, have an unexplainable fascination with my necklace. It's an open circle with a picture of Clint. It's covered by a solid metal circle. Every day, Tanner jumps onto my lap, pushes the solid circle aside with his chubby little fingers, points, and says "Kwint." He knows him. My heart feels good.

## GARRETT

Garrett's changes were dramatic. In fact, he might have been the one who changed the most. He had to step into a life in which his older brother no longer left footsteps for him to follow. He also, inadvertently, had to pay the price for Clint's mistakes. Gar received some of the restrictions and punishments Clint wasn't here to receive. For instance, even though Garrett is a very careful hunter, he wasn't allowed to hunt for years because of Clint's carelessness. Even though I had been super careful before, now I was "careful on steroids." Gar and the other kids couldn't do anything safely enough.

Garrett went from being my loving little baby boy to a teenager I barely recognized. Not long after losing Clint, Gar started hanging out with older friends so he could still feel close to Clint. At the time, I thought this was good for Gar. With hindsight, I know better. After a while, Gar didn't want to do much with either his family or other kids his age. He just wanted to hang out with his older friends. I had no idea that they were helping him to cope in illicit ways with alcohol and sometimes, prescription drugs. Honestly, I wonder if I did know but didn't want to face it. Maybe I couldn't deal with physically losing Clint, and now I couldn't emotionally deal with losing Garrett. Gar was distant and snappy all through high school. He was only a shadow of the boy he had been before the accident. Once in a while, there'd be rare glimpses of his former self. I still wrote in our journal, and I would place it on his pillow. Once in a while, I'd find it back on my pillow. In those moments, my heart would jump because he'd written back. Even as a teenager, Garrett has been the deepest thinker I've ever met. That says a lot because I've had the opportunity to work with some pretty deep and critical thinkers in my field of work. I can honestly say they're no match for my Garrett. So, when I'd find the journal on my pillow, I always knew he was going to give me some insight into his heart and soul. My little boy lived in these journal entries. He was still inside that teenage body. His innocent heart that was filled with love was beating strong. I learned that it was a different Gar I'd have to approach after reading the journal. Everything in me wanted to find and hug the boy who'd returned to me within his journal entries. I quickly learned that this would only suspend any future journal entries. It was ok if I knew his heart, but I was not allowed to acknowledge it. He wanted me to know it was still there, but in no way could I verbally translate that into him caring.

Gar also found peace in memorializing Clint with several tattoos. The first is simply Clint's name with an infinity sign and the German words "Wiedergeboren in Größe" which means "Reborn into Greatness." Beneath it are these words by William Blake: "I sought my soul, but my soul I could not see. I sought my God, but my God alluded me. I sought my brother and I found all three." The second is simply the word *chaos* down the inner side of his arm. The third, a quarter sleeve filled with all of his favorite memories of Clint: their little army men, lilacs they used to pick for me, Clint's headstone, and so much more. Through these tattoos, Gar is able to show that he cares.

As his high school years progressed, so did the ugliness that was brewing both inside and outside him. One night, it exploded into a situation that made me face the fact that my baby was all but gone. It looked like him, sounded like him, and even smelled like him during infrequent hugs, but for all practical matters, he was no longer there. That night, it became abundantly clear why. Those older friends, who *helped* him live through the early days after Clint's accident with the assistance of alcohol and prescription drugs, had introduced him to a life that was now his. He was a *user*. He was a user of whatever made him feel better . . . alcohol, drugs, and people. That night, Tim and I made the most difficult decision of our lives. We called the police and turned him in. When they came for him, Garrett begged me not to make him go. He begged me that he'd be better and that he'd listen. When that failed, he told me he *hated* me. Those were the last words he spoke to me as we made arrangements with the deputy to secure a place for him. Time was suspended, and my heart was broken.

Once again, Tim called my brother Kyle and Kyle's wife, Pam. They along with my nephew, Ethan, came immediately to my side. It was reminiscent of the day we lost Clinty. Kyle was the first person Tim called when we lost Clint, and in true big-brother fashion, Kyle was also the first to arrive when Garrett was taken away. Once again, he was there when my heart was breaking. This time, it was different. This time, my heart was breaking to save a son. They quickly reassured me that we'd made the right decision. They told me what my heart knew and hoped for. They told me that when we dug the old Gar out from the layers of despair, he'd love me again and that I would have him back.

Gar spent his senior year of high school in intensive outpatient therapy. He went to three-hour meetings three nights a week. We went with him one of those nights for family night. It was in treatment when Garrett met one of God's true servants here on this earth. He met Coleen. She would become Garrett's rock and salvation. She demanded transparency from him, and somehow, he was transparent with her. She could see through his layers of denial and pain and would hold him accountable to others and his heart. When Garrett said he didn't care, she made him see that he did. Coleen was able to make Garrett touch parts of his soul that he had buried with his brother. Through their talks, Garrett discovered that there's no drug that can numb the love you feel for the ones who are gone or the ones who are standing right in front of you. He was forced to face that there are no guarantees in life and that all love comes with the risk of being hurt. Coleen helped him discover that having that love, if even for a short time, is worth the risk. Slowly, Garrett returned to us.

Right before high school graduation, Gar successfully completed outpatient therapy. Although he made huge progress, things weren't perfect. We had a new Garrett that was close to who he used to be. Yet the new Garrett was different because, in a way, we all left that day with Clinty and have had to recreate ourselves. As with all of us, the new person is not exactly like who we were before. It's the same with Gar.

He's proud of where he's been and where he's ended up. He knows that you don't have to be perfect to have a perfect life. Gar's been a lot more open about his situation than I would've liked him to be. I've learned from him that if anyone is going to learn from our struggles, they have to hear about it in its ugliest form with nothing left out.

The fall after his senior year, Gar headed to off to college. I thought it was a mistake, but it was his life. Growing up, all he'd ever talked about was being a cop. Suddenly, he was going to school for business. I started to worry even more because he was going to a place known as one of the worst party schools in the nation. I could only pray for him.

Gar struggled in his first semester of college. Although it's one of the only things we've never directly discussed, he's hinted that the dark side crept back into him during this time. At the end of that first semester, he made the decision to move back home.

After a semester of construction work, Gar decided he'd give back to a world that had seemingly taken so much from him. He applied and was accepted into one of the most elite law enforcement programs in the nation. This program helped Gar to respect and understand others. Gar is clearly a man who has remorse about a troubled past in which his treatment of others was less than perfect. He's a man who wishes he wouldn't have taken from others to feed his ego in an attempt to cover his own pain. My son is now a man with a new perspective. He once again loves and trusts God, loves his family, and has the utmost respect for others and the law. He's a man that takes time on his trips home to visit his grandparents, siblings, nieces and nephews, and younger cousins. Even though I'm being selfish, he once again has time for "Mother", as he lovingly calls me. Our times together are deep and meaningful. It doesn't matter if we are privately journaling to each other, visiting over a cup of coffee, or watching a movie among piles of pillows.

There were times during those dark years when Gar would rarely touch me or say he loved me. As a mother, those were lonely years. I am elated to say this has also changed. Once again, Gar rarely leaves without hugging me and telling me he loves me. He almost always gives me a kiss on my cheek. Funny thing is he no longer cares who sees him do it. He appears proud to love and be loved.

Then there are times, mostly when we are alone, when he will speak Clint's name and share a story. These times are precious to me. I don't push for them anymore, but now I patiently wait for them to occur. In those moments, I feel complete. For just those few seconds, Clint, Gar,

Meg, the other kids, and I are together in the same room; united in our memories.

## BRIANA

Briana came to live with us full time in the fall of 2006 after months of custody negotiations. Life was seemingly perfect. She was finally able to live out her dream of being on the farm with her dad, the other kids and me. She was close with both of her brothers, Garrett and Clint. They'd taken on the big-brother roles of making sure that no one picked on her or thought about dating her. She really was more like them than the other girls; she was an absolute tomboy.

After Clint's accident, Bri was lost without Clint. He had always been there to fill in the gaps of silence with his jokes and laughter. Our home was now so quiet. There would be no more antics while waiting for the bus or diversions to put off homework after school. All of the silliness was gone.

Briana has always loved being at home, but this grew stronger in the months and years after losing Clint. She never wanted to leave. Not even to hang out with friends. She took great comfort in being here and knowing everything was ok. She also threw herself into doing well in school and at home.

Bri was the one who took over Clint's caretaking of all of the farm animals. It mattered to her that he loved them. It was an unspoken commitment to him that she'd take care of everything for him. She would love and name every cat just like she used to with him. She would carry the torch of getting Clint's cat, Smokey, permanently moved into the house. Along with me, she cares for her and is always aware of Smokey's need to occasionally sneak into Clint's room and lay on his bed. She believes Smokey is the queen of the house just like Clint would've expected her to be. Bri is loyal to this cat that was so loyal to her brother.

For months after the accident, Bri would sit silently with me and watch me. Rarely did she speak a word, but she was always there. Honestly, I've often thought that she could sense my thoughts of wanting to die. At times, I could see the fear in her eyes. She was afraid that she could possibly lose me too.

She tried to help in whatever way she could, whether it was through doing chores, working on tasks around the house, or giving me spa nights. Spa nights were a special thing we used to do. All of us (boys included) would do facials, pedicures, and manicures. Whenever Clint gave me a foot massage, he'd sneak his fingers between my toes and tickle me. There was never a warning. There was only the shocking jolt from my relaxation and a quick scolding from me. One night long after Clint's accident, Bri was giving me a foot massage. I was totally relaxed when, all of a sudden, she stuck her fingers between my toes and tickled me like Clint used to. My eyes popped open as I sat up and glanced at her. She simply stared back awaiting a verbal response. As our eyes exchanged looks, I could tell she wanted to know if I remembered. She wanted to know if it was ok to resurrect that memory. She wanted to know if we could laugh. After a moment of gathering my thoughts, we both began to giggle. It was in moments like this when I began to feel Clinty again.

As the months passed, Bri became the one that allowed Clinty to live. She was the only one in our home that would talk about him with me, and she did it often. She did it if I needed it, or if she just needed to hear his name ring through the air. As a mom, I've always talked about all of my kids. I've been so proud of them. Suddenly, I wasn't allowed to talk about Clint anymore. I wasn't allowed because people couldn't handle the pain of hearing the stories or even his name. It was different with Bri. With her, he became alive in our conversations. Many times, we've even rejoiced over what a glorious reunion Clint is preparing for us. We've rejoiced about what we will say and do when we see him again. She's been strong in her faith knowing that the day will come.

Bri's all grown up, but she will forever be my little Breezy. When she was little, she used to follow me everywhere. One day, I told her that I felt like Peter Pan and that she was my shadow. From that day forward, she began to refer to me as *Peter*. Even to this day, she will refer to herself as *Shadow*. It's heartwarming.

Today, she is all grown up and runs a daycare. She loves children and is extremely good with them. Although she likes having her own home, she often asks to move back to the farm. We remind her that she runs a home-based business and needs to be in town. She reluctantly agrees. It helps her to know that she lives in what was my Grandma Weber's house. It's the same house where I spent endless hours performing in personal spelling bees and learning Latin. Yes, it gives Bri comfort to know her house holds a piece of family history, which makes it feel more like home.

Bri still comes to the farm several times a week to check in on the animals as well as her dad and me. She needs to know we are safe. She hates it when we travel because she misses us greatly when we're away. She often begs me to find a job that won't take me from home. I'm afraid she's become much like me: a bit of a recluse with a big heart.

## KAYLA

Nearly a year before Clint's accident, Kayla had moved to the farm. She'd settled in, and all was well. Kayla has always been a girly girl, so she wasn't as active with all of the outdoor activities as the other kids were. Mostly, her time was spent with me. We'd fill our days with long talks, craft activities, or baking. Clint and Kayla were in the same grade and got along well. Being eight days older than Clint, she'd often joke that he was her *little* brother. That drove Clint nuts.

Kayla's grieving process was quite different than the other kids, yet it was much the same. It was the same because grieving can be very ugly, and it brings out the worst in a person. For her, it was different in the way it was ugly. Kayla has always been an attention getter. She likes to be the center of attention, and she will seek it no matter what it takes. Growing up, she always liked to cause a high degree of unnecessary discord between her two families. This was something that all of her parents worked hard to abate. After Clint's accident, her primary way of coping kicked in. The attention-getting behaviors escalated dramatically. It goes without saying that the loss of a child brings a great deal of attention to that child. The stories are endless, and the remembrance gifts are plentiful. Without conscious awareness or understanding, I believe this was really hard for Kayla. She was used to having a high level of attention. More specifically, she was used to getting a great deal of my attention. It goes without saying that after losing Clint, my reservoir for giving her attention was depleted. I had three other kids to take care of and little energy in me to do it with. No longer could Kayla get the lion's share of my time. I know this had to be hard on Kayla. She was used to having something that she was no longer getting. To be fair, the reason didn't matter to her, but things must have just felt very different.

Kayla sought attention from school staff with dramatic episodes of crying during school, and she began acting out at home. She began a relationship with a boy that took a great deal of our time to manage. Once again, our attention was hijacked by the necessity to get her back on track. Upon her 18th birthday, it became clear that our efforts had failed; she moved out. Not only did she move out, but also she told terrible lies about both of her families. We allowed her to move back shortly before her high school graduation, but she moved out immediately after the beautiful graduation party we threw for her. Once she moved, the negative stories and unfounded accusations resumed again. These lies were devastating not only to our immediate family but also to the entire extended family. It left many members of her father's family estranged from each other. It would be years before any type of reconciliation would come. Eventually, Tim and his family began navigating their way to the truth and reconciled with each other.

Then, in the fall of 2010, when all hope of having a normal relationship with Kayla had faded, she began to call me. She and I talked for months before we attempted to integrate her back into our family. You see, Tim and the other kids felt as though she'd used and abandoned the family in their darkest hour of grief. They also felt her crazy antics had caused unnecessary strife and pain. They feared this was another manipulation to gain something. I can't say I disagreed with them, but my heart missed what we used to have. Whether they wanted to admit it or not, she was a part of this family.

It wasn't long until Tim's entire family discovered that Kayla had been the root of the devastation in their family and that the stories she perpetuated were indeed fabrications. As a result, Tim and I, his father, his stepmother, his sister, and many more have never been closer. Grief is a mysterious thing.

Today, Kayla and her son are again a part of our lives. It isn't the way it used to be, but we are hopeful and on the road to recovery. We still need to remind her that we're part of her life even when she doesn't need something. She is slowly learning to understand. Regarding Clint, Kayla rarely utters his name. The grace in me wants to believe that she's recovered to the point of feeling guilt for what she did to us during that painful time. My heart fights to believe that she cares for Clint and not the unhealthy attention his loss brought to our family. She has offered, for lack of a more appropriate term, a *half-assed* apology, but she hasn't offered one with depth. The depth that I know exists in her is absent from our discussions. As she matures and grows, I only hope that she'll understand the cavern of pain her abandonment gouged within her dad and me, her siblings, her cousins, and her grandparents. I don't hold any ill feelings against her and have forgiven her. Because she's now a mother, I pray that her *mommy* heart will provide her with a wisdom that's been missing. This wisdom will define the unnecessary pain she created for so many people. It's also a wisdom that can bring learning and healing. I wait for the day when we, as mothers, will have that conversation. I miss the way we were.

## KAYDEN

Kayden is Kayla's son. He's a smiley and happy young boy. We don't see him as much as the other grandchildren, but we're all excited when we do. He loves being at our house and makes himself right at home. We've all had to constantly remind ourselves that Kayden is not part of the situation his mother created. We remind ourselves that *he* is innocent. We remind ourselves that he needs us in his life as much as the other grandkids. We remind ourselves that he needs our stability and endless love. He's also a reminder of the necessity to repair all that went so horribly wrong between his mother and her family. He should never see or know of the ugliness that was between us. He needs to grow up being proud of everything she is, who he is, and who he will be.

## SO MUCH MORE LOVE TO SHARE

I've always said that the single greatest gift in my life is being a parent. Back in the mid-90s, I made a decision to expand my family beyond my biological children, so I sought a permanent foster-care placement. I wanted a permanent placement so I could make a difference in the life of someone who hadn't been as blessed as I. That brings me to Sherreiea and Beth. They've both been my daughters since the mid-90s. They have been blessed additions to my family, and I love them with all my heart. Growing up in the foster care system changes a child. It can make them suspicious and untrusting to the point where they often feel that even love is questionable.

## SHERREIEA

Sherreiea was staying with us on that horrible day of Clint's accident. She was training to be a nurse and tried desperately to save Clinty. We were both aware too much time had passed and that her efforts were in vain, but we both knew that trying would lend some sense of hope. I can still see her lifting his beautiful head and trying without reservation to breathe life into his body. My heart anguished knowing his chest would not rise and fall on its own. That air wouldn't flow freely from his nostrils again. Yet, Sherreiea tried to make it so. After that day, I didn't see much of her for several months. I didn't understand how she could abandon us. Why?

One day, she gave me an answer. We sat at the kitchen table, and she spoke of feeling guilty for not being able to save him. She spoke of another loss that, in my shock and fog, I had not yet fully discovered. I knew I felt myself die on the front lawn with Clint, but I never imagined others would have also thought that I was dead. This day, I learned something. She spoke of losing the mother she used to know. She said that the Tanya she knew no longer existed. She told me that I'd always been her point of strength. She said I had always been positive and filled with laughter, and now I was blank. She shared how she desperately missed me and wanted me back. How she couldn't stand that I sat before her but was gone. I learned about another ugly face of grief that day. I learned that grief is an abductor lying in wait to steal a mother from her children. I learned how that additional loss made her withdraw from my life because of the pain of missing the mother that was taken on the front lawn. I learned how the yearning to have her back was unbearable. I learned how horrible it was that I looked the same on the outside when the inside had been replaced with a woman she no longer knew. I so badly wanted to tell her that I miss that woman too. Sitting before her, I promised myself that somehow, someday, I would find my way back even if it were only part way.

I'm happy to say that Sherreiea now comes around more. Being with her reminds me of how very much I miss her when she's away. I cherish every time we're together. Sometimes, I catch us laughing and joking like the old days. I wonder if she notices. I wonder if she feels that momentary sense of peace that is unknowingly gifted from the old me.

## BETH

Beth, oh how I wish I could reach her. Beth came to me too late. She was a teenager hardened from spending years in the foster care system. Although I've loved her like my own, she's never been able to feel it or accept it. She will run from hot to cold. She will come around for a while, and then it will be months and maybe years before she'll return. The loss of Clint was hard on her. Clint's accident was during one of her absent times. I think she's struggled with not getting to know him when he was a young man. This will forever be a piece she can't get back or make up for. I'm not angry at her for this. I feel sad at the rare opportunity she missed: the opportunity to fully know Clint.

Beth has her own child now. I have no doubt she will be an amazing mother and give him everything she didn't get as a child. I only wish she realizes that she could've had it; she could still have it. Please forgive yourself and let yourself be loved. I'm still here loving you, and I will be long after God calls me home.

## TIM, MY LOVE

Tim, my husband and best friend, grieved even more differently than the others. He was stoic, he laughed, and he rarely cried. He ate the food people brought and even sampled wine. I was angry, dismayed, and disgusted by his actions. I thought he should be crying and incapacitated like me. Every time I heard his laughter, which translated to cackling in my mind, I wanted to duct tape his mouth shut and hurt him. It felt disrespectful. I felt betrayed because the gun wasn't locked up, because he thought I couldn't hear his whispers to others about me and my devastation. Over time, I've learned that grief is different for everyone, and that's ok. I don't have to understand it to make it genuine. I've learned that Tim's training as a law enforcement officer has beaten *calm* into him, which explains the stoic nature. I've learned that emotional discomfort can be expressed in laughter. I've learned that he felt he needed to be a host when the hundreds of mourners filtered into our home. Overall, I've learned that everything he did gave him the strength to provide us with the support we needed for maintaining our lives. I've also learned that he often suffered alone by shedding many tears in the shower and his squad car.

Research shows that very few marriages survive the loss of a child. When we lost Clint, we also lost the dream of having more children. Although Tim still wanted us to have more children, there was no way I could've had another child after losing Clint. The kids we had here needed us. Although it was our choice not to follow through with having more children, we've both said it will be one of our biggest regrets. So no, surviving the loss of Clint hasn't been an easy journey, but we've beaten the odds. Through every tough time, my love for him or his for me has never wavered. Our love has always been strong and abiding. It was our hearts that God needed to heal.

## FAMILY DECISIONS & CHANGES

After losing Clint, we all made the decision as a family that we wouldn't sell our farm. Even though we lost Clint here so violently, the loss of our home would've been another hurt that might have made the compilation of losses unbearable. No matter how hard it may have been to stay, *we* collectively determined that it's where our memories of Clint and our perfect family are the thickest. We will stay here forever.

That decision hasn't always been an easy one. Everything changed within our home. Slowly, we made it look a little different on the outside and the inside. That horrible spot of Clint's accident on the lawn became a beautiful tribute to him. It couldn't remain a spot of trauma and sorrow that many would even fear. This didn't happen by accident. It was in the early days of my grief when I knew that spot would have to change if we remained in our home.

One morning, Tim rented a sod cutter and removed every inch of traumatized soil. I told him that although it was a painful piece of earth, I couldn't bear to see it thrown. Deep in my mind, I knew the blood of my son had filtered through that sod and made its home there. I had Tim place the sod at another prominent place on the farm. To this day, it's a place only few people know about; maybe only Tim and I know where it is. After the sod was removed, the daunting task of computing the perfect infinity sign began. It started with my sketched vision, a tape measure, stakes, and some string. From there, the outline of where the cobblestones would rest was placed. We called upon family and a few of Clint's friends, and the transformation began.

The cement mixer was humming and shovels were striking soil. There, dry dust turned to concrete so that hand-poured cobblestones could be laid into a dirt path. Many carved their names into the wet cement. Slowly, the bare lawn with a few markers of devastation became a breathtaking infinity garden filled with beauty and tranquility. My father, knowing Clint's desire to serve in the military, purchased a flagpole and flag, which would come to rest front and center. On any given day, you can hear it snap with pride as the wind gives it life. Plants came from other gardens on the farm to rest here for Clinty. Other plants came from the gardens of friends. Over time, things would just show up. Beautiful plaques, a solar-lit cross, Clint's rock collection, his handmade army men, bird nests like the ones he collected, a bell engraved by his class, solar lights to illuminate the flag through the night, and a large stone foot to represent Clint's fearless feet. The list is endless. With all this beauty, nothing catches my breath more than the three beautiful perennials that silently hold vigil to where we found Clint that day. Few, other than me, even know what kind of flowers they are. That spot is much more than just a beautiful garden or tribute to Clint. It's where I know 100% that God has graced this earth. It's where He took the hand of my son because his work here was done. It was time for my beautiful little boy to go home.

So, when I open the door to my front porch, step down to his garden, and sit on the bench; I close my eyes, feel the sun on my body, and try to imagine what a great moment it must've been for Clint to see the face of God. I understand why one arm was across his chest and the other was outstretched when I found him. I understand why his blue eyes were glistening and why he wore a smile on his face. I understand that he had gone home. Even as I write this, tears flow from my face, and I scream, "No, no, no!" Even now, I want him back. I search my heart because I know it's selfish. As my mind argues with itself, I pray for God to take away my pain and to grant me peace and grace so I can face today.

My writing is interrupted by my cell phone. I think to myself, now who is it? It's Jean, the wife of Tim's old law enforcement partner. She's staying at the same resort. She wants to go shopping. I wonder if I should go. I'm not feeling well today, but my writing's back on track. I need to trust God. He always knows when I've reached my limit. Perhaps for today, I have reached that limit. I quickly pull on a pair of white sweats, an Alexandria Tech sweatshirt that I got when we took Garrett to college, and a splash of makeup to hide my most recent crying episode. Yes, perhaps this touch of powder and mascara will hide my sadness from Jean. There, that ought to do. That should hide the pain that the outside world can rarely handle. That should hide the hurt that's bubbling just underneath the surface. I take one last look in the mirror to ensure that she can't tell. I know she'll find me to be somewhat odd when I don't make eye contact. Tim always tells me that my eyes give me away. Today, I can't look at her. The pain is oozing from my eyes; my sacrifice will be that she thinks I'm odd.

As I arrive back at my cabin after shopping, I see that I've missed a phone call from Garrett. I call him back, and we make idle chitchat about my day and his. It was the kind of conversation that I, as a mother, knew was masking something deeper. Soon, I would understand. Gar told me he had to make a card in class today for a classmate. I asked why. He said, "Mom, because his mom died in a car accident back home." The purpose of his call became as clear as the moment when a camera lens focuses on an object. Gar was calling to see if I was ok. He was calling to simply hear my voice and know I was still here. I told Gar that I felt bad for the boy and that it'd be difficult for him. He responded by saying he knew and couldn't imagine what it would be like to lose me. With Gar, I knew that was as far as I could take the topic. It was ok if I knew what was going on, but it certainly wouldn't be to talk about it further.

**THE NEW US**

Grief is like an ugly oil spill of which the flow can't be predicted. In no way can the dark and murky layer spread without covering us and leaving a slick of devastation in its wake. Tim's layers of grief flowed to betrayal, Megan's to coldness, Garrett's to darkness, Kayla's to deceit, Briana's to a need for perfection, Sherreiea's to abandonment, and Beth's to complete isolation.

As a family, we're finding a way to repair and become whole again. It is with an amazing love and loyalty for each other that we are able to do this. It is by the grace of God that He guides us through the process.

Since losing Clint, Tim has been promoted to the county's Emergency Management & Court Security Director. No more working nights or weekends. The kids and I have joked that we don't know what to do with a father that is home during nights and weekends.

After years of traveling for speaking engagements, I received my last promotion within the university and attained the highest rank possible a few years back. With that goal achieved, my traveling has been reduced greatly and my time for research and writing has increased. Around the same time, I also started an international research company based here in Minnesota: the Center for Scholastic Inquiry. This company has really started to take off. Professionally, we remain very busy.

As I've shared with you, everyone and everything changed after losing Clint. Tim may be the only one who's fully changed for the positive. Our family is absolutely his main priority. He used to be a hunting maniac. Even in those early days after Clint's accident, Tim thought we'd feel better if we went hunting. His early insensitivity was breathtaking. Somehow, this has also changed over the years. Now, he talks to me months before *any* hunting season to see if *we* are in the right place for it. He's careful to double-check with me if the demons that haunt my thoughts have retreated enough to allow for joy from a sport that led to the loss of my son. He double-checks if the colors of hunting, camouflage, and blaze orange will stop my heart permanently. For Tim, nothing comes before us.

Each of the children has suffered tremendous pain from our loss of Clint. Watching them navigate this pain has caused me pain that is nearly equal to my loss of Clint. Unfortunately, I have experienced the full spectrum of emotions as a mother. I've felt the complete joy that comes from instances such as watching a daughter have her own child, and I've felt complete devastation as I stood over the casket of a son. For me, there is only one emotion that comes close to this latter experience, and that is watching my children anguish in pain. Not just any pain, but it's a pain I can't take away no matter how hard I try. I've hated these moments and years of watching my children hurt. I hated the first day when we lost Clint, and I've hated it as recently as today. I'm sure this is a pain that, much like the pain of losing Clint, will never go away. Regardless, I'm here for them. I'm once again the strong and confident mother they need and have missed. I will do anything and everything to ensure their full recovery and happiness.

The children are all grown now and have lives of their own. No matter where they are, they try to come home for supper every week or two. I guess it depends on if I can break away from my office to cook for them. Yes, I can cook again. I have returned to preparing lavish meals and an extravagantly set table. These are some of the nights we all look forward to the most. They are nights when we are together. The dining room looks slightly different than when Clint was here. We took out a wall, built a new table, and changed its position. There would be no more need to avoid Clint's spot or his chair. Sometimes, these nights are crazy with noisy grandchildren and chaos, but I love them. Even though their bodies have grown into full adulthood, my babies are home.

When people see us or drive by our home and say or think to themselves, "That's the family who lost a son, a brother. How sad is that?" They have no idea of the true magnitude of our loss. We lost Clint that day, but we lost nearly everything else including each other. Because of the persevering spirit that rages strong within each of us, I'm proud to say we are finding each other again.

# CHAPTER 21

## *Our Roots Run Deep*

*"This family . . . laughs and learns, prays and protects, apologizes and appreciates, dreams and discovers, fights and forgives, teases and trusts, gives and grows, believes and belongs, loves and lasts . . . forever."*
~Author Unknown~

We lost having our Sunday dinners at my mom and dad's . . . Grandma and Grandpa's. They came to an immediate end. Everyone who loved me lost the sister, the friend, and the mother they once knew. Our family lost its innocence and its wholeness. The closeness that made us special has yet to fully return. Perhaps it's unrealistic to expect normalcy within such an abnormal situation.

We were like the Waltons, the Ingalls, or the Cleavers. We grew up close and intertwined. Whether we'd ever admit it, not one of us wanted to move far away. We wanted to stay close and near each other even as adults.

I've been told that I'm the glue that binds our family together. I'm the one who likes to help Mom organize the family events so everyone can be present. I'm the one who tries to make sure that no one is left out and that no one's feelings are hurt. I was the one who planned the Sunday dinners at Mom and Dad's house and made phone calls to let the rest know. I had been strong, organized, and confident, but that was gone. The new me was weak, scattered, and lost. It was as though I was a vase that had fallen onto concrete . . . I was broken. They all had a part in desperately scurrying to gather all of the pieces in an attempt to put me back together. The fight to find their mother, their daughter, their sister, their aunt within the fragments must have been hard for my entire family to bear. In the past, I would have taken the helm, pulled us together, and collectively charted a course. Not this time. This time, we were a ship without a rudder. This time, an intricate part of the navigation system was missing. It was me that was missing. For all practical matters, I was shipwrecked . . . my mind and soul were dead. My family would have to withstand the crushing hits from wave after wave without the ability to steer its way home. Adrift in unchartered waters, my family would have to find their way back to "us" without me.

**MOM & DAD**

What more can I say about parents that are perfect. At least they've been perfect to me. They are full of love for all of their kids as well as their grandchildren. They like having us around, and we all like to be around them. Their family farm is the nucleus from which none of us lives too far away. They are loving and generous to a fault, sharing what they have with whoever needs it. They are both highly educated professionals: Dad was an engineer, and Mom was a registered nurse. Yet, their passion remains with operating and preserving the family farm. They are workaholics that scold me often for working too hard. Because of this, they are hard to take seriously. I have never known them not to have multiple jobs and endeavors. Even now, with Mom in her late seventies and Dad in his eighties, they run an Angus cattle operation and a gravel corporation. I have no doubt they will both die working.  Although I hate to even think of losing my parents, that is how they would want to go–working.  They work hard and have never been really good at play.  When we were young, however, they did buy a cabin on our favorite camping lake.  Somehow, even during the farm crisis, they were able to hold on to it.  To this day, it's one of my favorite places in the world.  To me, it's where our amazing family comes together under one roof just like when we were young.  Except now, there are many grandkids and great grandkids as well.  There at our family cabin, we dine together, sit by bonfires, enjoy nature, partake in water sports, and watch outdoor movies.  On some late nights, my dad and I talk into the wee hours of the morning like we used to when I was a little girl.  Other times, he wakes me so we can watch the sunrise over the lake.  These are some of my best memories.

The family cabin is a symbol of perseverance for our family.  Through all we've endured, there she stands proudly among the trees, faithfully awaiting our return.  She welcomes us in and we return to a time of togetherness and joy.  It is the place Clint and Grandpa would proudly raise the American flag each 4th of July.  Yes, this is our favorite place and, to no surprise, it was also Clint's.

**HOLLIS, VERA, & FAMILY**

My oldest brother, Hollis, lives four miles away on our grandparent's homestead.  He's a wise man who, only second to our father, is the next patriarch in line.  Everybody likes Hollis.  He's a man of integrity, and he's well known for it.  Hollis is quite a bit older than me, so we weren't close growing up. As adults, we both try. Since the loss of Clint, there are times when he tries even harder. I'm sure he hates to see me hurt because he's my big brother. Clint and Garrett used to work for him on the farm. He was known as being a tough boss, but they loved it. They loved it because he was also carefree with them. He let them do things their mother wouldn't such as having BB gun wars with snowsuits and helmets, riding the hay bales up on the semi while it was moving, climbing the highest of trees, running wild with the baby animals, and chasing the bulls back into their pen. Oh, he drove me nuts with his careless, oops, I mean carefree way with my boys. The madder I would get at him, the more he would laugh. Like the time Garrett climbed to the top of a tree and hit nearly every branch on his way down. It was the last branch that poked his chest and caught a rib that saved him from hitting the ground. You see, that was funny to Hollis because Gar didn't get seriously hurt. Actually, Gar and I laugh about it now. The incident left a perfect heart-shaped scar on his chest. I wonder to myself sometimes if that was God's way of letting me know how much my brother loved them deeply even though he had been wildly carefree with them. Maybe we could reminisce about the day Garrett's arm snapped after Hollis let the big boys wrestle with the little boys. Oh, it could have been worse; after two orthopedic surgeries and six pins, Gar recovered. Then, there was the famous chick incident when Hollis put Gar, who was just a toddler, down in the midst of a barn full of chickens and baby chicks. Of course, Gar recovered from this too but not before several doctor appointments and one psychiatrist session. Or perhaps we could point to the day I called Hollis to tell him I was bringing the boys their lunch. He told me not to bother because Clint and Gar, 15 and 13, were on their way home. I shrieked at him, wondering how they were making the four-mile trip. It wouldn't have been unlike him to build their character by having them walk, which would have been ok with me. However, that wasn't the case. He had given them a four-wheeler without helmets and sent them on their way. There had been no consideration that they could get hurt or picked up by a deputy. Again, he laughed. I jumped in the car and met them halfway between the farms and told them to turn their little butts around and head back to Hollis' house. When we got there, Gar just shook his head, but Clint had words for me. Words that were, in part, inspired by my brother's spirit of carefree carelessness. Clint turned to me and said, "Mom, I love life to the fullest so when it's my time to go . . . it will be a great day!" Then, as though realizing he'd just sassed his mother, he sheepishly stepped away to eat his sandwich. I could see he was also filled with pride for sharing his philosophy with me. In that moment, I knew what he just said was profound. What I didn't know was that we would choose to carve these words into his headstone in just a few short months.

After Clint's accident, Hollis struggled with the feeling that his time with Clint should've been different and that perhaps, in an effort to teach him responsibility and work ethic, he'd been too hard on Clint. His wife shared with me that he called her for a ride when he went to check a hay field. She explained that when she arrived, she was frustrated with my brother, who is famous for his lack of planning. He said he needed a ride, yet there he was in the field with someone. When they saw her, they turned to go meet her. There they were side by side. She said she froze as they got closer because Clint was by Hollis' side. When

Hollis got in the vehicle, he told Vera there was no one with him in the field. Even as Vera shared the story with me, she shook. She knew Clint had come to comfort Hollis that day. Even if just for a few moments in time, my baby had come to comfort his uncle, my big brother. Clint undoubtedly wanted him to know that he hadn't been too hard on him and that he was loved.

To sum up, Hollis is carefree with all the nieces and nephews, and they love him for it. He's a big kid disguised as a grown man. He's generous and has a heart of goodness. After losing Clint, he came by often, and he also called me several times a day. He'd always referred to me as Tanya. One day, we were about to hang up the phone and he said, "I love ya, Tan." Only my friends call me that. It'd happened. Even with our age difference, we had become friends.

Happily, he lives on the family farm with his wife, Vera. Vera is an educator and a technology specialist. She's outspoken, yet she values her privacy. All of their kids are grown and enjoying their own lives.

As a boy, Erick was much like Clint: energetic and mischievous. As a grown man, he's channeled this into hard work and success. Erick works with wind tower energy and travels quite a bit. Although it's been less in recent years, he stops by to visit when he's home. He's intelligent and has a great sense of humor. I enjoy our visits.

Blaine works on the family farm with Hollis. He was my first nephew. Oh, how I loved to babysit him. He grew up to be mischievous but quiet. He is that dangerous kind of mischievous that sneaks up on you when you don't expect it and gives you a pinch under the arm. It's a pinch that triggers instant rage, yet when he smiles at me, my heart finds it so difficult to be mad at him. After all, he will forever be my little Blaine. Inside, I know his quirky pestering is his way of showing me he cares.

Sam is a child-support officer and lives nearby. He's always been quiet around me but is never too busy to stop what he's doing to talk. I find him to be quite intelligent, yet he seems uncomfortable with his smarts. He's always sporting some mountain-man look such as a scruffy beard and shaggy hair. I'm proud of him. He's always his own person unconcerned with what the world expects or demands. He finds what makes him happy. Isn't that what we wish for all of our kids?

Lyndsey was my first godchild in a line of many. Pooh, as I lovingly call her, has always been special to me. She is the same age as my daughter Megan. They were close as children, but their busy adult lives have taken them in different directions. Today, Lyndsey works at a local company. I've always thought she'd own a company. I still have no doubt that she will one day. Lyndsey is beautiful, smart, and confident. She means the world to me. I wonder if she is fully aware of the many gifts that still lie dormant within her. She is so talented and gracious. I wait with great anticipation to see what big things God has planned for her.

After losing Clint, Lyndsey, fully aware of Clint's plan to join the Army, ordered him a flag that had been in Kuwait. The day it arrived, it brought me to tears. She wanted to remember and honor her cousin for a future that would never be his.

## TODD, DIANE, & FAMILY

My second oldest sibling is my brother Todd. When I was really young, I remember him feeding us when our parents were working. He would take care of us and make sure we ate. Sometimes it would be fried bread; other times it was tuna fish and rice crispy bars. It didn't matter what it was. To him, it mattered if we ate. In later years, we had a love-hate relationship. To be honest, it was mostly hate. He thought us girls didn't work hard enough. The truth is he was hard to grow up with. He partied hard, drank too much, and was unforgiving of noise if he was trying to sleep off a hangover. He sobered up decades ago, but coldness remained between us. It wasn't until after losing Clint that things changed. The day after losing Clint, I was sitting on the couch barely able to raise my head or open my eyes. There was Todd busting through the crowd of people and taking me by the hand. He said, "Let's get out of here." I had no instinct to stay or go. I was with my brother. I knew I'd be safe. It was uncannily warm, but it was still November. He took me outside. Barefoot with just a tank top and thin pair of sweats, I felt no cold. My body and mind were numb. Maybe they were frozen and feared the ugliness I needed to face. What Todd said to me during that walk forever changed my view of him. He was soft inside. My tough, strong, bull-headed brother was showing me his heart. He was hurting. I could tell he missed Clint and that he loved me. I felt something. For the first time in 24 hours, I could feel. I could feel my brother's love infuse me with a little life. I could feel the coolness of the grass under my feet. You know that crunchy grass that is still green but has a little frost engulfing each blade? We walked down to the horses. Of course we would; Todd loves horses. There we stood. He smoked a cigarette. My eyes couldn't focus because they were swollen and sore from crying, but they could make out rings of smoke in the air. I watched as he put a cigarette to his mouth and drew in air. I could tell that it hurt when he drew in air. That kind of hurt when a deep breath stings a little after you've been crying. As he blew through his pursed lips, a perfect ring of smoke entered the air. I watched it catch a breeze and disappear. He dropped his cigarette into the grass and put his cowboy boot over it. I watched his foot push the grass down and his ankle shimmy from side to side to extinguish it. As he did, he told me that I was a good mom and that he couldn't figure out why it had to be me. Why did it have to be one of my kids? He shook his head and spoke no more. He must have been able to tell that a chill had run through me. Or maybe he was uncomfortable sharing emotions. In either case, he put his arm around me and said we should go back inside. I didn't care. All I knew and needed to know was that my brother Todd thought I was a good mom.

Todd has been a pleasant surprise since losing Clint. We are close. I can't believe I'm saying it, but yes, we are close. He called me nearly every day for a year. Then, the calls became a little less. This fall, they started again. It warms my heart. Todd once told me that Clint was always different than the other kids in the family. He said Clint made him feel normal. Even though Todd could sometimes be gruff and tough, Clint always made time for him. This past fall, Todd called to tell me that Clint is never from his mind and that he misses him.

Todd is married to Diane. They have five kids. Unlike the rest of us who live relatively close to Mom and Dad,

Todd moved a whopping twenty miles away. He lives in a gorgeous historic home on an acreage that borders the river. Diane works at the local hospital. We used to be very close. In recent years, I don't see much of her. I tell myself it's because she's very busy with her job, the kids, and the grandkids. The truth is I miss her. She loved Clinty. When we do see each other, she's not afraid to talk about him. I like that.

Jackie, oh, Jackie. Jackie is the oldest of their kids and is also the oldest of the grandchildren. She is stunningly beautiful with a constant goal of perfection, whether it's for her house, her kids, her husband, or the way she looks. All those things are great, but I hope she realizes that her perfection comes from within her heart; a heart that has been perfect all along. I see it when she smiles. I recognized it when I walked through her house and saw a picture of my son, Clint, on a shelf. Her heart is big. Her heart doesn't forget. I'm so proud of her and the life she has created for her family. She's had a lot to overcome in life, and she has done it with grace. We were close when she was little. I have no idea what happened. Maybe it was nothing, or maybe it was just life. At times, many times, I yearn for being close again.

Troy is handsome beyond words and tenderhearted to a fault. I can see that the bad in this world has weighed heavily on his heart and caused unnecessary struggles. He is another one that has no idea what his smile brings to a room. From the first day I met him, he was everything a little boy should be. I only hoped that, one day, I could have boys like him. Now, he is grown up with a beautiful daughter. Delaney couldn't be more perfect. When they are together, anyone can see what a good dad he is. He once told me his goal as a dad was to make her feel like the most important person in his world. I have no doubt that she feels it. Like all of us, Troy isn't perfect. He has had his bouts with his dark side. I only pray he doesn't think those things define him. He has so much more to offer this world. He also makes me very proud.

Kolten is a cowboy through and through. If I were to ask him what happiness is, he'd probably say it's the smell of horse crap. I chuckle as I type it because it's probably true. Kolten has a temper from years of being raised to be a rough cowboy, but beneath it he has a heart of gold. What I love about him is he's not afraid to show it. One smile at him buys a huge smile back. There has never been a time when he hasn't hugged me when we see each other. He doesn't just hug me, but he squeezes me tight. When he does, I feel absolute love.

Kasidy is another godchild. She will kill me for writing this, but she's a lot like her dad. She has a chip that sits on her shoulder, but unlike her dad, it easily crumbles. She loves kids, she loves being with family, and she too loves to give me hugs. It is rare when I see Kasidy and she doesn't hug me twice. Once for when I first see her, and once for when we part ways. Her heart is an open book.

Dakota is a mystery to me because she doesn't leave anything to the imagination. What you see is what you get. What she thinks is what you hear. She has a filter but doesn't always use it. She's high-spirited and uncensored. She makes us all laugh. To top it off, she's sharp as a tack. Like Kasidy, I never see her when she's not sharing her heart through a big hug. Then, we have another one just before we part.

Clint used to love to go to Todd and Diane's house to spend time with their kids. They were each very special to him.

## KYLE, PAM, & FAMILY

Kyle is married to Pam, his high school sweetheart. Pam was an upperclassman and a good friend of mine when they met. I like to remember being the one who set them up together. A few years back, I even found a card that she gave to me in high school. In it, she called me Cupid, her pet name for me for setting them up. I like to call it evidence of a job well done.

After losing Clint, they came over every day for the first year. When we were apart, they'd call me several times as well. They knew, much like my husband did, that I wanted to die. They knew more than most what my children meant to me. They knew the kids were my life. They knew that finding a way to navigate the loss of Clint would be nearly impossible. They knew it could happen only through God. Then, the unthinkable happened; they watched me cast Him from my life. I no longer went to church. I no longer prayed to a God I loved. I spewed hatred to a God that was a hoax! They knew I was lost. They knew the light within the sister they loved had all but faded to black. Even so, they kept coming. They kept hugging me with the hopes that they'd feel some life from me. I don't know how they did it. I had to have been such a drain. I can only imagine that my emotionally dead body sucked the life right out of them when we held each other. They did this willingly all in the hopes that, one day, they'd see a flicker that represented the sister they had loved.

Along with them were often their boys. Those beautiful boys who couldn't feel more like my own. They really were. You see, Kevin and Ethan and Clint and Garrett were the same ages. They were nearly inseparable. If they weren't at our house, they were all at Kyle and Pam's. I know the loss of Clint was wearing down on all of them as well. No, he wasn't their son or brother, but he was the closest thing possible.

Kyle has always been and will always be one of my absolute best friends. That's all there is to say, yet there is so much more to say. I could write a book about the two of us. Some might find it unbelievably boring. In our entire lives, I don't think we've even had a serious fight. The closest he and I ever came to having a fight was after losing Clint. They were having a party, and I called to say I couldn't come. He was mad and called me back to let me know it. The one thing about Kyle is he'll tell you how he feels. When he called me back, he told me he was sick of me not showing up at their gatherings. He explained how it hurt them both. Inside, I flared with anger. He knew me! Why couldn't he understand how painful it is to go those gatherings and listen to all of the happy families talk about their kids? Yes, all of their kids. I didn't have all of my kids. It wasn't fair and I wouldn't and couldn't go. I called him back and told him just that. Before I could finish, he apologized and said he didn't want to see Pam hurt by me declining all the time. He said they just missed me and wanted me back. I told him I was trying to find my way back, but I needed time. He was sorry.

From as far back as I can remember, Kyle has been rescuing me no matter whether it was me coming home late, coming home drunk, dating a bad guy, hanging out with the wrong crowd, or dealing with town gossip after my divorce. Kyle has always stood by my side. If ever there were a modern-day hero, to me, it's him. Losing Clint was no different. He was the first one who entered my mind. He was the one I needed. I wanted my big brother to fix it. He had always fixed everything, so of course he could fix Clint. That day, I asked my brother to do the impossible. In hindsight, I put a pressure on my brother that was unreasonable and unfair. All he could do was hold me while my son lay lifeless in front of us. All he could do was find the courage to tell me "he is gone" and hold me down.

Clint used to love to tease Pam. He often played dead to scare her. There was the time we were tubing and he fell off his tube. There in the lake, he lay lifeless with his head in the water and his arms outstretched. After screaming, Pam was about to jump in to save him when he popped his head up giggling. Or there was the time when he dove off the dock after being instructed to be careful because it could be dangerous. He never came up. You see, Clint was an outstanding swimmer and could hold his breath for nearly as long as I. When he didn't come up, Pam screamed and ran to the end of the dock. Well, when he did come up . . . he was all laughter. Auntie Pam was not happy. He got an earful. Then there was the time they were jumping dirt bikes in the field at their house. Pam was watching from the window when Clint had a horrible crash. Again, he lay lifeless. Her heart filled with fear as she ran to him only to find that he was fine. From that moment on, she swore he wasn't allowed to do anything dangerous at her house ever again. She told him she couldn't take it. So, on that horrible fall morning, Pam's fear became a reality. I'm sure she, like me, just wanted him to wake up. There would be no more leaping to his feet or breaking the surface of the water and giggling uncontrollably at us worrywarts. It was real. My beautiful boy's laughter was silenced and replaced by sirens. There was nothing left to do but pick up the pieces both metaphorically and literally. They rarely miss anything; they don't miss his birthday or the anniversary of his accident. They're faithful in their support of me.

Kevin is my handsome and fidgety godson. Kevin has held a special place in my heart long before he was born. He arrived just five days after my Clinty. They grew up together as cousins and, ultimately, as best friends. They were inseparable most of their lives. As with many best friends, Kevin and Clint had their little spats. They would madly stomp away from each other, but they always made a quick return. Before we'd know it, the disagreement would be over just as though nothing had ever happened. They always knew no matter what faced them in this world, they'd always have each other. Kevin was one of the first to arrive that horrible day. I remember the look of horror on his face when his worst fears were confirmed to be true. He looked so lost. He just walked around in circles as though he had nowhere to go. He walked around as though he was looking for his best friend for comfort . . . his best friend that was now and forever unable to help him. In Kevin's words, "chaos" was born.

Ethan is the same age as our younger son, Garrett. They too became the best friends and inseparable. Unlike Kevin and Clint who had their squabbles, Ethan and Garrett have never had a serious fight. There was one time when Ethan made Garrett cry. Ethan felt so bad that he cried too. Ethan is quiet but smart. He is methodical and purposeful in his thinking. He is independent and wise for his age. In family pictures, he could easily be mistaken for my son. He's always looked more like me than his parents. On the inside, he feels like my son as well. Unlike Kevin, Ethan and I don't have close talks about Clint or about life for that matter. But we do have our silent exchanges. I know, at times, he sees sadness in my eyes. I know he cares. At times, I see that same longing for Clint in his eyes. There is an unspoken understanding between us that is deep and purposeful. Although it's silent, that unspoken language screams that if ever I need him or if he needs me, all we need to do is ask. Sometimes, it's enough just to be in each other's presence that makes things feel right again.

One thing that has always bothered me was the fact that Ethan was somewhat overlooked when we lost Clint. He wasn't technically Clint's *best friend*, he wasn't technically his *brother*, and he wasn't technically one of his *friends*. Yet, he was *all* of those things. The four boys were everything to each other. Rarely were they apart. The loss of Clint had to be extremely hard for Ethan. I hope he knows that I know.

After losing Clint, the boys didn't come to sleep over anymore. That ended nearly instantly. Rather, Garrett would and still does go to their house. This was another unspeakable loss for me. Not only did I lose Clinty's voice within our home, I lost their voices as well. To this day, I miss having them with us. Kevin and Ethan will forever own a piece of my heart. For months, they came to see me every single day. Their hugs provided an infusion that must have been similar to giving a blood transfusion to a person who is injured and bleeding out. Those hugs infused me with emotion. Emotion was something that was nearly dead within me. Slowly, these two boys helped to breathe life into me again.

## BOBBIE, TIM, & FAMILY

Bobbie is the youngest of us and my only sister. There have been times in life when we have been very close and times when I wish we had been closer.

When we lost Clint, Bobbie tried to be a big sister for her big sister. It had to be a difficult role reversal for her. My little sister, although she doesn't know it, is wise. She's painfully quiet and rarely shares her thoughts in a room full of people. I'm one of the rare ones she has let inside. I like being there in that place where my sister and I find comfort and deep trust in each other. It feels safe.

A few years before Clint's accident, Bobbie and her kids moved back from North Dakota to be closer to the family. These would be precious years . . . the last years we'd all be together. During this time, Bobbie and her children, Britta and Steehl, would grow close to everyone, especially Clint. He loved to spend time with Britta and Steehl. As for Bobbie, she always had a special affinity for Clint. He was kind and took time to seek her out. You see, Bobbie is probably the shyest among all of us. She prefers to be by herself rather than interact too much. When she would do this, Clint would go find her just to visit. Usually, he would fill her with joy and they would end up laughing hysterically. Bobbie also found Clint to be a great older cousin for her kids. He always made time for her kids, especially Steehl.

Steehl is much like his mother. He is painfully shy and very much a loner. Both of my boys have always been fantastic at seeking him out and finding things they can do together. It didn't matter if it was going to his house and playing video games or getting him to go to a movie with them. They liked doing things with Steehl. Clint loved showing him his model army tanks and his intricately built array of other military models. About a year before his accident, he made the decision to give Steehl some of his army planes and ships. In the moment, he was happy to do it but soon had remorse. He wanted them back. As much as he wanted to have them back, he cared so deeply for Steehl that he let him keep them. He wanted to see Steehl smile. Clint told me that when Steehl outgrew them, he would get them back. When I asked Clint why he thought Steel, who was younger, would outgrow them but not himself, he said he wouldn't outgrow them because he'd like them for his future classroom. He planned to hang the bombers from his classroom ceiling.

Britta was little when we lost Clint, but he also made time for her. Again, he would find things that made her happy. If she wanted to swim, they would. If she wanted to play dolls, he would. If she wanted rides on the go-cart, he would take her. Britta grew to look up to Clint and admire him. Britta is beautiful and kind. Unlike her brother, she is a chatterbox and will talk your ear off. She is a social butterfly and likes to hang out with friends. Yet she always makes time for family.

A few years ago, Bobbie met her husband, Tim. Why she had to marry someone with the same name as my husband, I guess I will never know. It's funny at times. We can get ourselves into trouble fairly easily if we don't use phrases like "my Tim" or "your Tim." Tim has been a great addition to our family. He is a faithful servant of God, supportive, well educated, funny, and has great integrity–all the things our family requires of its members. Tim has four boys that are also a great addition to our family: Ty, Dalton, Landon, and Riley. We don't see them as much as we'd like, but they are part of us.

## AN ABIDING LOVE

No matter who you were in our family, you probably had a sense that Clint was your favorite or, at least, among your favorites. He went out of his way to make us all laugh and feel loved. He was our smile . . . he was the family sunshine.

Clint would never want us to give up. He and Garrett used to do a lot of cattle fencing with Grandpa Weber. Some days, it was nearly unbearable with the heat, poison ivy, and mosquitos. It was on one of those days when Clint's positive attitude and wisdom shined through. They were about to give up on a tough section of pasture when Clint looked at Grandpa and Gar and said, "Shut up and keep rowing." Surprised by Clint's statement, Grandpa said, "What?" Clint said, "Grandpa, when times are tough we need to dig in harder. We need to shut up and just keep rowing." Clint told me that Grandpa burst into laughter, nodded, and told him that was exactly right. So, when times without Clint are tough, we try to do it Clint-style: "Shut up and just keep rowing."

With our family, there is still a coldness that lies deep beneath the surface. It's a coldness that stands watch from its post over our hearts. This watch is needed to protect the vulnerable spot deep within each of us. That spot that never knew the depths of the indescribable pain of losing a grandson, a nephew, a cousin, a sibling, or a child. That spot that never knew the despair involved with watching those we love live in anguish without relief. It's because of that spot that we will never completely return to each other. It's that spot that makes the first glance between a brother and a sister one that seeks to know if she's alright today. It is that first glance between a mother and her child that wonders if she hurts or smiles inside today. It's that first glance of each encounter between my parents and me that simply screams to their hearts to run from any interaction with that spot inside of us. It's that first glance of every encounter with my babies that I wonder if they are truly ok. It's that spot that has made this silent interaction our unspoken greeting each and every time we meet.

Although there is a coldness that lies beneath the surface, there is a strong and abiding love that lies just beneath it. I would imagine it's like the molten lava that burns hot at the center of the earth, and it only emerges with a push from somewhere deep within. That push is a desire for our closeness to return. Yet the fear that comes from such vulnerability is strong. At times our love, much like that molten lava, cannot be contained, and it crashes through the layers of hardened stone as it rises to warm the surface. Yes, more and more, our love is bubbling through the protective layers of coldness. Finally, we are returning to each other.

## 2020 AUTHOR NOTE

It's been years since I wrote the proceeding pages and published this book. With the passing of time, life has taken me on many additional twist and turns. As a result, I no longer view or feel the same about many family members. Or, for that matter, the family itself. My perspective and perception of many I'd written so fondly of has changed. With the sudden loss of my father and the onset of dementia within my mother, true personalities were revealed. Some were pleasantly surprising while with others an ugliness emerged that exposed greed in a way I have never seen, heard, or imagined. A greed so great that for some, the honor and care of (and for) our parent(s) no longer existed. Although this selfishness has been a painful realization, my wish is to remember each of them as we once were… a family. For at that time, whether real or not, we were the Weber's. We were raised by amazing parents who provided us with more than anyone could ever ask or expect. Any challenge to that memory or reality feels like an attack on the Father Himself. After all, He calls us to honor our father and mother.

Forgiveness has been called a gift to oneself. The truth about forgiveness is that it extends far beyond a gift to self. Rather, it is one of God's greatest expectations. As I understand it, He commands it. So, although I will never respect or condone what has transpired, with time, I have fully forgiven. I loved these certain family members when we were the Weber's, and although our lives will likely never blend again, part of me always will.

# CHAPTER 22
## Ray of Hope

∞

*"Hope is not dead, it is just larger than our imaginations; its purpose extending far beyond our comprehension."*
~Kathy Hobaugh~

Flashbacks are like flash-spark flares or hay bales that have spontaneously combusted. They blow up in my mind when just one small thing triggers them. This is where real pain lives. This pain, my pain, could easily make me even more of a recluse. Each time I relive the experience, it only drives the pain deeper, and then I retreat further into my own private world. I wish those around me could understand this never gets easier. It's a continual fight within me to be strong, to be positive, and to be grateful. It takes a great deal of internal work that is never ending.

Sometimes, my ability to analyze my own thoughts and behaviors becomes paralyzed. I can't see whatever is right before me clearly. I must learn to control my own thoughts because they're not always real or true. Sometimes, reality needs to guide my internal voices, who naturally tell me to be sad or depressed. At times, I need to force an override and hit the reset button. I need to *choose* to be happy until I really am.

There is a difference between talking yourself out of something and talking yourself through something. That difference has been difficult to discern. To me, talking myself out of something seems like denial or avoidance.

Talking myself through something is healthy and promotes internal growth and wisdom. For instance, there are times when my mind wants to believe that Clint will come back one day. Talking me out of this would be telling myself that I don't want to think about this right now, and I simply push it out of my mind. Talking me through it would be telling myself that I know Clinty is not coming back to me in this world, and reminding me that I'll see him again in Heaven. Don't get me wrong, there are times when it's best to get out of something and not through it. An example would be if there were physical dangers involved. For instance, if I were in a burning house, I better get my ass out of it. It's different when you're dealing with emotions. There's a sense of peace and understanding that comes with a true honesty you can only find within yourself. Others have good intentions, but their goal is almost always to get you *out* of the moment of pain. It's more comfortable for them. In doing this, they say things like "it will get better with time" or "let's think about something else now," or they simply don't mention the person you've lost. Navigating through these good intentions with your own best interests in mind is difficult. The ability to talk yourself *through* something versus *out* of something is a profound indicator of a positive mental prognosis. You see, some wisdom is not unlocked until an experience (good or bad) produces a key that opens that door. Give yourself the key!

**PHYSICAL PAIN**

No one ever told me that parents who lose their children experience a physical pain that has no explanation. The entire body hurts as though it's been caught in a grain auger: twisted, torn, and spit out. There is a choice to make; you can either wallow in this pain or move through it. I have chosen, daily, to move through it. In the early years of my loss, I often thought I was ill. My chest would hurt, my limbs would ache, and none of my bodily functions operated to their full capacities. The emotional pain wreaked unspeakable havoc on an already stressed and overloaded system. No, nobody had told me this was normal and to be expected. I fought the pain. I tried to get enough sleep, to eat right, and to exercise. Finally, after years of battling fatigue and an array of grief-induced physical pain, I see additional rays of hope. I no longer feel a hundred years old but rather, more appropriately, middle-aged.

**OUR RELATIONSHIP**

Our relationship hasn't ended. It has changed. Although the beautiful body that held Clint is gone, Clint is still with me every day. Everything inside of him lives. I feel his presence. I feel him with me. I feel I have a special relationship with him that no one else has. It's as though he's on a vacation or an extended trip, and he is preparing for the day I go to stay with him. Until that beautiful day, I will live here.

Acclimating to this new reality means choosing to focus on and cherish those around me and the many gifts I have been given. There is a Bible verse I have always loved but never fully understood the depths of:

> "... When someone has been given much, much will be required in return; and when someone has been entrusted with much, even more will be required."
> ~ Luke 12:48 ~

    I used to believe I was blessed because I had a beautiful family including loving parents, amazing siblings, out-of-this-world children, and grandchildren that warm my very soul. In an effort to give back, I've been kind to others, I've volunteered my time to help the needy, and, through foster care, I've provided a loving and stable home for those who haven't had one. We've also done well professionally and financially. It hasn't come easily, but we've been blessed. I've shared our blessings through donating generously, organizing foundations, giving cash to needy family and friends, or giving away our own things just to bring a smile to the face of another. Yes, I had been given much, and I knew much was expected. I thought I was doing well with it. Then after I lost Clint, I realized there is so much more I could give. Even though I've lost part of my very being, my son, I've been able to see through the thickness of pain and realize I'm still blessed. God had not stripped me of all the gifts He had granted to my life. He simply took our beautiful son home to enjoy for Himself.

    Today, I still want to be angry at God for taking him home, but I can't. I now know how very much He must have missed him while he was here with us. I now know I was blessed even if I had a short time with Clint. I am still blessed. Since losing Clint, God has gifted me some extraordinary experiences. He has restored my faith, He has granted me moments in His presence, and He has granted me moments when I can feel my son. In an instant, He granted me the ability to write and chain these words together. He has given me much, and He still expects much. How could I take these gifts granted by God Himself and not share them with the world? After all, as stated in Luke 12:48, He *requires* it. Until the day I leave this earth and join hands with Clint, I will share what God has given me.

## HAS SADNESS BECOME ME?

Some ask, "Will you always live so sad?" The answer is simple; I am *not* always sad. There have been periods in my life when I'm extremely happy. However, my mind is like a spilled glass of water on a sloped floor. The water naturally runs toward the lowest point. My heart and mind are much the same. They naturally want to flow to the lowest point, to my sadness.

Losing Clint is not a life sentence of sadness. It is, however, a conscious choice to not only live but also to *really* live. It's a choice I make every day, many times a day, and, sometimes, many times an hour. This takes faith. On my office wall, I have the following statement painted. It provides a complex yet simple definition of faith to me: "Faith is the strength by which a shattered world shall emerge into the light." That is the faith God has given me. He has provided me with a faith that has given me the strength to live. And yes, I am beginning to live again.

Where does this faith come from? It comes from promise and prayer. It comes from the promise to Clint that I will live a good life, and it comes from a promise from God that He will not leave me and that we *will* be together again. It also comes from the prayer I have said more times than I can count; it's a prayer for a peace that surpasses all human understanding.

## SO WHAT HELPS?

People often ask me what helps us to cope with living without Clint. Well to be honest, as a family, we have tried nearly everything. We have tried medication for lack of sleep, medication for too much sleep, medication for depression, medication for anxiety, therapy for depression, and therapy for grief. You name it and we have tried it. I don't really know what helps other than knowing it is not just one thing. Perhaps a better question is "What gives us hope?" First, I would have to say our faith and the knowledge that we will be together again. For this to happen, we have to live a good life with Christ. Prayer and knowing another life awaits gives us focus. Before we get on the plane, we have to make sure we have a ticket, right?

What helps with the pain? People who *really* care and remember help the most. One needs to realize that it doesn't matter how many years have passed. Even though several years may have passed, at the same time it's as though it happened yesterday, but it also feels like it happened a hundred years ago. The tragedy may feel like yesterday, but the last time you were with your loved one feels like an eternity. So, when people show us they still care, we appreciate their acknowledgement.

The things that actually help are so very different for each person. The truth is most mourners don't know what helps because the things that help might change from day to day. To address this, self-understanding is critical for overall understanding. This deep self-awareness is necessary for each of us, but it's difficult to attain. It only comes from very hard, introspective self-discovery. Exactly how one is able to reach that level of discovery is both individual and personal. For me, it has come through writing and through pushing myself to revisit and touch parts of my pain that would've otherwise remained buried. Digging at these scabs that aren't yet fully healed can be horrific. It can resuscitate sadness and flashbacks. To protect itself, the mind wants to take the easy way out. It wants to run from the pain by omitting the truth. We need to face these lies of omission. Otherwise, these lies we tell ourselves invite the Devil to come inside us. He promises relief through depression, alcohol, and other drugs. Even when a person is strong, these things are tempting. It would be so very easy to lose myself in a bottle of alcohol for just one night. This is a lie the Devil whispers to me. The truth is it wouldn't be for just a night. It would be every night thereafter until my soul was lost. God didn't promise us an easy life, but He did promise that He wouldn't leave us. So, do I have hope? Yes, there are rays of hope beaming down on me, and from me, every day. Had I lost myself forever, any learning and discovery would've been buried. For me, Clint's loss was worth more than a lost, undiscovered lesson.

    Through my sadness, the world had become a place I no longer knew or understood. Oftentimes, *rays of hope* came in the form of people. These were people that I have no doubt God placed in my life. I felt a deep love and affinity for some of these people whether or not I had known them previously. It was as though my very soul knew them. They saved me! These rays of hope allowed me to see the genuine goodness in this world with more clarity. These rays of hope allowed me to see a kindness and welcoming that resonates in people. Whether they were my children, my parents, my sister, my brothers, my friends, or complete strangers, the rays surrounded me and engulfed me with hope. It was a hope that I would live each day a little better than the last. I hoped to live each new day without crossing it off the calendar at 5:30 in the morning. I hoped to live each new day without taking a single second for granted, and instead, treat the day as if it were my last. I treat each new day as a day I will never get back because the truth is, I won't. Unlike Clint and me, you may get a chance to see your loved ones again, but you will never be able to recapture that moment in time. Please cherish as many moments as you can.

So, are there rays of hope? There absolutely are!

## CHAPTER 23

## *Holding On*

∞

*"Your life was a blessing, your memory a treasure . . .
you are loved beyond words and missed beyond measure."*
~Renee Wood~

There've been many things I've done to *hold on* to our sense of family and sanity. Mostly, I've made promises that needed to be kept and done things to keep Clint's memory alive both within us and around us. It has been a goal of mine to live a life that not only would make Clint and my other children proud but also a life from which others might know God by interacting with us. We are far from being a perfect family, but we're one that has held on because of Him.

I started to occasionally watch *Dr. Phil* after losing Clint. I didn't watch it because it was an intellectually stimulating program, I watched it for a much more simplistic reason. I watched it because it highlighted people with lives that were more messed up than the new one I must call mine. One day while watching the show, I heard Dr. Phil say something that inspired me. He said that a bad situation needed a hero. I wanted our hero to come from within my family. I didn't need it to be one of us. I needed it to be all of us taking turns when the others were beaten down. I wanted that strength to solidify our connection and bond. Without each other, we were weak and vulnerable, but together, we found strength and perseverance. We found a hero for our messed-up situation. That hero was me when the kids were down. It was Gar when we just wanted to sit on the couch. It was Tim when Megan wanted to slip into negativity. It was Briana when we just needed to hear Clint's name. It was Megan when she would share a story about the brother she missed. The hero was a compilation of each of us. We, collectively, became our own hero.

It wasn't always easy for us. Some days it was more like being the cheerleader. I've found that it's both difficult and draining to be another's strength. That is where absolute and unconditional love lives. A hero is the person that jumps in to hold you when you emotionally can't navigate through the pain to comprise a coherent sentence. That hero tells you it's ok because there are brighter days ahead. That hero stands in for you until you can stand alone. Proudly, we can all stand again. We are all at different stages; some are still learning to walk while others can run. It's alright because we still have the hero. This hero, our hero, will leave no one behind. We will move forward together!

## HOLDING ON BY KEEPING HIM PART OF US

To hold on to our Clinty while moving forward, we have done many things to include and remember him. Some of these things have been for just us, and some have been for everyone. Even though some of these things are private remembrances, I feel a need to share them with you. I need you to know how much we love our Clinton.

### The Jewelry & Shirts

There were so many things created by Clint's friends and family. There was no limit to their love for him and their efforts to keep him alive. There were the beautiful and witty pink bracelets with Clint's picture that were made by my Pooh Bear, Lyndsey. There were the T-shirts, the sweatshirts, and the sweatpants that were created by his friends. Then, how could anyone forget Kyle, Kevin, and Ethan's beautifully designed and hand-poured sterling-silver crosses. Realizing that $70 would not be affordable for everyone, they solicited local businesses to cover most of the cost so each of Clint's classmates could have one if they wanted one. To do this day, I see the cross hanging from their necks if I run into one of his friends.

Each of these items wasn't created without planning or love. My heart is still warmed over their generous outpouring of effort to keep Clinty visually with us. They've been successful.

**The Gatherings**

During all of those "first" events without Clint, his friends and our family never left us alone. They would always join us to celebrate Clint. Whether it was at the bonfire that first fall, the party for his 18th birthday, or the remembrance party at graduation time, they were with us.

**The Garden**

There were several things that I instantly knew needed to happen. The first was changing our front yard from a place of tragedy and sadness into a place of peace and solitude. We did this by cutting out the sod and building a garden. Not just any garden would do. We hand poured stone pavers and placed them in an infinity symbol pathway. Within this garden, Clint's friends, their parents, our family members, and our community members placed plants, plaques, and other tokens. This was no longer a place of sadness. It had been transformed into a place of peaceful reflection. To me, it's also a spiritual place. Without a doubt, I know Jesus was there when he took my son home. That makes this garden a powerful place of peace.

**The Scholarship**

From the beginning, I also knew we wanted to establish a scholarship in Clint's memory. Not just any scholarship, but one that would recognize others for their acts of kindness and humanitarian efforts. The only exception to this was Clint's graduating class. Each and every one of them received a $100 scholarship whether or not they were college bound. There was no way Clint would've singled out anyone. We knew we were doing what he would've wanted.

To date, our family and friends have given over $20,000 in scholarships. This may not seem like a huge amount, but when you consider that we don't solicit money through campaigns or special community events, it's a considerable amount of money. We strive to honor how Clint lived through his silent acts of kindness. These are the kinds of acts that do not ask for recognition; therefore, donations are given from the heart and not through public channels. Since the majority of the proceeds from this book will be given to Clint's Foundation, those purchasing this book will be supporting his scholarship as well.

In January of 2007, several people joined together to hold a benefit for Clint's family and the family of his friend Nick. Even our portions of the donations from this benefit were directly channeled into Clint's scholarship.

**The Website**
As an effort to promote the scholarship, we initially developed a website. Since then, it has become so much more. It's a compilation of Clint's life. There are several pictures of him, several videos of family and friends, and a video of his memorial service. The site not only offers access to the scholarship's information but also access to who Clint was and the way he lived his life. When you get a chance, visit the site: www.clintmccoss.com.

**The Memorial Site**
A grave site? No, a grave site seemed too sad for Clint and wasn't fitting for his upbeat personality. Knowing that people needed a place to memorialize him, I didn't know what to do. With the help of the kids, we designed a memorial headstone. We didn't know where to put it. Then one day, my mom and dad came to me. They reminded me of how Clint so badly wanted to grow up and live on their farm. Dad asked if it would be alright to place Clint's memorial site within their pines. My heart smiled as tears fell from my face. That would be perfect. Clint's memorial would be in a place he loved. It was even more perfect that it would be next to a private entrance to the farm where visitors could feel free to come and go without being watched. Even better, it would be right across the road from the end of my driveway. It was accessible; it had meaning, and it was a happy place. It was perfect.

We decided to build a pergola over the site. It is large and made from rustic pine. It stands proudly over the headstone, which was lifted into place by crane. As a gift, our good friends Art and Billie asked if they could have a landscape crew help to make it perfect. I have such gratitude for my gracious and generous friends. They were careful to ensure perfection even when selecting plants that were wild and crazy like Clint. Some are native grasses, while others have beautiful blooms. None were as beautiful as the Wisteria that have twisted and curled their way to the top of the pergola where the huge purple blossoms now fall through and fill the air with a sweet aroma.

In the middle, there is a stone path weaving through so visitors can enjoy all of it. I added a bench so people could take their time and reflect. There is also a mailbox that holds a black leather journal. In it, friends and family write their thoughts to Clint, share stories, and reminisce. Reading this journal has given me strength. It doesn't matter when I go there, for I always find something left behind by a friend. Sometimes it's a flower; other times it's a not-so-obvious item that must only have meaning to Clint and the person leaving it. These things are usually placed at the base of his stone. It's a memorial stone that should make you sad, but it doesn't. The first thing you see is a beautiful colored image of Clint smiling back at you. I've even challenged myself to look at it and not smile. It isn't possible. His smiling face is surrounded on the stone by many of his favorite things and some precious words of his own wisdom. If you haven't been there to see it, consider this your standing invitation.

**The T-Shirt Quilts**

Clint was famous for his T-shirts with their witty and humorous sayings. I couldn't leave these in his drawers as the hands of time ticked past. With the help of my sister, we cut them into perfect squares with precision. I took each of the squares and carefully made quilts. I was able to make three. They turned out perfectly and have come to be a part of our daily snuggling.

## Our Adopt-a-Highway

As a service to the community and as a visual reminder that he was really here, we have adopted the section of highway that runs the two miles in front of Clint's home. Three times a year, we call together family and friends. On those days, our official purpose is to pick up trash, but all of our hearts feel a bigger purpose. We are together to remember our Clinty. We laugh, joke, and focus on this service. We honor him by doing what he was so good at: helping others

## The Writings

Writing has become somewhat of a therapy for the many individuals who were impacted by the loss of Clint. They write their thoughts on his Facebook page, in e-mails, in letters, in school papers, and on their bodies in the form of tattoos. The written word is everywhere.

I have used writing as a means for healing as well. I have written to all of Clint's classmates, I have written to family and friends, I have written on Clint's Facebook page and on my own Facebook page, I have written in his journal, I have written in my journal, I have written in Gar's journal, I have written a letter to the editor, I have written scholarship messages, I have written a funeral good-bye, and I have written this book. These are all important, but there is one more thing I didn't mention. I have written annual remembrance memorials. People often ask how we are doing, but they don't *really* wait for a response. It's more of a passing greeting than anything else. I'm certain that these people do not mean to hurt me, yet they do. So early on, I decided that for those who care, really care, I would take the time to write to Clint once a year and put what I wrote in the newspaper. I do this not because I like to shell out the roughly $75 to $100 it costs, but I do this to let others know what really goes on with a family, our family, as time passes. These writings can be found in the appendices of this book, and they are lovingly called "Infinitely Ours."

## Our Clinty Christmas Gift

Every year, Christmas is a time of both excitement and dread for us. There is excitement because we'll be celebrating a glorious event as a family. There is dread because not all of us will be together. There is the obvious gap of one person missing. It doesn't matter if we're celebrating the holiday at my parents' or at home with the kids. There is the unspoken absence of my son, Clint. Since the very first Christmas of his absence, we burn a candle for the entire night. The candle is rustic; it's made of black iron and antique bubble glass. Even before I arrive with the candle, my mom prepares a place for it. She polishes the coffee table so it shines. She also surrounds the empty spot with the Christmas figurines Clinty used to help her set up. The container and the candle are beautiful, and they boast his picture on the front. The flame burns hot while we enjoy our Christmas together and is not extinguished until we leave for the night. Clint is always with us, always remembered.

When it's just the kids, the grandkids, and us on Christmas morning, we remember him differently. The candle still stands watch from its home on the fireplace mantle, but it isn't lit. The way we remember and include Clint on Christmas morning is with his Christmas stocking, which is hung each year. It always holds a card and a gift from Clint. There are a few simple rules for this gift. It has to be something we can all enjoy together, it has to remind us of Clint, and it has to bind us together. Although our Christmas tree is buried with presents each year, this is the gift the kids look forward to the most. Here is a list of our Clinty gifts:

> 2006: 52 inch flat screen TV. Some of our best times were watching movies together. Now we could have a small theatre to share.
> 2007: Hot Tub. Clint wanted a hot tub so badly. He thought we were going to put it outside his bedroom window and attach a slide so he could open his window and slip right in.
> 2008: Mazatlán Trip. Clint loved Mexico. This was our first trip without him.
> 2009: Swimming Pool. Clint was an amazing swimmer and would have loved to have a pool at the house. This year, the family received his pool.
> 2010: Pepsi Vending Machine. Pepsi was Clint's favorite pop. We decided that the pop machine proceeds would all go to his scholarship.
> 2011: Sauna. This was something we could all use.
> 2012: Silver Rings. These rings were engraved on the interior with "No farewell words were spoken, no time to say goodbye. You were gone before we knew it and only God knows why."
> 2013: Clinty Bears. The kids were the first to receive them.

These were all things that reminded us of Clint and drew us even closer. They were things we could have with us and use to build more memories for us.

**The Clinty Bears**

One of the most recent ways I've chosen to keep Clinty with us is to make bears. Not teddy bears, but "Clinty bears." The motherly instinct in me wants to hoard everything that is and was Clint's. It's hard to give things away because there are only a few things of his that still remain. Each week, I go into his room and see all of his beautiful clothes. A smile crosses my face but quickly fades as selfishness fills me. Although Clint was mine, he also belonged to everyone. He was full of life and loved to share. If he were here, he'd tease me by asking who the real hoarder was. You see, I used to tease him about hoarding everything just like his Grandma Weber. So this past fall, with Clint heavy on my heart, I decided to share what little we have left of him. I decided to make Clinty bears for all of my family members. Not just for each of my children but also for Clint's grandmas and grandpas, aunts and uncles, and cousins.

I've found time to be a precious commodity. Until this point, everything I've done to remember Clint has been with my own hands. This time, I decided to hire someone to do the sewing. Of course, I couldn't let all control go; I gave plenty of instruction. Like everything else we've done for Clint, I wanted them to be perfect.

The first of them would be made from clothing that has been long since locked away for safekeeping. The first bears would be made from the clothing Clint wore the day of his accident. Until this point, these clothes had been scary. I didn't want the kids to find them one day and become afraid. I wanted them to cherish their bears as they do with everything of Clint's. So, the seamstress and I began the daunting task of designing these first very special bears. I decided where his jeans, his sweatshirt, his socks, and even his boxers would be placed. We used nearly everything, and the bears turned out beautifully.

There is one bear that is slightly more special than the rest. He wears a heart over a very scary hole. There is no way to say this without causing me pain. The heart covers the hole from the shot that ended his beautiful life. Yes, there is a small fabric heart that has symbolically mended my Clinty bear. This bear sits in my bedroom, standing watch over a mother whose broken heart is also slowly mending.

So far, the bears have been given to my parents, Clint's paternal grandparents, my children, my grandchildren, my siblings, and several nieces and nephews. Each of them was carefully selected for whom they would be given to. It's strange, but each bear, much like Clint, is filled with personality. It's easy to choose who they should go to.

When the seamstress asked me to select one of her poems for attaching to the bears, I just couldn't. The poem for the Clinty bear had to be customized and written by me. Here is what it says:

*These are the clothes I last wore.*
*Just as I liked them all tattered and tore.*
*I don't want this gift to make you scared or sad.*
*I'd rather you hold it and think of the fun that we had.*
*Please accept this gift that was once mine.*
*Know where I live now, I am more than fine.*
*My old duds now weaved into something new with this bear.*
*Hopefully, it makes you feel like part of me is still there.*
*Keep this bear close and hold him tight.*
*Hang on to our memories with all of your might.*
*When the absence of me hurts and on your heart tugs,*

*Snuggle your Clinty bear and send me some hugs.*
*Love, Clint*

**HOLDING ON IS PERSONAL**

Although we've done many things to remember Clint, it doesn't mean that those who do nothing don't remember him. Nor does it mean that the things we've done are the right things. Remembering and honoring someone is a personal and difficult decision that shouldn't be taken lightly. These are the ideas that have worked for us, and I simply wanted to share them.

We have another means of remembering Clint that we are going to implement. After losing Clint, one of his teachers brought over one of Clint's unfinished projects. Clint had been working on an assignment that required him to list 100 things he wanted to do in his lifetime. This was an assignment Clint had been working on at the time of his accident, so it is incomplete. He was able to get as far as number 61. We are left to imagine what might have filled the other blanks. Receiving this list is a rare and special gift, because we now have insight into many of the things Clint wanted to accomplish. As you can see from the list, Clint knew how to dream big and had huge plans for his future. In honor of him, our family has decided to accomplish as many of the things as possible. As we accomplish them, we will document the events and cherish the memories in a scrapbook of our journey. He wasn't able to experience all of his dreams, but as a family, we can and will do it for him.

# 100 Things Clint Wanted to Do in His Lifetime

1. get car
2. get house
3. go to college
4. get job
5. Go to Scotland and see my cousins
6. Visit every state of the US.
7. learn to play the bagpipe
8. become rich
9. buy an AK 47
10. I want to see the R Kings Wings
11. I want to be the president
12. I want an Island
13. I want RPG
14. I want to be in the army
15. I want to be the Russian Pres
16. I want to go to all the contests
17. go to europe
18. see russia
19. I want to ride an elephant
20. I want to go to hawii
21. get a kilt
22. by jeep
23. By pass
24. Dove man pincher
25. buy Tank
26. Buy plane
27. get big house
28. own 1000 acres
29. Visit jamaca
30. go on cruise
31. go sky diving
32. go to australia
33. Piña Coladas
34. become 100 years old
35. become famous
36. be on TV
37. go to france
38. go to mexico
39. get M16
40. go scubadiving
41. fly a plane
42. I want a German Shepard
43. I want a pit bull
44. 
45. I want to drive a tank
46. I want to win the lottery
47. own a paintball park
48. own AK 47 paintball gun
49. meet the pres
50. visit stocks as a millionar
51. go elk hunting
52. moose hunting
53. Grizzly hunting
54. go to a blue collar comedy concert
55. I want to go to spain
56. go to the Bahamas
57. get a cadalac divl
58. by a truck
59. I want to own the vikings
60. I want to own the twins
61. I want to own the Timber wolves
62. 
63. 
64. 
65. 
66. 
67.

# CHAPTER 24

## So What Happened Anyway?

*"If you spend time praying for people instead of talking about them, you'll get better results."*
*~Author Unknown~*

So what happened anyway? That's what you want to know, right? Well, I suppose we could ask the woman who told my daughter that she was part of the ambulance team that responded to the call. She would know the facts, right? This is the same woman who told my daughter gruesome details about that morning. Oh wait a minute, you can't ask her because we confirmed with the ambulance service that she was not part of the ambulance crew, let alone part of any crew, that responded. Ok. Well then, maybe we could ask the officer who called his daughter to tell her what happened within minutes of us finding Clint. He would certainly have the facts, right? Wait, it turns out that particular officer was never at the scene. In fact, he didn't even work for any of the local departments. Hmmm. Now why would people do such things? You might think these are isolated examples. I'm sad to say they're not. Unfortunately, these types of individuals created mistrust between us, the community, and the responding agencies/departments. I'm glad to say personal conversations have since taken place with the heads of those departments. Although we may not perfectly agree on procedures and protocols, I can honestly say that I have the utmost respect for them, their departments, and what they are called to do.

People fixate on the details of someone's death: when they died, how they died, and so on. I've come to realize these are surface questions posed by those of a simple mind. Upon even cursory reflection, one should realize that it's not important how a person leaves this world but it's important that they are gone. As a family, we have found that the reactions of others can extend and exemplify a person's grief. Their need to make it exciting and give themselves something to talk about only causes pain to those who love the person that is lost.

Inevitably, it matters very little how a person leaves this world. We put far too much emphasis on it and way too little concentration on how they *lived* and what they left behind.

Why do people gossip? I will never understand the concept. Being a voyeur into our darkest hour is bad enough, but to take it outside the walls of our misery and share it as if it were idle chatter causes even further pain ... crippling pain! When you consider that some of the gossipers were trusted community members, it's hard to imagine they could take our darkest pain and reduce it to "something to talk about."

## FACT OR FICTION

There are some who like to say we ignore the facts. Those who think they know "the facts" simply must not realize that facts are not truth–facts are interpretable through perspective. Unfortunately, facts are altered when they're filtered through multiple perspectives: from mouth to ear, mouth to ear, and yet another mouth to ear.

The process repeats itself over and over. The facts have shattered into a million perspectives. In the end, for many, perspective becomes reality. Now, the question is which reality do we believe? Mine? Yours? His friends? His family? One investigation? A second investigation? Each perspective holds its own set of "facts" about that fateful November morning. The only real fact is you can find anyone to validate or invalidate "facts." Just turn on the news and watch a court case. Every day, innocent people are found guilty and guilty people are let free. Not even top experts can agree with each other.

I want you to learn from our experience. My intent is not to chastise but to educate. It seems like the circumstances of death get misconstrued with ugly details. It doesn't matter what happened. If it's a car accident, they were driving too fast. If it's alcohol related, they were stupid and should've expected it. If it was a reckless teenager, the parents should've known better. There is always a way to spin the story into some form of excitement or blame. My sincere prayer is that no one ever has to experience the pain of losing a loved one compounded by such heartless behavior.

**DENIAL?**
**NO, THAT'S JUST A LONG RIVER IN AFRICA**

I feel very compelled to tell those of you who think you know everything that, quite simply, you don't! Those who say I am in denial clearly enjoy making things up. Until this moment, I have never spoken publically about the loss of my son and the way he left this world, be it by accident or by suicide. I have no dog in this fight. Yes, I Tanya McCoss-Yerigan, Clint's mother, do not know what happened nor do I care. If he committed suicide out of sadness for a lost friend, my heart is at ease with that. If he had a horrible fall with a firearm, I've also come to grips with it and my responsibility in it. Whatever caused his death, I have decided that I will call it an accident when I reference it. It's an accident either way people want to see it because if he fell, it is an accident. If a young boy, with a brain that is not yet fully developed, made an impulsive decision by himself, it's an accident. Of course, the latter scenario has an ugly name attached to it, and it's associated with a stigma that gossipers feed off of. It makes for much more exciting chatter. The fact is whenever someone has an accident precipitated by an impulsive, self-inflicted act, the focus and lesson becomes lost in sensationalism. The focus becomes the "senseless act." Shouldn't it be on that person's underlying issues such as depression, drugs, or alcohol?

In short, my official stance is my son had an accident. Beyond that it doesn't matter. If it doesn't matter to me, the woman who bore Clint of her own flesh and blood, perhaps these gossipers should examine why it is a fixation for them or their neighbor.

What I am about to talk about next fills me with anger and a sense of betrayal. When I taught my boys about journaling, I promised them an expectation of privacy. In fact, I expect the same for my writings. They were told if they wanted me to read it, they could leave it out for me and I would. If not, it was for their eyes only. Just days before the accident, Clint came to me. He had been journaling. He said he felt sad for a girl involved in a recent accident. He said he was worried she might be at risk of hurting herself. He said they'd just had a Yellow Ribbon presentation at their school on suicide prevention.

He hoped she would use the card she was given if she felt too sad. Clint brought up anger toward an extended-family member who often talks of suicide. He wanted to know how anyone could possibly hurt those who would be left behind. He said he wanted to tell this guy off but didn't dare. He asked me how we could help. He wanted to know how someone could hate this world so much that they'd be willing to leave such pain in their wake. I have learned so much from Clint and my other kids. There was and still is a closeness between us that allows us to share anything and everything. Whether they were written words or verbal conversations, their private thoughts and our private conversations should have remained between us.

In an effort to educate and silence gossipers, I feel like I am betraying my oldest son by sharing his most private thoughts. I hope the gossipers find it worth it. I hope it quenches their despicable, sinful, and senseless need to know that to which they are not entitled.

**NOTES OR OTHERWISE**

People talked about a note. There was a note that was in one of Clint's pockets in the same pair of jeans he had worn to his friend's prayer service where they announced his passing. The slip of paper was handed out for the congregation to write a message that would later be read to Nick. One of Clint's friends, who was sitting next to him when Nick's death was announced, said he watched Clint scribble on it and put it in his pocket. The same pocket we would find it in later. For those who have fixated on what it said, this next part is for them: "meet me at the gates of Heaven." There, the mystery is over. That is what it said. This is the same endearing thought that was read aloud at Clint's funeral. It was a simple vision of the day they would see each other again. A suicide declaration? Most likely not. To me, this isn't evidence; it's coincidence. For instance, there's a chapter in this very book called "See You Soon." If I were to die tomorrow, it could very well be misconstrued as a suicide declaration, but for the record, it is not.

The second note was a page from Clint's journal box. You see, my daughters have always been talkers, but my boys were always too busy running and playing. In an effort to have real "talks" and be close to the boys, we would journal, write to each other, and sometimes just jot down our thoughts. Garrett had a book (actually we still use it) that we write back and forth in. Clint had many pages of printer paper that he kept in a blue writing box. This was a box I had given to him when he was a young boy. He would write and show me his writings. It wasn't uncommon for him to leave them on the table or in my room. After I was done reading them, I would keep them or he'd put them back in his box. When the box was full, he would take his writings and put them in tablets. Not long before his accident, I was helping Clint with the unsurmountable task of cleaning his room. His journal box was overflowing, and dozens of tablets were scattered everywhere from previously emptying the journal box. He was such a hoarder of everything; I suggested he should throw some of them. That was a suggestion I will forever regret. With little thought, he emptied his journal box and made the haunting decision to throw away many of his journals. Oh, how I wish I could have them all back. So on that day, there was another journal entry. It was from his journal box. I don't recall the exact words because it has been a long time since I saw it. Basically, he wrote about being sad about the divorce between his dad and me, the loss of his grandpa the preceding summer, and the recent loss of his friend. He wrote about how these things had been difficult for him, and how he wished we could all be together in a better place. He wrote that he was sorry for feeling this way. It wasn't much different than some of his previous writings.

Was this just another page from his journal box, or was it a deliberate suicide note? To be blatantly honest, I guess we will never know. Although some may *think* they have the answers, the truth is much more complex, and the answer isn't clear.

Clint was a beautiful letter writer, and over the years, he'd written me many. I know how his letters look and sound with my name scrolled at the top, "Mom," and his rough signature at the bottom, "Love, Clint." Clint never wrote a note or letter without these two pieces. Most of the time, he would throw in "I love you" too. The piece of paper from his journal box wasn't one of Clint's letters. It was, as with all his journal entries, more like a list of thoughts. It wasn't addressed to anyone, and it wasn't signed. There was no goodbye. Not once in Clint's life did he leave the room, let alone the house, without hugs, kisses, and good-byes. No, there were no notes saying good-bye, telling us he was going away, stating he was going to shoot himself, or stating he was going to be dead that day.

## OUR INTENTIONS ARE ONLY A PERSON'S BEST GUESS

In many ways, it would be easier if such a note existed. The plain and simple truth is that there wasn't and there isn't. I ask myself if it's possible that the entry from the journal box could have been a suicide note. I guess maybe, but it would have been totally out of character for how my son wrote and so would be taking his own life. Suicide is the most selfish act known to man, and Clint just wasn't selfish. So I doubt it, but maybe. I wasn't there that day. What I have learned since that day is that anyone can have a selfish moment. The day of Clint's accident, I never intended to live to see the sun rise the next day. My plan was simply to be with Clint and hold him again as quickly as I could. Endless options for suicide crossed my mind. What didn't cross my mind were those I loved. Not my children, my husband, my siblings, or my mom and dad. Only relief from the unspeakable and gut-wrenching pain crossed my mind. I couldn't see through my own pain to even consider others . . . I was being *selfish*.

As I've told you, I raised sons who journal avidly. They did not fall upon it by accident because I also journal on a regular basis. In fact, after the gossip over Clint's journaling, I burnt years of journals. Also, I have been careful to destroy even current journal entries that appear to be sad. I have written hundreds of pages that could be construed as "a note". Again, for the record, those are my private thoughts and not suicide declarations.

When I was in that state of sadness, I can't even say that I was my true self. It was my flesh, of course, but the mind operating it was absolutely not me. It was as though a terrorist took control of my mind, strapped a bomb to me, and set me loose. I was in a full-fledged battle for survival against this invisible enemy. I can't help but think that the kids or adults who actually commit suicide are in such a state of sadness that their senses and decisions are hindered and controlled by this intruder named grief.

## DOES IT REALLY MATTER?

Is it possible that my son could have acted totally out the ordinary and had a selfish moment that would have never come again but in that second? Was it a single second he wouldn't be given a second chance to fix? Could he have been that sad about the recent loss of a close friend? Maybe . . . I just don't know. It could just have easily been an irresponsible boy with an untied shoe, a loaded gun, a scope that just retracted and broke his nose, a stumble on frosty grass, and a horrible fall that caused the accident. Could it have been an innocent boy who had just woke up; brewed fresh, hot apple cider; and filled his hunting thermos? Could it have been an innocent boy trying to win a big buck contest between his mother and a few close friends?

Clint has many very loyal and steadfast friends and family who have never wavered in their belief that he had a horrible fall with a deadly firearm. This vast group stands staunchly behind the belief that he had an unthinkable accident. In fact, with the absence of a video or signed note, they will never believe otherwise. These people take comfort in knowing him through how he lived.

Probably everyone has had their moments of pause and wondered what the "truth" is. Not only is that ok, it's good. The importantthing is that you find peace in whatever the reality is for you. I also know that sometimes we can be so arrogant that we think we know the truth when, in actuality, we simply know very little. So, to those who believe he had a horrible fall, let go of trying to defend the way your brother, your cousin, your nephew, and your friend lived. There is no need to defend anything. Take comfort in knowing him through how he lived his life. To those who believe he did it himself, please ask yourselves why it matters to you. Does it really matter?

## WHY SO FASCINATING?

I have pondered deeply why Clint's death is so fascinating to so many. I had the opportunity to talk with one of the officials who responded to the scene on that horrible morning. He told me Clint's accident is the one he's been asked about most in all of his years of service to the community. When I asked him why he thought that was, he told me, "Because he had the perfect life." For a second, as a mother who misses her son, I felt flattered. When you lose a child, there is no chance to ask him or her if they were happy, if the love you gave them was enough, and if they loved you. In that second, that man gave me a gift he did not realize he had given me. He said Clint "had the perfect life." He affirmed what my heart knew to be true. He went on to say that is what people can't wrap their head around. It's what they fear. If people had the option to believe Clint's accident resulted from either a fall or was self-inflicted, they could not comprehend that latter option. If Clint could do it, then anyone could. Other than the recent loss of a friend, he had no signs of sadness. He was happy, interactive, involved, loving, loved by many friends, and a complete joy.

He was right, for if you believe Clint did this to himself, then brace yourself. If it could be my son, then anyone and everyone is at risk. In a nutshell, that is what the community fears.

## REALITY IS THE ABSOLUTE TRUTH

The reality is you can't live in that place, or you'll become sick with worry. I choose to base my memories and focus on how he lived his life instead of how it may have ended. As I said earlier, the truth is I don't care if he had a horrible accident or if he planned it himself. The fact of the matter is that he is gone, and I will never again hear him say "Mom," get to kiss his cheek, or get one of his famous hugs. The way he left this world does not change that in this world, he was a beautiful, happy young man. He was a gift! So, for those who have made an obsession out of how my son left this world, the absolute truth is. . . it doesn't matter.

My heart aches for humanity due to the people who actually live their lives without regard for the hurt their words and actions can create. The fact that my baby and the horrific end to his life became someone's entertainment, something to talk about while sitting around couches or cafes, is unfathomable to me. It wrenches my brain. These people have caused a dual traumatization. First we lost Clint, and without the strength to face it, we have also had to face such gossip. I don't loath them for it, I weep and pray for them. May God never let you see this from the other side as I have had to.

# CHAPTER 25
## Clint's Life & Legacy

*"...The goal isn't to live forever,
the goal is to create something that will."*
~Chuck Palahniuk~

    This is a difficult chapter to write. What can I write to encompass the life and legacy that Clint leaves behind? How do I summarize my son and what his life stood for in one simple chapter?

    Everyone lucky enough to know Clint loved him and loves him still. He was and is easy to adore . . . completely unaware of his magnificent beauty, his effortless kindness, his acceptance of every person who crossed his path, his carelessly charming approach, and his nonchalantly mischievous demeanor.

    As parents, we would say he loves history, Pepsi, canned ravioli, and teasing me by talking like a mobster. Clint's grandparents know that he adores and named every single barn kitten ever born on their farm. They would also say he was always the first to offer a helping hand. Clint's sisters would rave about his scrambled eggs–the best they've ever eaten. Clint's brother would brag that Clint is an unrelenting paintball warrior. Clint's aunts and uncles would say how much he loves the family cabin, that he is the first cannonball off the dock, and that he builds elaborate army camps in the sand on the beach. Every single person who knows Clint could attest to his spontaneous goodness. He was the most satisfied when he was helping others through his generosity, understanding, and compassion. Clint always extended himself to others through kindness.

Clint McCoss was just a few weeks shy of celebrating his 16th birthday when he was tragically lost to his family, friends, and community in a hunting accident. As profound as it has been to navigate the aftermath of losing Clint, his loved ones have been immeasurably healed by learning what a secret blessing Clinton was and continues to be to so many of his schoolmates, teammates, family, friends, and community members. It would be entirely fair to say that we have learned as much about Clint since he was called to Heaven as we did when he was traipsing around in his witty T-shirts, wrinkled jeans, and untied shoes.

It's unclear if Clint realized how impactful his private habit of reaching out to lift up others was. But it has become the joyful task of those closest to him to lovingly preserve the legacy of Clint's genuine concern and generosity toward others. Hearing about the innumerable ways in which Clint interacted with others has already enriched scores of people's lives. It has inspired everyone from those who knew him best to those who barely knew him at all. It's this unquestioning celebration of Clint's spirit that sustains his family and friends in his absence.

The measure of one's love for humanity does not manifest itself through words or feelings but through behavior. Thus, one's demonstrated generosity, understanding, compassion, and kindness evidence his or her willingness to love his or her fellow humans. I believe that humanity begins with children and their realization of how valuable their actions, words, or even smiles can be toward individual growth and the everyday well-being of the people surrounding them.

Occasionally, we meet someone harboring the spirit of genuine, fundamental goodness. These individuals can be difficult to recognize because their gifts of kindness are often given through private acts rather than through established, public channels. Such a person loves and honors almost everyone not to please him or herself but simply to enrich the world's goodness.

To extend Clint's legacy of kindness, we have established the Infinitely Clint Foundation. Each year, we seek to find a recipient who makes the act of giving a fun-filled adventure. Clint was such a rare individual. To him, helping others was automatic; it was fun. It was the reason he was born. Everyone Clint encountered became a recipient of his simple goodness. The examples of Clint's genuine concern and generosity for others are virtually endless as demonstrated in the dozens of stories shared with us during and after his memorial services. In memory and honor of Clint, the scholarship committee endeavors to emulate the positive impact he has made on so many people by awarding a recipient who embodies the same giving spirit as Clinton.

The Clint McCoss Kindness Scholarship is not based on perfect class attendance, exemplary academic performance, or financial need. One's acts of kindness serve as the sole indicator of an individual's qualifications for this scholarship. The recipients are chosen for their humanitarian efforts. Thus, it is one's behavior and willingness to love—their generosity, understanding, compassion, kindness, and guiding hand—that exhibits the unique and rare qualifications for this award.

This scholarship is void of any considerations regarding sex, race, religion, national origin, sexual orientation, and other similar attributes. The recipient, harboring a heart of simple and profound goodness, is destined to enrich scores of people's lives.

The Clint McCoss Kindness Scholarship was created to recognize those who are doing good work and deeds for others. Because we value purposeful efforts to extend kindness toward others and because Clint was very generous in all of his interactions with others, we look for these qualities when we review applications to select deserving recipients. There are no specific requirements related to intended college major, grade point average, or class rank. Our selections focus on evidence of an individual's kindness to others in daily life.

So, I guess summarizing Clint's legacy in one chapter wasn't so hard. As it turns out, I can summarize Clint's legacy in one word: *kindness*. We will keep Clint's legacy alive by seeking out kids with similar hearts of goodness and by shining a spotlight on them.

# CHAPTER 26
## *See You Soon*
∞

*"So I will hold you as close as I can longing for the day*
*when I see your face again but until then*
*God must need another angel around the throne tonight."*
~Jenn Bostic~

Those are the words of a beautiful song. Not just any song, but a song that my four-year-old granddaughter, Maddie, sings to me several times a month. Although it's a complex song, she knows the words, she knows what they mean, and she knows the impact they have on her grandma.

My beautiful, beautiful boy. I will see you soon. In the early hours, days, weeks, and months after Clint left us, those words had a different meaning for me than the meaning they have now. You see, during that time, I *was* going to see him soon. I so desperately wanted to know what happened during my absence that morning, and I needed to hold him. What would cause my loving son to break the rules and take out his shotgun? He had always been a respectful boy, but he was filled with impulsivity. He could be so careless. I both loved and hated this about him. I admired his carefree attitude toward life, but I hated that he was going to live life recklessly and fully. So many times, I've wished I could have just one more chance to stress the danger of guns or the importance of tying his shoes. I wish I could stress that my rules weren't to limit him but to protect him. How I'd like to apologize that we missed locking up his gun that afternoon because a coat had been laid over it in the corner. I have felt that I'm to blame. The phrases "what if" and "if only" fill my every waking hour. These questions used to cripple me. They crippled my actions and thoughts. Now, I know better. I know that God was fully aware about what would happen that day long before Clint was ever born. I don't believe God planned it or even allowed it, but He knew about it and expected it. I've found peace in God's plan.

"I will see you soon." Those words bring a smile to my face even today as I type. I can't wait for the day when I see Clint again. It'll be a glorious reunion. Although I write "I can't wait," what I really mean is I'm excited for that moment, but I'll wait for my time. I'll wait for a time that has already been written in the scrolls, for a time that only God is aware of. I wanted to hurry to that time and make it happen even if it meant taking my own life. I no longer feel that way. I also wanted the end of the world to happen so we can all be together again. I also no longer feel this way. It's not that I don't look forward to that day, because I most certainly do. It's just that I refuse to waste away what precious time God has given me here with the others I love. I'll cherish this part of the journey. I'll cherish those who are here so it'll be that much more special when we return to Heaven together.

When I think "see you soon" to myself, it absolutely has a different meaning than it used to. Like Gar once told me, "Our time here is like a blink of an eye and we will have eternity together." I know Gar is right. I won't wish away this life for that life. But make no mistake; I'm certainly looking forward to it.

So, my precious Clinty, I love you; I will miss you every second we are apart, but I'll live a good life to ensure that we'll be together again. Although there undoubtedly will be days when it doesn't feel like a blink of an eye, I know that Gar's words are true. Before we know it, I will be sitting by your side at our Father's feet, and it will be as though we were never apart. My baby, I will see you soon. Until then, as I fall asleep each night, I will close my eyes, feel your cheek upon mine, and kiss you good night. Until then . . .

# CHAPTER 27
# *A Son for a Son*

*"The great use of life is to spend it for something that will outlast it."*
~William James~

This book is coming to an end. It's a good thing, because another piece of me gets taken away every time I sit at this keyboard. It hurts. I've learned that God sometimes asks us to do much more than die for others. He asks us to live. I hope my pain has been worth it for each and every person who has read these pages.

One of the many lessons in this tragedy is if it can happen to my son, it can happen to anyone's child. I'm a woman who takes parenting seriously: I love my children, I have kept them safe from harmful people and things, I have checked out parents before they could stay somewhere overnight, and so on. Another great lesson is that no matter how careful we are, we're not in control of our time on this earth. Even though we have free will and limitless choices, God still knows the outcome. Yours, mine, and Clint's day to go home was written by God long before we were born.

While writing this final chapter, I experienced something called *deus ex machina*. It's Latin and references a seemingly unsolvable problem that leaves no way out but still surprisingly results in a happy ending. It could really be described as an outside force that enters the picture and changes everything. I can't think of a better term to describe what I'm about to share with you. What I'm about to describe to you is deus ex machina; for all other reasons, it's a *miracle*.

In the early days following Clint's accident, I begged God to let some good come from losing him. When God put the need to write this book on my heart, I argued with Him. What did I owe Him anyway? He had just taken away my son. When I told Him I was a horrible writer, He gave me a tremendous gift. That gift is the ability to write. It's the ability to transfer the lessons I've learned and my scattered thoughts into words that might help another person. When He gave me the gift of writing, I told him I wouldn't do it. What would I call such a book anyway? He told me it would be titled *No Ordinary Son*. In defiance, I succumbed and told God that He was finally right. I told Him that my son was not ordinary and that he was *mine!* I told Him I would write His stupid book just to prove it would fail, because His idea was just like the book: stupid! That conversation took place years ago. As I write, I'm ashamed of my defiance and insubordination to my Father in Heaven.

In my hatred for Him, He only pulled me closer. When I fought Him, He wrapped his arms around me and held me tight. When I was weak, He held me up and was my strength. When I was sad, He caressed my cheeks and dried my tears. No, I never saw Him, but I felt His presence engulf me. As hard as I tried, He wouldn't let me go. A thread of my heart wouldn't let go of Him either.

In the beginning, I prayed that Clint would bring me comfort in my pain. Somewhere along the way, I turned my prayers to God. My desperation changed from begging to have Clint back to wanting my Father back. I longed for His grace.

The tears are pouring from my eyes so profusely that I can't even see my computer screen to type. As I wrote this book, I found my Heavenly Father again. As it turns out, He was never gone but always right here steadfast in His belief in me.

The process of writing this book is how the Son of God breathed an undeniable faith in me so I could live again. Yes, God and others He purposely placed in my life breathed faith into me. He used the loss of my son to bring good into this sometimes ugly and unforgiving world. The love I feel for Him is so profound that the mere uttering of His name fills my eyes with tears.

I used to wonder why this *bad* thing happened to us. I thought we did something wrong for which we were being punished. I now realize it's not because we did something wrong. It's because we did something right. God entrusted me with the knowledge that good would stem from it. He knew that with His help, I'd know what to do with this knowledge and also that I could handle it.

**THE ANSWER HAS BEEN WITHIN ME**

As I finish this book, I am sitting in my office. It's a beautiful office, and its walls are lined with pine boards from trees that the kids, including Clinty, helped lumber. The sun is shining through the stained glass panel hanging in the window, and the snow is falling ever so lightly outside. In this moment, I realize that the length and depth of my love for Clint is not measured by the depth and length of my grief for him. I am determined to spend my time in the way he *lived* and not in the way or on the day he left this world. I realize in this moment that I am truly healing. I know it will be a lifelong process, but I understand it and am well on my way.

This process, this journey has been such a profound learning experience. I think to myself that God selected such a simplistic name for *our* book. It just doesn't seem to fit anymore. How will I argue this point with a God I now trust wholeheartedly? Of course, Clint was not ordinary; he was extraordinary, but is that really what God wants highlighted? For goodness' sake, this is prime real estate; it's the cover of the book. Then, as though God places His hands on my shoulders and speaks directly into my heart, the words hit me so hard that I fall to my knees. I whisper "no ordinary son" to myself. I can no longer speak. I can't raise myself up from the floor. I can only weep. My mind flashes back to so many years ago. No ordinary *Son*! He wasn't talking about Clint. He was talking about His Son, Jesus. How could I have been so arrogant? My head is spinning in circles from the realization that should've been so clear all along. He was speaking about His Son! Of course! It's only by the grace of God that I've survived the loss of my son. It was because of no ordinary Son! How else could a woman who lost her son, a woman who planned to die at the first chance she had, come through this better and not bitter? How else could this woman's faith, which had faded to nearly denying God's existence, become a faith that fills her and surrounds her like armor? How else could this woman find gratitude and love in a life without one of her babies? How did this book become a reality? It has been Him all along, the Master Shepherd, guiding and protecting His lamb: standing vigil every moment until she was safe, standing watch until her heart could heal and open again. He was keeping her safe from herself and a cynical world. He was keeping her safe until she was strong; until she was strong enough to defend against all who would take joy in her fall from the Heavenly Father.

Not today, world, *not today*. I am that woman. My son is extraordinary, but Jesus is no ordinary Son. My heart and soul belong to God. I now fully know that Clint is safe in the arms of my Father in Heaven. He is His. Thanks to this book, *No Ordinary Son*, and the Man it's titled after, I am also His. I have been lost a very long time. Dear Lord, it feels good to be home.

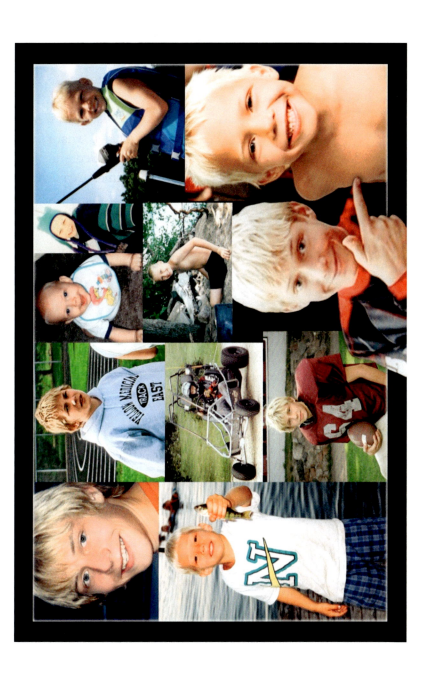

# AFTERWORD
## *Our Family Would Like to Hear from You!*

*Dear Reader,*

*Thank you for taking the time to read about our journey. Thank you for traveling with me to a place that is hard to go. It is a place where I live alone with my thoughts. Taking you to this place has been difficult. It is difficult because I'm used to going there alone. It's difficult because the memories and thoughts that live there are not always understandable or happy. In fact, because I am a private woman, they can be downright embarrassing for me to share. In the beginning of this book, I told you that I bare everything within these pages; I am emotionally naked. In the hope that you will think differently and more deeply, I have done something I do not do well: I have trusted you. I have trusted you to view those who have lost someone with new understanding, compassion, and grace. For you, I went back to that place within my mind. Today, I leave that place and, ever so slightly, close the door behind* me. Although the things that ease the pain can be different from day to day, there are a few constant sources of relief: one is God, and the other is you. Knowing that our loss has somehow made a difference gives us hope. It is a hope that something good has or will come from the absence of our precious Clint. It is in your stories that we are reminded that Clint was, and remains, a gift. If our journey has helped you in any way, big or small, we would love to hear from you. Thank you for making our story yours.

*All My Love,*
*Tanya*

Infinitely Yours Publications
Attn: Dr. Tanya Yerigan
4857 Hwy 67, Suite #3
Granite Falls, MN 56241
tanya@mvtvwireless.com

# EPILOGUE
## *Do You Still Hunt?*

*"Courage does not always roar. Sometimes it is a quiet voice at the end of the day saying . . . 'I will try again tomorrow'."*
~Mary Anne Radmacher~

Every so often I am asked, "So, do you still hunt?" At first, I was embarrassed to answer; it's as though it would have been a crime to hunt. They look at me like I am unaware that I lost a son in a hunting accident.

What these people fail to understand is that Clint's day to return to Heaven, as well as yours and mine, was written in the scrolls long before we were born. If not a gun, perhaps a fall down the steps or a car accident would have taken my son that fall day in the November of 2006. So, do we hunt? I offer you this explanation.

**A SEASON OF HOPE**

It has been three years since Minnesota's hunting season has occupied a space on our calendar. Even so, the seasons have not come and gone without being noticed. I've been painfully aware of these days, and I've avoided them like I avoid drinking cold water against my fillings. This year, we decide to leave our local hunting area for a new landscape. Maybe somewhere farther away from here will soften the striking blows of harsh memories that batter my mind. We decided to make our way out of the shotgun zone and into the rifle zone. Perhaps even the simple deviation in weaponry might ease this first step. The decision was made. Park Rapids, which is in north-central Minnesota, was our destination.

The day began with the screeching pitch of our hotel room's alarm clock jolting me from my unsettled slumber. As I rubbed my eyes, I thought to myself, "No way is it that time already." Begrudgingly, I rolled over to look at the time. Yes, it was 5:00 a.m. Before I could reach the snooze button, my husband had already leapt from the opposite side of the bed at the speed of light and turned off the alarm. Chipper as a chipmunk, he greeted me with "Good morning, sweetheart." I let out a growl that half surprised me when it escaped my lips and said, "Wake me up in ten minutes." I knew I should have just gotten up. There'd be no sleep with Tim buzzing around the room. His excitement rivaled that of a five-year-old boy with a new Erector construction set.

We ate breakfast together in the hotel dining room. Lots of hunters were getting ready to head out. Everyone was gathering their food, discussing the day, filling their bellies, and hurrying to their trucks that filled the parking lot. The hotel workers were so accommodating. They opened breakfast two hours early so the hunters could eat and were rushing to keep the food counter replenished as they helped fill thermos after thermos with piping hot coffee. Finally, we were dressed, fed, and in the truck on our way to our deer stands. My husband was nervous when we were among the last ones to leave the parking lot. I joked that he was getting soft in his old age. Years ago, we used to sit in our stands an hour before sunrise surveying the darkness. Although he joked back, I could tell he secretly wanted to be there already, and next year we would probably be in our stands even earlier. All the way to stand, he tried to justify the early departure of the other hunters stating that they must have farther to drive. If I razzed any further, I knew he'd have me up even earlier tomorrow.

We arrived near my stand but had to walk part of the way. It was a beautiful morning—about forty degrees. It had been zero degrees with two feet of snow for so many of the previous seasons. Not this year. The grass was still green in some areas, and the forecast was calling for sunny skies with a temperature nearing sixty. In the cloak of darkness, we walked to my stand.

My husband sat with me until sunrise. I guess he made this decision when he realized that I would drive to my stand if he didn't walk me to it. Apparently, driving right up to one's stand is a big no-no. I didn't ask, but the lecture came anyway. I guess the vehicle spooks the animals because it's out of place—something new in their world, and they become leery of it. My mind wanders back to a few years ago when I drove the four-wheeler to the base of my stand in Wisconsin. To me, it seemed to attract the deer. Many walked right up to the machine, sniffed it, and slowly walked away. It gave me an idea to pour liquid corn scent on the four-wheeler's tires prior to driving it the second day. I drove the machine up my shooting lane and parked it at the base of my stand again. Wow, did that defy the advice of the hunter who said to leave the vehicle on the road. A 190 pound, 8-point buck picked up the scent roughly 200 yards away and followed it right to my four-wheeler. Today, his rack hangs on the wall of my great room. Because of that, I remain curious why I need to walk to my stand instead of driving to it.

Maybe my husband thinks I need the exercise. Tim headed to his stand just after sunrise.

I'd seen six deer so far, including a few bucks, but I decided to let them walk. It's too early. I'd be patient. I thought to myself that I don't want that six-pointer. I want his grandfather. After all, that would make Tim proud, and maybe then we could go home.

The squirrels thought they were being quiet, but the noise they made was disruptive to the normal serenity of the woods. I liken it to a baby crying incessantly in church. I couldn't help but imagine how they must drive the birds, deer, and other wildlife crazy with their constant chattering. The sun was falling fast in the west. The temperature fell along with the falling sun. I lit the pilot light on my Mr. Heater and couldn't help but think of the staunch, more serious hunters who would say I was casting a scent into the woods that would be a dead giveaway to the deer that humans were near. As I struck the starter, my only thought was that my feet would soon be warm.

My eyes continually scanned the terrain. Pasture to the north, east and south bordered by woods, and all woods to the west. As the sun began to set, I noticed different shadows and landscapes that weren't there just moments ago. The woods seemed to come alive with other creatures as the darkness covered everything. I watched. I waited. I watched. I waited. What patience this hobby takes. As the end of shooting time drew near, I wondered if letting those bucks go was a good idea. Should I have been satisfied? Should I have let them walk? Would we even fill our tags today and begin our journey home? The bucks from earlier this morning are unaware of the gift I gave them. What an easy shot they would have been. To me, they are DBW . . . dead bucks walking. Just then, I looked to the north and saw a buck standing 275 yards away. I didn't know how many points he had, but I didn't think it mattered when even though it was nearly dusk, his rack was clearly visible and standing over a foot above his head. His horns were white as snow, his body was huge, and he was standing still. I guess they call it a broadside shot. As he looked to the highway behind him, I put my rifle up and glassed him through my scope. I had to turn my scope up three times before I thought I could take the shot. I pondered about taking such a long shot with the highway 150 yards behind him. Quickly, I looked for traffic and saw a small stack of asphalt 100 yards directly behind him. If I missed, there was a backstop. No cars were coming, so I braced my knee on the chair. With my hand as a cushion, I placed the gun out the window and wedged it tightly against the window frame's corner. The crosshairs were behind his shoulder. I wondered if I should aim higher at this range. As he stood with his flank to me, I pulled the trigger. The roar of the rifle ripped through the silent woods. The deer jumped as I ejected the brass from the chamber. I quickly had him in my crosshairs again. As I watched him lope slowly across the landscape, I thought, "Do I shoot again? Could I make a good shot at a loping deer?" I'd never tried. Just then, he stopped and looked toward me. He looked as though he might lie down. Was he hurt? I was instantly filled with sadness for him. I set my crosshairs on him and started to pull back the trigger. The refuge of the woods was only thirty feet away from where the deer was currently standing. Just then, bang! A neighbor to the north shot at a deer. My deer jumped the fence into the woods. He ran the fence line for twenty feet and then disappeared. I didn't know if he went down a ravine or crashed to the ground. I just couldn't be sure. My cell phone rang. It was my husband. He heard the shot. Before I can say "hello," he asks, "What'd you get?" He said he could tell from the impact that the bullet made contact, but my account of the event made him believe it wasn't a solid hit. He said we had to let the deer settle down. We had to wait.

    Twenty minutes later, I pondered whether to make my way to where I thought the buck was when I shot him. It was hard to remember where that was. I've learned that once you're down from the vantage point of your stand, you often can't gain your bearings enough to know the exact spot where the deer was hit. I quickly repositioned my rifle like I had it when I shot—tightly against the left and bottom of the window frame. From that position, I was able to determine a more specific area for where he was when I shot him. With that information, I got down and made my way to the area. As I did, another buck ran across my path. He looked as surprised as I did. I didn't shoot at him. I already had my buck. It was getting dark. The sun had set. I found myself a little scared of the woods. I hurried to the area and quickly discovered very large prints on the ground. I was surprised because I'd never seen prints that big. It was hard to see. I couldn't find blood, but I quickly found a small piece of bone. Bone? Instantly disoriented, I staggered and felt ill. It was as though a movie screen covered the landscape while scenes from the 2006 hunting season flashed before me. While I tried desperately to push the images from my mind, the sharp taste of salt filled my mouth and jarred me to consciousness. Suddenly, I felt the warmth of the tears that had been streaming down my face and entering my mouth unnoticed. As I wiped the tears away, I felt nauseous from thinking about the 2006 season and the loss of my son. I uttered to myself, "No, not today!"

I was certain I had hit the deer. Was it in the leg? I should have shot him again. I should have put him out of any misery. I called my husband on his cell. He arrived in a few moments. Quickly, he also found the tracks and bone. He backed off from the woods. I wondered why. After all, Tim is the best deer tracker I know. Why was he backing off? He whispered to me. Why was he whispering? You can't spook a dead deer. It didn't take long to realize that he doubted I leveled a lethal hit. He decided that we would leave the deer overnight explaining that if he was dead, he'd be dead and waiting for us tomorrow. If he was hurt, pushing him that night could push him off our land, and we would lose him. If we left him, he would lie down, stiffen up, and be either dead or unable to move in the morning. The thought of a deer in pain kept me awake most of the night. In my mind, I rationalized that the deer was dead or would be soon, and the kids could enjoy their favorite venison jerky.

The second morning passed quickly. That afternoon, Tim sat with me. We were cold from tracking in the rain. Tim picked up my buck's trail right away in the morning. He called to say he'd found blood. A half hour later, I saw him through my binoculars taking aim at something. I later found out it was my buck. He was a huge 10-point buck with a white rack nearing 18 inches above his head and a very dark body. Tim called me over to cover the mouth of the ravine. My buck, now referred to as the Phantom, was on the run again. Tim continued to track him, and I waited to cut the Phantom off. My nose was running due to the cold.

It had been thirty minutes since we returned from tracking the Phantom. My nose was still running. I tried to be quiet as I repeatedly wiped it. I wondered to myself what Tim would do if I just blew my nose. I would have if he wasn't there. However, even though he was with me, I decided to go for it. I blew my nose. I reluctantly looked his way. Yes, he'd noticed. His eyes quickly darted at me as though I'd jumped out of the deer stand, waved my arms, and yelled, "Run, bucks! Run!"

More time passed. Now I had to go to the bathroom. Too much coffee, I guess. I decided not to tell Tim. He told me that would happen. I hate it when he's right. It's not fair. He always drinks too much coffee, and he relieves himself in a milk jug. When I drink too much coffee, I have to hold it or climb down from my stand and bare my backside to every creature around and, perhaps, any local hunters with binoculars. The better option was to hold it. After two hours passed, the old coffee can in the corner began to look appealing. In fact, it began to look like a suitable toilet. Finally, I dropped my drawers and positioned the can. Ah, no more holding it. I wondered to myself what I should do with a can of urine. Oh no, human urine. I'd been warned against dispensing that near my stand. After all, we go to such lengths to cover our odors. I recalled how I went at the base of my stand twice yesterday, and it didn't seem to bother the twenty-seven deer I'd seen. Wisdom told me maybe it was an attractant. So, I proceeded with dumping the urine out the window of my stand. I liken it to when I used cherry ChapStick. My husband hated when I wore it and thought it would ruin the stand. That season, I had several deer catch the scent and walk right up to my stand. It was like casting my line, setting the hook, and reeling them in. I'm not sure human urine is like cherry ChapStick, but then God didn't equip me with a milk jug adapter. A girl's got to do what a girl's got to do.

The afternoon passed with a few more deer sightings. The darkness came fast that night with the overcast sky and rain. My mind quickly switched to hotels. Where would we sleep? We'd only planned on staying two nights, and all of the hotels were filled. What a fine time for staying a third night.

I woke up still sick about the phantom buck. Feeling bad, Tim let both of us sleep in a while. What a treat . . . ten extra minutes. My thoughts quickly returned to yesterday morning and our search for the elusive buck. As Tim resumed tracking along the ravine, I posted myself at its opening. Forty-five minutes later, as I stood stoic in the rain, I saw the buck charging through the woods about 150 yards away. Before I could even blink, he made a ninety-degree turn and, without even slowing down, jumped a fence and disappeared over a ridge. That was when I called my husband so we could regroup.

Well, that was yesterday, and today is a new day. I fill our packs with peanut butter sandwiches and cups of coffee. This morning is colder than yesterday. There is frost on the truck. On the way to my stand, we make casual conversation about what we might see or hope to see that day. Yesterday, I discovered that when I closed the lid on my Caribou Coffee mug, it didn't spill when I placed it in my pocket. Yeah . . . coffee goes with me to my stand. My husband was not impressed. However, he must have been jealous of my warm coffee because he actually carries his own mug to his stand today. I wish his old hunting buddies could see him now. Rifle slung over one shoulder, a pack on his back, a flashlight in one hand,

and a steaming cup of coffee in the other. They'd be impressed at his preppy Caribou Coffee mug, too. Maybe he'd get points for its manly appearance of black leather and pewter. He could only hope they'd cut him that much slack.

As we walk, I quickly realized the ground was frozen. It makes a crunching sound as my steps break through the top layer. It is slimy underneath, and my feet slide with each move. I know I have to be careful. Although we never walk to our stands with loaded rifles, I know a fall would cause a thundering bolt of noise that wouldn't go unaddressed. In the darkness, we make the quarter-mile walk to our stands. With every step, noise echoes through the air. I hear the loose brass for my .270 Winchester clanking in my pocket. I can tell by the way Tim looks at me that he wants to scold me, but he doesn't. At least not until I give him a subtle opportunity. I whisper to him to stop walking because I can hear something in the woods. Perhaps it was a deer hitting a fence. He snaps, "No, that's your coffee mug and the ammo in your pocket." I quickly respond, stating, "It was a deer." He resumes walking. I think about how humorous our friends would find this entire experience. Tim and I rarely argue or disagree with each other.

The fog is heavy in the meadow but lifts by midmorning. Not a deer so far. Maybe Tim's a jinx! He decides to head to his stand. Ah, maybe I can get a nap. Distant sirens breach the silence. Although Tim is a deputy, I hate sirens! Again, my mind begins to flicker with unwelcome images from 2006. I hope no one is hurt. According to the radio, there have already been several hunting accidents and deaths this season. It terrifies me! My mind instantly returns to three years ago when my son died during the hunting opener. Sirens screaming, an ambulance, blaze orange, running EMTs, camouflage, and the gun we'd bought him . . . horror! I won't let my mind go there; I can't. It has been three long years of trying to sort out this hobby, our lives, and my own guilt over that day. No, I will not let my mind go there today. Today, I will sit and remember what Clint loved so much—the quiet of the woods, wildlife, anticipating the next big buck, his family, and me. Yes, my mind gets a break. There will be plenty of time tomorrow. I try desperately to change my thoughts just like yesterday when I found the phantom buck's tissue and bone. When I picked it up, my mind instantly flashed to the grass where we found my son. Long after the emergency workers had gone, I remember gathering his tissue and bone fragments. After all, it was all I had left of him, and he was too precious to be left that way. Would anyone understand why I had done that? Why I needed to do that? Yesterday, I also struggled to change my thoughts. It happens several times, hundreds of times, or maybe even thousands of times each day. I have to change my thinking. If not, I might lay myself down and wait for my own death. I truly believe the pain that settled in my heart after losing Clint is lethal and fully capable of drawing out my last breath. So, yes—for now— I will change my thoughts. This takes practice and is a skill I have not yet mastered. I will continue to concentrate on remembering the way my son lived in this world and not the way he left it. So, why am I still hunting? It's simple: my husband loves it, and I love him.

 My cell phone vibrates, and I realize my mind has taken me on another journey that stole my nap from me. Still no deer in sight. I open my phone to read Tim's text. He says it's lunch time and is heading my way. Our messages are brief because Tim hates the idea of having a phone in the woods. You never know . . . he may miss a deer while composing a text. We exchange a few texts so I know his position. Safety first, right? Is this it, I wonder to myself? Will he want to head home, or will he want to hunt more? I miss the kids, I miss my bed, and I miss home. This time, I secretly hope he says, "Let's pack up."

After a long lunch visit with the landowner and a tour of his property, Tim decides we might as well stay for an evening hunt. Even that terminology is misleading. When you hear a hunter say evening hunt, it really means hunting all afternoon. I didn't know how much more I could handle this season. I wonder to myself if the prolonged visit was intentional. Did it matter? We'd enjoyed our time with the landowner and the visit. I quickly decide that it doesn't matter. If it makes my husband happy to be out in the woods, I want him to have that peace. We sit together the rest of the day but don't see even a single deer. My earlier hypothesis that Tim may be a jinx was looking much more likely. When he was with me, our deer sightings were minimal. When we are apart, my luck was much better.

As we prepared to leave our stand for the last time, there was a lot to pack: used Kleenex, several empty tanks from the heater, backpacks, rifles, chairs, and more. Tim joked that he felt like a pack mule. I thought to myself that if we would have driven to our stands, we wouldn't have to make the quarter-mile hike back to the truck weighed down like beasts. Arriving at the vehicle felt like a major accomplishment. As we cased the rifles for the last time, I noticed a sadness come over Tim's face. I knew he was thinking about the 12 months he'd have to wait until he could uncase his rifle again for the 2010 hunt. As we quickly stripped off our outer hunting clothes and packed them into our duffle bags, my mind felt victorious for surviving our first return to the Minnesota hunting season since losing Clint. I could tell Tim's thoughts were on me. He asked, "How are you . . . you doing ok?" Without even a thought or plan, I had minimized the pain during the last three days. I didn't want him to know the hurt in my heart. I kept telling myself it wasn't his hobby's fault that my son wasn't with us today and that his hobby wasn't the reason our daughters and younger son decided to sit this season out. I tell myself it was just Clint's day. It doesn't matter that his Remington was missed when the guns were checked and locked up that Saturday evening in 2006. It doesn't matter that someone threw a coat over his gun that was standing in the corner. It doesn't matter that he decided to sleep in Sunday morning to rest up for the evening hunt, woke up before our return, and went out hunting without us. It doesn't matter that his shoes were untied or that he chose to run on frosty grass. It doesn't matter that everything went so perfectly and resulted in something so tragically wrong. Did it even matter that he knew the rules, defied them, and made a decision that would destroy all who loved him? No, it doesn't matter! God says He knows our paths before we are even born. So there! It was just Clint's day. However, if he had to go, why did it have to be that way? Why did it have to be through a hobby that meant so much to him, my husband, and our younger children? I have gone from wanting to throw away all of our guns and hunting gear in a huge dumpster to forgiving a hobby Clint loved. Would I harbor the same resentment about driving if he'd been killed in a traffic accident? Would I have driven again? Would that have been looked at differently than a family who resumed hunting after one of them died as a result of a hunting accident? Do people judge us? Do they judge me? Do they think Clint's life didn't matter to me? Should I hold onto a hatred of his hobby as a vigil to him? I don't know the answers to any of these questions, but I do know that they occupy my mind daily. This dichotomy in my thoughts is consuming.

We buckled ourselves into the truck, and then made our way down an entanglement of highways through the woods. Soon, we would be back on the prairies of southwestern Minnesota. Before we got far, our oldest daughter called to see if we were safely out of the woods. I could tell she'd been filled with worry; she missed us. It's like the old game of telephone we used to play with paper cups and string when we were kids. She texted her brother, he texted his younger sister, and soon they all knew we were on our way home.

Yesterday, when he took the ninety-degree turn and jumped the ridge, the Phantom went into a pit. We searched up and down the fence line, the gravel pit, and searched the nearby woods. Our phantom buck had simply disappeared. We couldn't find a trace of blood or prints, and he never resurfaced. On this trip, we would be heading home without the phantom buck. He lived for another day. Another day for the neighbors to tell stories, glass their woods, scan the fence lines, dream, and talk big.

The gap between us and home quickly closed as we traveled down the winding highway through the darkness. It was a long drive ahead of us. My heart warmed and a smile filled my face as I pictured the yard light's glow bouncing off our log cabin in the heartland. I couldn't help imagining my kids safe and asleep in their beds. I was filled with excitement! I couldn't wait to see them again. This is a gift many parents take for granted. Not me! One day three years ago, I left my children fast asleep in their beds. I thought they were safe, but I've never seen my oldest son's smiling face again.

# APPENDIX I
## *Infinitely Ours*

> *"Your vision will become clear only when you look into your own heart. Who looks outside, dreams; who looks inside, awakes."*
> *~Carl Jung~*

Even though I proudly call him "My Clinty," I clearly know he was loved by many and belongs to them too. In this life here on earth, he was a gift. He left us with several lessons. That beautiful boy saw no colors and felt no prejudice. He was the perfect friend that we should all strive to be. He had an uncanny knack for making everyone feel like they were special to him only because they were. He saw the good when others saw the bad. Last but not least, he loved shamelessly! With such a tremendous loss, people often ask how you're doing but often do not wait for an answer. It's more of a greeting than an actual question. Even worse, if you say you feel "terrible," they say things like "super" and "great." I now know they haven't done this to be hurtful. They just don't know what to say. In not knowing what to say or do, they do exactly what they shouldn't do. They do not listen. Why can't they just listen?

Because listening can be difficult and uncomfortable, I decided to let everyone know how we are doing once a year in our local paper. This update is formatted as a letter to Clint. In these letters, I let him know about everything he missed that year. I don't do this for Clint, because I don't believe that he misses anything. I do it in an effort to show others the magnitude of our grief and the progression of our healing. So, for those who *really* care, I have included the past letters for you.

## REMEMBERING CLINT ~ 2008

*Clint,*
*It's been two years since you went away.*
*Our lives have been forever changed since that day.*
*Your friends remember with hugs, visits, balloons and flowers by your stone;*
*And in the letters to you, their love is still shown.*
*A senior class picture with a banner and snapshot of you…*
*They've planted a tree and made a homecoming slideshow of thee.*
*The community remembers with an occasional card, an email or a smile.*
*For them, it maybe feels like it's been quite a while.*
*Even though they go on, it only takes a visit to see*
*That you touched their hearts, and they pray for the family and me.*
*The family remembers, with sharing, how you made us all laugh.*
*We try to fill the emptiness with jokes on your behalf.*
*No matter how hard we try, nothing's the same.*
*Because of your loss, we've all sought someone to blame.*
*It's taken some time to seek out the truth--that*
*God needed you home in the prime of your youth.*
*When we're all together, there's just something missing.*
*Where's that floppy blonde hair and that beautiful face we'd all be kissing?*
*We start each day with the hope that the past months were a series of bad dreams,*

*But soon are forced to realize it is just as it seems.*
*Each day we let ourselves fantasize that you will walk through the door,*
*All the while knowing, your job's in Heaven with the angels to soar.*
*With all that we've lost, we look to each other and know our gifts are still great.*
*Here, there's much love around us…we'll get to Heaven, but we'll arrive late.*
*We talk of you often even though it hurts for some.*
*We want them to remember your name and where you came from.*
*You lived with our family, and "YES," you really were here.*
*Just for a while, rather than you, it's your memories we'll hold near.*
*With the beauty of fall comes such a horrible pain,*
*But we must remember that this was for Heaven's gain.*
*We thank God for your presence, even though only for a short while.*
*You brought to this Earth your incredible heart and that smile.*
*Not a person who met you will forget your love and that look.*
*To change our lives and this world for the better was all that it took.*
*So on this 2nd anniversary, we look at it not as though you're gone.*
*For we believe you are living with God, his angels and singing a song.*
*Keep watching over us and comforting us, too,*
*As we ask God for grace to help us live without you.*
*We love you,*
*Mom & Family*

## REMEMBERING CLINT ~ 2009

*Clint,*
*It's been 1095 days, 156 weeks, 36 months or three years.*
*No matter how you look at it, it's been filled with tears.*
*As more time has gone without you here; how years past have become so dear.*
*Our memories keep you close but yet so far.*
*We can only dream of where you are.*
*This year, there were many more milestones for us to face,*
*but you weren't here to ease the pace.*
*We'd barely get through one event and another was here.*
*Each time I'd pray..."Please be with us, my angel dear."*
*Your 18th birthday, prom and graduation were just a few*
*we had to face without you.*
*Your kindness scholarship inspired those with a giving heart.*
*Your work continues because many contributed from the start.*
*Each classmate was given a Clint McCoss Scholarship gift.*
*Their thank you notes shared that it offered an incredible lift.*
*Summer flew by and soon all were scattering to college and such.*
*I remembered our talks and how you had planned so much.*
*College to study history and serving your country you'd planned.*
*We should have known that your future by God was manned.*
*As your friends went their ways, many came to say*
*that part of you was leaving with them that day.*
*In September, the first of your friends was married.*
*How happy you'd have been and how your laughter would have carried.*
*We wonder to ourselves if you miss us, how you are and what you do.*
*We want you to know our relationship and love grows infinitely for you.*

*Eyes closed, I wake each morning asking God to hold you near.*
*I dream it's me and feel your whiskers against my cheek so clear.*
*Yearning to see your beautiful smile,*
*or hearing your door close with your not-so-quiet style.*
*Hearing a sound in the room or on the breeze that I'm sure is you,*
*just to realize it's only my desire and isn't true.*
*Though unimaginable that life could go on without you, it reluctantly does.*
*We've been forced to create a new us and face that we can't have what was.*
*We are learning from the way you lived and from your loss;*
*it's hard to accept we are not in control or boss.*
*The promise of eternity has me delighted;*
*knowing the perfect blend of my children's laughter will be reunited.*
*A person once asked me, "What good has come from the loss of Clint?"*
*Good? Initially my anger raged as if sparked with flint.*
*As time has passed, I've been able to ponder;*
*but to find the answer took me on a journey to yonder.*
*The anger has subsided, and the answer is clear;*
*it was hard to see but was always right here.*
*I've had to pray, dig deep and ask God to share with me;*
*and now I know the good from losing you was He.*
*To survive the pain of such a horrible thing,*
*so many have turned to our Lord and King.*
*You see, for the love of God to grow in so many hearts,*
*it took a son...that's how it starts.*
*Love, Mom & Family*

# REMEMBERING CLINT ~ 2010

*Dear Clint,*
*Four years have come and gone since that day;*
*Looking back leaves me with much to say.*
*We once thought life would not go on;*
*After all, it's just not right with you gone.*
*You'd of been nineteen and soon turning twenty.*
*Nearly every minute, I have to face that I'm missing plenty.*
*Life does not slow down for us to heal.*
*In fact, it barely gives us time to know what to feel.*
*Your niece, Maddie Rae, was born and soon will be one.*
*What an uncle you'd have been ... filled with such fun.*
*Garrett and Bri are seniors this year and soon on their own.*
*This will add to the quiet you left and create a total silent zone.*
*We've done some things I never wanted to do.*
*Yes, we've put away some things that belonged to you.*
*Your things are no longer scattered about your floor;*
*They were put away for new carpet to replace what your*
*chinchilla tore.*
*Your smell no longer lingers where you laid your head;*
*So I've washed your sheets, blankets and made your bed.*
*We want your room to be a place everyone loves to be.*
*Even this week, Maddie went in, played with your toys, turned*
*and smiled at me.*
*She kept hugging your bear and kissing its face;*
*I couldn't help but wish it was you in its place.*
*She'd have been crazy about you—such a fun-filled lad.*
*But instead, we'll share the memories; and for that, we are glad.*
*Many quilts have been made from the clothes that you wore.*
*Soon I will wash those in your basket tucked by your door.*
*Grandpa and Grandma celebrated their 50$^{th}$ this year.*
*Flowers from your garden filled a vase to make you feel near.*

*We've adopted part of Highway 67 in your honor.*
*Two miles of picking up garbage, and your aunt was nearly a goner.*
*For she walked every inch hoping to be thin later,*
*While your siblings and cousins drove the Gator.*
*More money was given from your kindness scholarship fund.*
*The students and families continue the work that you'd done.*
*An act of kindness, a smile or a helping hand —*
*They spread your legacy through the land.*
*Though not physically here, you are in every thought, tear and smile.*
*We remind ourselves we'll be with you in just a while.*
*We love you, Baby, and are not forgetting;*
*But for now we will live in a separate setting.*

## REMEMBERING CLINT ~ 2011

*Clint,*
*It's been five years…so hard to believe.*
*Although time passes, we still do grieve.*
*Garrett, Bri, and Ethan are high school grads.*
*They've moved away with their own college pads.*
*Meg & Pooh graduated college and are done with school.*
*It was a long road but still so cool.*
*There are no more kids here at home.*
*Just Tim, I, and Smokey your cat that roam.*
*Grandpa turned 80, Hollis 50, Bobbie 40, your buddy got married and baby Kayden is here.*
*We have no doubt that you, from Heaven, also did cheer.*
*Your friends still come to visit, email and call.*
*It's such a comfort to us all.*
*Megan and Garrett each got another tattoo.*
*All inked up in honor of you.*

Garrett's with the lilacs you picked as young boys,
the sun, your headstone, bagpipes and your army man toys.
Megs, simple as can be.
Your name on her wrist...a silent memory.
Your niece Maddie is nearly two.
She's growing up but not without you.
She reaches into the air and takes your hand.
She waves and says "Clinty" as though there you stand.
She's able to see what we are not.
Oh, the lessons this precious child has taught.
We're learning to live and feel real joy.
Yes, I'm learning to walk this earth without my oldest boy.
It's not easy to do but each day I shut my eyes and imagine you.
I see your beaming face and the sun glisten in your hair.
A tear falls down my cheek as you smile without care.
I smile in return as I shut my eyes because I know the Lord has heard our cries.
And one day, when they close for the very last,
As promised, all this pain will be part of our past.
Love, Your Family

## REMEMBERING CLINT ~ 2012

Clint,
It's that time...school resumes, colors change, the air grows crisp, harvest begins...it's fall.
Once again, time to face that an anniversary is coming that no one likes to recall.
People often ask "How long has it been?"
I think, "yesterday", but utter "Six years since then".
Again, so many things changed this year.
All things that make us want and wish you were here.
Your nephew Tanner was born and, in part, named after you.

Meg got married and said "I do".
Bri and Garrett are at college. Bri to teach and Gar a cop.
It feels like their schooling will never stop.
Kayla moved away but now is back.
She is in school with life on track.
This year we remodeled houses for Gar, Meg and Bri.
Yes, we are crazy. We worked on three.
Maddie Rae talks about you nearly every day.
She calls you "my friend Clinty" and says you come to play.
It's a mystery that she really knows who you are.
She asks to come see you but we explain Heaven's a bit too far.
More of your friends were married and having babies, too.
Each and every time, we think of you.
Twelve more scholarships given as your kindness legacy.
The recipients and families were honored. That was plain to see.
We've launched an international company that's growing fast.
All the countries and accents...you'd of had such a blast.
Our book about you, the family and change will be done this year.
All proceeds to your scholarship, my handsome little dear.
Our hearts still ache and we miss you still.
The stories keep you alive and the babies help the cracks to fill.
We're learning to live and find where you fit.
Life goes on and our scars are healing just a bit.
For now, you live strong in our stories and hearts.
Then one day, God will gather the parts.
As Gar reminds me, the day will come sooner than we think;
And our time apart will seem like just a blink.
We love you, Clinty!
~Your Family~

# REMEMBERING CLINT ~ 2013

*Clint,*
*Seven years without you now placed in the past.*
*Your flawless love has managed to last.*
*I feel your presence as though you're still here.*
*I'm not crazy. Believe me, reality is clear.*
*I watch friends and family build their lives.*
*Although happy to see, it still cuts like a thousand knives.*
*All things we are wishing, missing, and felt God should have known.*
*This, too, has settled as our understanding of Heaven has grown.*
*Those words "life goes on" are painfully true.*
*It goes on for friends, for family, for me but also for you.*
*Each of us carries a symbol or two to hold you near.*
*Something to help us hold back even just one tear.*
*It might be a decal, a tattoo or necklace, such as your cross.*
*Something to prove you were here and not just a loss.*
*All who love you wear it somehow.*
*Yet, no symbol is stronger than the memories still with us now.*
*Ah...those memories...so many, so rich and so deep.*
*They're what we hold on to. They're what we keep.*
*As we hold you close, soar high my son.*
*Know we haven't forgotten, not for a second, not even one.*
*We ask God to grant us grace and peace while we finish here.*
*Then, in Heaven, we will hold you forever my dear.*

# APPENDIX II
# *Discussion Questions*

**DEDICATION**
1. Where did the mother find the strength to make the promises that she did? Did she really plan to keep them?
2. With those same circumstances, could you have promised not to drink, to get out of bed each day, and to live a good life? What would the alternative have been?

**FORWARD**
1. What made this boy look up to his mother?
2. What did journaling do for him?
3. What did he mean by his quote "Ask not what time has taken from you but what time has given you"?

**INTRODUCTION**
1. The author says, "It's through the writing of *No Ordinary Son* that the buckle has been released, opening my heart." What does this mean?

**CHAPTER ONE**
1. How do you imagine their family?
2. How do you think the kids in this family looked at their life?
3. Did what they had or have now come easily, or did/do they have to work at it?
4. Does their family make you think of your own family? How?

**CHAPTER TWO**
1. Do you believe it is possible for God to speak to us?
2. Should she have done something differently with all of the signs and communications from God?

3. Has there ever been a time when you felt God might have been speaking to you? What did you do? Did you tell anyone? Why or why not?

**CHAPTER THREE**
1. Would things have turned out differently if she had stayed home that morning?
2. If it had been you, would you have wanted to be the one to find a loved one's body? Why?
3. This was a horrible scene. What will you remember most when you fall asleep tonight?
4. If this happened at your home, could you ever find peace there again?
5. Each time your kids leave, do you hug and kiss them goodbye and say "I love you"? If you ever forgot to, would they seek you out for it?

**CHAPTER FOUR**
1. How would the feeling of your home change if you knew one of your children would never return?
2. What were you feeling when she described the last trace of his kisses being washed from her? What about when his blood washed off of her?
3. What happened before she fell asleep that first night? Did Clint really hug her goodnight? Was he actually there comforting his mother?
4. Explain how you think she felt when she woke up to realize her son Clint was nowhere to be found.
5. Would you be prepared to make the vast array of decisions for one of your children? Organ donation, obituary, funeral, and so forth?
6. What were you thinking when she went to lie where he took his last breath and desperately searched for traces of him? What about when she collected his fragments and blood from the grass?

**CHAPTER FIVE**
1. If you lost one of your children without warning, would you know without a doubt that they loved you?
2. When saying good-bye in the back of the church, Clint's mom nearly crawled into the casket with her son. She struggled with the lack of privacy and people watching her. What do you think about this?
3. Clint's mom had a need for people at the funeral to know him as she did, so she wrote a letter. Would you choose to say good-bye to your child? How?
4. She talks about part of her mind closing with the casket lid. What did she mean by this?

**CHAPTER SIX**
1. Do you believe in God, or is He a hoax?
2. Do you think you can earn your way into Heaven by being a good person?
3. Do you expect favor from God, or can bad things happen to good people?
4. Can you feel her father's pain? How would you feel if your child hated God?

**CHAPTER SEVEN**
1. What do you think about the six-month promise?
2. Would you be able to offer the same promise to a grieving loved one?
3. If you were grieving for a deceased loved one, do you think you could have kept such a promise?

**CHAPTER EIGHT**
1. The reclusive mother is surprised at needing people around her. The impact of grief is powerful. Does the extent to which it changes her surprise you?
2. Have you ever been selfish or done a poor job when someone you know has been grieving?
3. She talks about a grief-induced shock that creates a numbness that lasted for years. What do you think about this? Why?

**CHAPTER NINE**
1. What would it be like to wake up over and over to the worst day of your life? How would you handle it?
2. Have you ever experienced the type of peace she repeatedly prayed for? What do you think about the prayer she often repeated? Do you think it helped?

**CHAPTER TEN**
1. The author shares an experience of hearence when her son gives her a glimpse of Heaven. Do you think God can allow this?
2. Until this incident of hearence, the author did not have a gift for writing. She believes God granted it to her. Can God do this?
3. Have you ever experienced what she calls hearence?

**CHAPTER ELEVEN**
1. In this chapter, it is clear that the author is angry. What does she have a right to be angry about? Do you think it was really anger or something else?
2. She learned a great deal about the Bible and how she could use it. How were you taught? Were you allowed to write in your Bible, bend the pages, or do anything else to your Bible?
3. She sounds so lost and alone. Does it surprise you that much of this pain was induced by a church?
4. What did you take away from her Thanksgiving message that was never shared?
5. Did you understand her anger at her son? Explain.
6. Were you surprised by her anger at the *death* of herself? What are your thoughts on this?

**CHAPTER TWELVE**
1. Does she paint a picture of what she feels happened to her life?
2. How was her life "hijacked"?

**CHAPTER THIRTEEN**
1. Are you one of those parents who always has to know where your kids are and that they are safe?
2. Can you even imagine what it would be like to have your child ripped from you and be left with no right to know where he/she was? What would you do?
3. Some of the pastors gave poor spiritual advice. What do you think of this?

**CHAPTER FOURTEEN**
1. The author ascertains experiencing something that she made up a word for: hearence. Share your thoughts about this word and what it stands for. Do you believe what she and others experienced? Why?
2. What would you do if God wanted you to do something you didn't want to do?
3. Do you think God was working through the author in that discount store? Explain.

**CHAPTER FIFTEEN**
1. After the author loses her son, she is filled with several fears. If you had these same crippling fears, what would you have done?
2. She shares powerful examples of God's power. Do you believe He is this powerful? Have you ever experienced His power?

**CHAPTER SIXTEEN**
1. The mother explains a dichotomy between loving to hear about people and the pain it caused due to Clint's absence. Would you have realized this would be an issue for a parent who lost a child?
2. What could you do to support a friend who felt this way and still enjoy your own family being alive?

**CHAPTER SEVENTEEN**
1. The chapter is called "Don't Hurt the Money." What does this mean?

2. She explains trauma-induced brain damage. Did you know it was possible to hurt your brain without a physical injury?
3. The author talks about losing the ability to do many things. Did any of these things surprise you?
4. How was it possible for her to navigate the loss of her son and these brain injuries? Why didn't she tell people what she was going through?
5. What could this information mean for anyone who loses someone? A student, a coworker, etc.?

**CHAPTER EIGHTEEN**
1. She clearly wanted the reader to understand her son. What did this chapter leave you thinking about her precious Clint?
2. The infinity symbol meant a great deal to Clint. Now it means a great deal to many. After reading their story, what will you think when you see this symbol?

**CHAPTER NINETEEN**
1. It is clear that Clint's friends helped the family. We often overlook the good in our youth. What do you think of the things they did to lend support? Share examples of your own.

**CHAPTER TWENTY**
1. This family not only lost its son and brother but also each other. Did any of this surprise you? What was the most impactful?
2. She fought to save her family. Where did she find the energy and wherewithal to do this?
3. How would you deal with children who, all at once, began to self-destruct? This includes children who abandon the family, become bitter and defiant, turn to drugs, and seek either perfection or isolation.
4. Was she successful in saving them? Were they successful in saving themselves? Could they have done it without love and support?
5. After losing Clint, grandchildren came into the picture. What did they bring to the family?

6. She says her husband is the only one who 100% changed for the better. How?
7. What did she mean grief is like an oil spill? Have you experienced what she depicts?

**CHAPTER TWENTY-ONE**
1. The author explains how each of her family members were helpful but in different ways. Would you know what to do if there was the loss of a child in your family? Explain.
2. She shares how her extended family changed. Did you feel their desire to return to each other?
3. How do you balance loving deeply and the vulnerability it creates?

**CHAPTER TWENTY-TWO**
1. What did she mean by "Sometimes my ability to analyze my own thoughts and behaviors becomes paralyzed"?
2. She shares, "There is a difference between talking yourself out of something and talking yourself through something." What is the difference? Is one healthier than the other? Share examples.
3. What does she mean by "I feel I have a special relationship with him no one else has"? What is her intention of quoting Luke 12:48?
4. What things did she say helped? How can you use these things to help someone else? What caution did she give?

**CHAPTER TWENTY-THREE**
1. What did she mean when she said they would be their own hero? What did they do?
2. They did many things to keep Clint part of their everyday family. What stood out to you?

**CHAPTER TWENTY-FOUR**
1. The author starts this chapter by making it clear that some people falsified information and supported the validity of these stories by saying they *were* at the scene of Clint's accident

when, in actuality, they weren't. Why would anyone do such a thing?
2. The author clearly struggles with the fact that *gossip* took precedence over their *loss*. How would this make you feel if it were your child? Would you care?
3. She talks about a lot of confusing *facts* that would be validated by one and then disproven by another. Would you have come to the same point as her?
4. The author seems to almost laugh at the assertion that she is in *denial* over how her son passed away. Why do you think this is?
5. She feels betrayed by the sharing of Clint's private writings. Having promised your child an expectation of privacy, would you have felt the same?
6. The author addresses suicide head-on. She makes it clear that she believes there is no shame for those who commit this act but only shame in the unaddressed pain that leads to it and how the public responds. What are your thoughts?
7. The author shares that even with her perfect life (kids, parents, etc.) she still wanted to be selfish and leave it all in a second of uncontrolled pain. Have you ever felt this way?
8. Is it fair to judge anyone for something they do in a single second of pain and selfishness? Would you want your worst decision to define you?
9. The author clearly wonders why the loss of her son is so fascinating to gossipers. Why do you think it is?
10. The author refers to an *absolute truth* about her son's loss . . . she doesn't know and doesn't care. What does this make you think? Would you *need* to know? Would it matter?

**CHAPTER TWENTY-FIVE**
1. The family has created a scholarship in Clint's memory. How do you feel about acknowledging kids for their silent acts of kindness?

**CHAPTER TWENTY-SIX**
1. The author explains going from wanting to die to wanting the world to end, and finally, to wanting to live. How did she make this transformation? Why?

**CHAPTER TWENTY-SEVEN**
1. Have you ever heard of the term *deus ex machina*?
2. Do you believe our time to return to Heaven was written by God long before we were born? Explain?
3. Do you think we are in ultimate control of our children's safety?
4. The author claims God asked her to write this book. Has God ever asked anything of you? Have you been listening?
5. In the last pages of the book, the author depicts the shocking realization that *no ordinary son* was not Clint but Jesus Himself. How did this realization make you feel? What does it make you think?
6. She refers to God as the master "shepherd." Why?

**EPILOGUE**
1. After losing her son in an accident with a firearm, she was able to let her family hunt again. Could you have done that?

**INFINITELY CLINT**
1. Is there anything to learn about the progression of grief from reading the mother's annual letters? If so, what?

# APPENDIX III
## *Donation Form*

I would like to make a donation to
**Clint's Kindness Scholarship**
in the following amount:

$

### CHECK DONATION

Please mail check donations to:
Clint McCoss Scholarship
4857 Hwy 67, Suite #1
Granite Falls, MN 56241

### PAYPAL DONATION

Please make PayPal donations through Clint's website:
www.clintmccoss.com

# APPENDIX IV
## *Book Order Form*

| SHIP TO | |
|---|---|
| First & Last Name | |
| Address | |
| City, State, Zip | |

| Number of Copies | $20/Soft Cover $30/Hard Cover | S&H $5/per book | Total |
|---|---|---|---|
| | | | |

| CREDIT CARD ORDERS | | | | |
|---|---|---|---|---|
| Type of Card (Visa, MC) | | | | |
| Name on Card | | | | |
| Card Billing Address | Address | City | State | Zip |
| | | | | |
| Card Number | | | | |
| Expiration Date | | | | |
| 3-Digit Code | | | | |
| Card Holder's Signature | | | | |

| CHECK ORDERS |
|---|
| Please mail check orders to: |
| **Infinitely Yours Publications** |
| 4857 Hwy 67, Suite #3 |
| Granite Falls, MN  56241 |

| ONLINE ORDERS |
|---|
| www.iypublication.com |

*Credit card orders can be emailed or called into 855-855-8764*